lonely planet

POCKET
SAN FRANCISCO

Alison Bing, Dylan Lalanne-Perkins
& Margot Seeto

Contents

Plan Your Trip 4

Top: Fish & chips, Fisherman's Wharf (p43)
Bottom: Alamo Square Park (p109)

Explore San Francisco 41

San Francisco Toolkit 191

FROM TOP LEFT: BENJAMIN HEATH FOR LONELY PLANET, RAULCANO/SHUTTERSTOCK

★ Top Experiences

Worth a Trip

The Journey Begins Here

No matter what else is happening in the world, know that flowers are blooming year-round along alleyways named after radical poets – if San Francisco didn't exist, you'd have to make it up. The little city that launched free speech, organic cuisine, gay and trans rights, the internet, fortune cookies and AI is already onto its next big dream. Adventure is a given, and free spirits always welcome. Hop onto a cable car, and prepare for the wild ride to San Francisco's next peak moment. - *Alison Bing*

Alison Bing
@alisonbing.bsky.social

Alison has survived booms, busts, live-action robot wars and performance-art potlucks to tell only in-San Francisco stories for global media outlets.

Dylan Lalanne-Perkins
in linkedin.com/in/dylanlalanneperkins

Dylan is a writer in love with his hometown of San Francisco.

Margot Seeto
@beyondmeato

Margot is a third-generation San Franciscan, food and travel freelance writer – and the dumpling columnist for SFGATE.

California cable car line (p72)

UVL/SHUTTERSTOCK

Van Ness Ave. California
59
& Market
Streets

THE BEST

Dining Experiences

With 46 global cuisines packed into 7 sq miles, San Francisco is like a greatest-hits compilation with no skips. SF holds the most Michelin stars of any US city – taste the next breakout star now.

Dine on art at **Atelier Crenn**, where global megastar chef/owner Dominique Crenn draws inspiration from SF seafaring legends and Sonoma landscapes. (p56; pictured)

Feel clever by association with **Rich Table**'s ingenious Californian signature dishes, like *cacio e pepe* pasta with *uni* (sea urchin). (p170)

Dip into an artist's palette of chutneys and scoop up scrumptious Kerala curry shrimp with sculptural *appam* (pancakes) at **Copra**. (p117)

Try some of everything at the **Ferry Building**, SF's local food landmark – featuring SF star chefs and three bountiful weekly farmers markets. (p66)

Brace for maximum flavor at **San Ho Won**, where tasting menus feature Korean filet and soul-satisfying sides. (p135; pictured)

Taste the Mediterranean in **Dalida**'s sumptuous dishes, showcasing trade-route flavors and seasonal ingredients. (p56)

Right: Ferry Building (p66)

THE BEST

Off-the-Wall Art Experiences

Art explodes from frames and jumps off pedestals in San Francisco, where murals wrap around entire buildings, immersive shows envelop you with sound and vision, and interactive art installations make you part of the art.

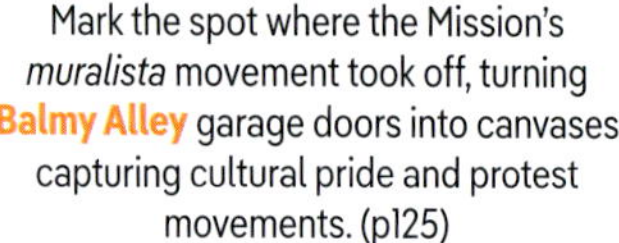

Mark the spot where the Mission's *muralista* movement took off, turning **Balmy Alley** garage doors into canvases capturing cultural pride and protest movements. (p125)

See how many women trailblazers you recognize in the magnificent *Maestrapeace* mural covering the **Women's Building**. (p125; pictured)

Jump into artwork already in progress at **Edge on the Square**'s participatory community art shows. (p96)

Catch poster art fresh from the silkscreens at **Haight Street Art Center**. (p166)

Deep dive into SF's arts scene at **Minnesota Street Project** with eye-opening gallery shows, indie art fairs and First Saturday openings. (p131; pictured)

Walk among local legends captured in larger-than-life murals along **Calle 24**, San Francisco's designated Latino Cultural District. (p126)

Right: Balmy Alley (p125)

THE BEST

Out & Proud Experiences

Over 175 years of trailblazing LGBTQ+ history, iconic moments and legendary looks, San Francisco puts in the work as the world's best place to be out and proud. If you're here and queer, welcome home.

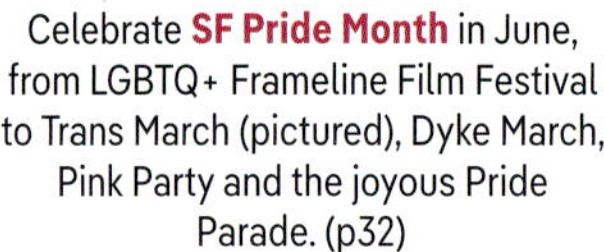

Celebrate **SF Pride Month** in June, from LGBTQ+ Frameline Film Festival to Trans March (pictured), Dyke March, Pink Party and the joyous Pride Parade. (p32)

See how far we've come along Castro's **Rainbow Honor Walk**, with 68 sidewalk plaques honoring LGBTQ+ icons. (p146)

Witness history in the making in August, SF's official Transgender History month, ending with the Riot Party in the world's first **Transgender District**. (p75)

Meet San Francisco LGBTQ+ icons who changed culture around them at **GLBT Historical Society Museum**, with historic artifacts that show exactly how they did it – and leave with plans for your own future. (p149)

Get spanked for charity at **Folsom Street Fair**, the massive annual kinkfest in SF's official Leather & LGBTQ Cultural District. (p75; pictured)

Right: Participants at Pride Parade (p32)

FROM LEFT: SHEILA FITZGERALD/SHUTTERSTOCK, NEVSKII DMITRII/SHUTTERSTOCK, SHEILA FITZGERALD/SHUTTERSTOCK

THE BEST

Outdoor Experiences

San Franciscans love the outdoors, and it shows – historic SF conservation efforts have protected thousands of acres of parks, beaches and woodlands across the city for all to enjoy.

Do what comes naturally in **Golden Gate Park**: sniff flowers at SF Botanical Garden, race turtles around Stow Lake (pictured) and rock out at epic concerts. (p178)

Picnic at driftwood-shaped benches perfectly positioned for sublime Golden Gate Bridge views at **Tunnel Tops**. (p48)

Hike **Lands End** to reach a secret sea cave and breathtaking blufftop vistas framed by wind-sculpted pines. (p182)

Fly kites along **Crissy Field**, then chill at the scenic bayfront beach. (p48; pictured)

Laze away in **Dolores Park**, surrounded by semi-professional tanners, birthday partiers, and kids swarming the play pyramid. (p128)

Climb the rocky red crag of **Corona Heights** as city lights flicker on, and watch rainbow lights twinkle welcomes across the Castro. (p148)

Right: Lands End trail (p182)

FROM LEFT: SUNDRY PHOTOGRAPHY/SHUTTERSTOCK, ARTYART/SHUTTERSTOCK, VENTU PHOTO/SHUTTERSTOCK

THE BEST

Counterculture Experiences

Feel free to entertain wild ideas in San Francisco – this city is living proof they might actually work, and change the culture around them.

Wander **Haight** sidewalks where Flower Power took root in SF's Summer of Love – like rogue dandelions, counterculture movements keep popping up here. (p158)

Watch underground art explode from the shadows in **Clarion Alley**'s graffiti showcase, curated by a collective of SF street-art legends. (p125)

Plot screenplays, epic poems and Ferlinghetti-inspired protest slogans at **Caffe Trieste** over powerful espresso and jukebox opera. (p103; pictured)

Scratch that itch in your ear with punk on vinyl from volunteer-run, nonprofit **Thrillhouse Records** – stick around for free weekend shows. (p130)

Toast sheroes at iconic drag joint **Aunt Charlie's**, located at the crossroads where trans women fought police harassment in 1966. (p75)

Read up on permaculture, online privacy and radical comics at volunteer-run **Bound Together** anarchist book collective. (p165; pictured)

Right: Haight & Ashbury signpost (p161)

FROM LEFT: STEFANO POLITI MARKOVINA/SHUTTERSTOCK, LUIS VILLA DEL CAMPO, CC BY 2.0, VIA WIKIMEDIA COMMONS ©, SCAROLA PHOTOGRAPHY/SHUTTERSTOCK

1500
Haight
600
Ashbury

THE BEST

Futuristic Experiences

In blockbusters, Godzilla, aliens and genetically enhanced apes roam San Francisco streets. With its self-driving cars, cyberpunk fests and interactive science experiments, SF is a sci-fi fantasy come to life.

Explore the outer limits of science and art with mind-bending **Exploratorium** experiments designed by MacArthur Genius Grant winners. (p47; pictured)

Watch SFFILM Festival sci-fi movie premieres in the **Presidio**'s Letterman Theater, built by George Lucas as his *Star Wars* screening room. (p48)

Join the future already in progress at **Gray Area** events, showcasing futurist visions blending art, science and technology. (p128)

Imagine a world where art and technology aren't judged by sales or likes but by long-term impact over drinks at **The Interval**. (p58; pictured)

Look up at SF's night skyline: you can't miss Jim Campbell's **Salesforce Tower** digital art installation, featuring collabs with SF ballet dancers, high-school animators and drag superstars. (p78)

Right: Salesforce Tower (p78)

THE BEST

SF Handmade Experiences

Here in the global tech hub, there's a low-tech, high-craft creative movement underway. Delight your senses with handmade wonders at dockside fairs, hands-on arts in the park and arts makerspaces in repurposed downtown offices.

Catch the next wave of craft at the **Museum of Craft & Design**, where magic carpets capture climate change and buttons transform worn streetwear into royal regalia. (p134)

Indulge your senses at **West Coast Craft**, when tasty artisan foods, textural handmade clothing and fragrant hand-dipped candles by local makers overflow Fort Mason's ex-army warehouse. (p52)

Join the maker revolution underway at **ICASF**, where artists have taken over a downtown office space with art shows and a well-stocked makerspace to make your own prints, zines and more. (p74)

Capture SF inspiration while it's fresh at **Sharon Art Studio**, offering workshops in glass, watercolor and jewelry in the heart of Golden Gate Park. (p179)

Sharon Art Studio (p179)

FILEDIMAGE/SHUTTERSTOCK

THE BEST

Live Music Experiences

Hard to say what concert you're going to remember years from now – but shows at iconic San Francisco venues often end up on collectible posters, prized concert tees and DJ vinyl collections for a reason.

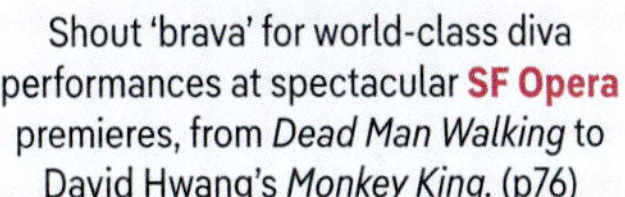

Shout 'brava' for world-class diva performances at spectacular **SF Opera** premieres, from *Dead Man Walking* to David Hwang's *Monkey King*. (p76)

Sway to the tempo of a contemporary classical music set by multi Grammy Award-winning **San Francisco Symphony**. (p76)

Witness jazz legends improvising live in extraordinary **SFJAZZ** collaborations with soul icons, tap dancers, skateboarders and more. (p167)

Bond with strangers over intimate shows by major talent, in the baroque former bordello that's now the **Great American Music Hall**. (p80)

Rock out at music-legendary **Fillmore Auditorium** – and score lifetime bragging rights with your free Fillmore concert poster. (p112; pictured)

Roar for more at **Outside Lands**, Coachella's cool cousin, with three days of headliners and partying in Golden Gate Park. (p180; pictured)

SHEILA FITZGERALD/SHUTTERSTOCK

Asian Art Museum (p73)

THE BEST

Museum Experiences

San Francisco's best museums are portals of possibility, providing glimpses of art and ideas from around the world and across time that seem right at home here at the creative cutting edge of the continent.

Step inside Yayoi Kusama's polka-dotted pumpkins, Olaf Eliasson's *One-Way Color Tunnel* and Agnes Martin's minimalist meditation corner – and exit **SFMOMA** with fresh perspectives. (p68)

Explore a world of inspiration at the **de Young Museum**, spanning cultures and art forms with basement blockbuster art shows, main-floor photography, top-floor textiles and outdoor sculpture. (p179)

Travel through time and across Asia in a single afternoon at the **Asian Art Museum**, wandering past ancient wonders, through futurist video-art installations, to the sunny art terrace. (p73)

Peek inside jewel-box galleries at the **Legion of Honor**, where thought-provoking contemporary art meets priceless paintings and dazzling decorative arts. (p184)

THE BEST

Architecture Experiences

Modern architects know better than to compete with the Golden Gate Bridge for attention – but don't miss SF's low-profile highlights, including splashy Painted Lady Victorians, alleyways graced with Chinatown deco design, and vintage movie palaces.

Photograph the **Golden Gate Bridge** end-to-end at Crissy Field or below at Fort Point – its deco design works from every angle. (p46)

Live the fantasy at Timothy Pflueger's 1922 **Castro Theatre**: behind the Mexican-Spanish facade, anything's possible in the Chinese-Italian deco auditorium. (p146; pictured)

See the sci-fi **Transamerica Pyramid** – William Pereira's concrete rocket is so iconic, Godzilla politely sidestepped it in the 2014 blockbuster. (p79)

Meet the Painted Ladies around **Alamo Square** – you won't believe the scandalous stories these elegant Victorians can tell. (p109)

Go deco at **Aquatic Park Bathhouse**, the ship-shape 1939 Streamline Moderne landmark lined with glittering mosaics. (p53)

Wander **Chinatown Alleyways** to see how the community revived their neighborhood after the 1906 earthquake with a signature deco style. (p90; pictured)

FROM LEFT: ALLARD ONE/SHUTTERSTOCK, CLA78/SHUTTERSTOCK

THE BEST

Wild West Experiences

San Francisco's Wild West days aren't over yet: bison still roam, Victorian circus acts still perform and tall tales are still swapped in SF saloons over potent drinks – only now, there's indoor plumbing and aspirin.

Start a Wild West saloon brawl and glimpse scandalous Victorian circus acts through a vintage Mutoscope for less than a buck at **Musée Mécanique**, SF's vintage arcade. (p54)

Find a home where the buffalo roam at Golden Gate Park's **Buffalo Paddock** – though technically, they're bison who can't be bothered to stampede. (p178; pictured)

Take a powerful Pisco Punch at **Elixir**, the Mission's original 1858 saloon and SF's first certified green bar. (p138)

Enjoy quack cures at Victorian apothecary bar **Devil's Acre**, where delightfully quaffable potions involving 'Gold Rush bitters' may yet save you from the dread perils of hysteria and ennui. (p102; pictured)

Sip spur-rattling cocktails at **Comstock Saloon**, where cowboys used to relieve themselves in the marble trough under the bar – now ragtime bands entertain bathroom lines. (p102)

THE BEST

Drag Experiences

Nowhere does drag quite like San Francisco, where performers have entertained in drag since the Gold Rush – and SF drag stars keep winning hearts and civil-rights victories with false lashes and true courage.

Catch **Oasis** drag shows so outrageous, you'll laugh, gag and cough up glitter – *Star Trek* spoofs, Alanis Morisette tributes, drag-superstar DJ dance parties and more. (p74)

Expect nothing and get everything from shambolic, wildly unpredictable drag nights at **Aunt Charlie's**. (p75)

Watch rainbows and towering wigs (pictured) break through summer fog for SF's **Pride Parade**. (p32)

Put down your drink and pogo for Punk Pride drag revues at **Chan National Queer Arts Center**. (p128)

Don your best Easter bonnet for the **Hunky Jesus Contest**, the fundraising drag contest by SF's charitable drag nuns, the Sisters of Perpetual Indulgence. (p128)

Get assists from **Piedmont Boutique**'s drag-couture experts to outfit your alter ego – whether that's a mermaid, sailor or both. (p172; pictured)

FROM LEFT: SHEILA FITZGERALD/SHUTTERSTOCK, PAULAAH293/SHUTTERSTOCK

BENJAMIN HEATH FOR LONELY PLANET

City Lights Books (p92)

THE BEST

Bookish Experiences

You can hardly throw a stone in SF without hitting a reader (ouch) or writer (ouch again) – but this isn't some sedate library. Join the lit local scene at cooperative bookstores and raucous literary events.

Celebrate your right to read freely in the designated Poet's Chair at **City Lights Books**, San Francisco's free-speech landmark. (p92)

Hear writers' stories too outrageous for print at LitCrawl, the delightfully uncensored grand finale of the annual **Litquake** literary festival. (p132)

Mingle with SF writers and artists loading up on inspiration at neighbor-supported, volunteer-run **Adobe Books & Arts Coop**. (p139)

Stagger out of **Green Apple Books**, laden with used cookbooks by SF chefs and just-released novels signed by local authors. (p189)

Stock up on spyglasses and freshly published literary magazines at **826 Valencia**'s nonprofit writing center and pirate supply store. (p139)

Get lit at **Booksmith** author signings, silent reading parties and writing workshops with an assist from next-door Alembic cocktails. (p164)

Best for Kids

Hang out with butterflies, penguins, alligators and real-life scientists at the **California Academy of Sciences** (p178).

Discover superpowers you never knew you had and explore weird science at the hands-on **Exploratorium** (p47).

Create a kid-triathalon in **Golden Gate Park** (p178): paddle Stow Lake, skate JFK Drive and attack the Children's Playground daredevil hillside slides.

Go wild at **Pier 39** (p54): bark back at sea lions, ride sea dragons on the antique San Francisco Carousel and brave Aquarium of the Bay's shark tunnel.

Meet comic-book heroes at **Cartoon Art Museum** (p54) shows, featuring the original drawings and iconic covers of collectors' dreams.

Best for Free

Catch **Hardly Strictly Bluegrass** (p180) headliners like Elvis Costello, Gillian Welch and banjo legend Béla Fleck plus 100 other acts for free in Golden Gate Park.

Take a good look at the murals DC censors didn't want you to see inside **Coit Tower** (p93), revealing what life was really like in 1930s San Francisco.

Follow smoke signals to **420 Festival** (p180) in Golden Gate Park, with free music and free giveaways for adults with ID.

Rock out in the redwoods at **Stern Grove Festival** (p184), where legends from funk to punk and pop to opera perform gratis in SF's natural amphitheater.

Watch 150-year-old steampunk machinery at work at the **Cable Car Museum** – and gain renewed appreciation for your next cable-car ride.

Perfect Days

A day or two in San Francisco will engage your senses with breathtaking art, foot-stomping concerts and mouthwatering meals – three days here may permanently raise your expectations.

Sea lions, Pier 39 (p54)

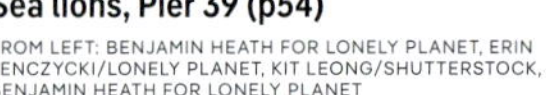

FROM LEFT: BENJAMIN HEATH FOR LONELY PLANET, ERIN LENCZYCKI/LONELY PLANET, KIT LEONG/SHUTTERSTOCK, BENJAMIN HEATH FOR LONELY PLANET

DAY ONE

Only Have One Day?

MORNING

Wander Chinatown for **Edge on the Square** (p96) eye-opening art and epic true stories at **Chinese Historical Society of America** (p97). Find your fortune at **Golden Gate Fortune Cookies** (p91; pictured), and go gourmet with **On Waverly** (p103) cookbooks and **Wok Shop** (p103) kitchenware.

AFTERNOON

Sample dumplings at **Osmanthus Dim Sum Lounge** (p100), then hop on a cable car to Fisherman's Wharf to meet **Cartoon Art Museum** (p54) comic-book heroes, battle Space Invaders at **Musée Mécanique** (p54) and bark back at **Pier 39** (p54) sea lions.

EVENING

Enjoy waterfront sunsets and SF's seafood *cioppino* at **Scoma's** (p57). End the day with spur-rattling cocktails at **Comstock Saloon** (p102), comedy at **Cobb's** (p98) or punk rock at **Mabuhay Gardens** (p98).

DAY TWO

A Weekend Trip

MORNING

Stroll Golden Gate Park, where flowers bloom year-round at **San Francisco Botanical Garden** (p178) and wonders never cease at the **de Young Museum** (p179; pictured). Hang out with penguins at **California Academy of Sciences** (p178) or beachcomb along **Ocean Beach** (p181).

AFTERNOON

Feast on piping-hot *piroshki* at **Cinderella Russian Bakery** (p187), then head to the Mission for murals and galleries, disco-naps in **Dolores Park** (p128) and **Calle 24** (p126) bookstores and cafes.

EVENING

Order the definitive Mission burrito at **La Taqueria** (p135). Don't miss showtime at **Chan National Queer Arts Center** (p128), **Roxie Cinema** (p128) or **Oasis** (p74). Follow rainbow-lit sidewalks to Castro clubs or toast to new friends at legendary Mission bars.

DAY THREE

A Short Break

MORNING

Be experimental at the **Exploratorium** (p47), where hands-on exhibits dare you to stop time, sculpt fog and dive headfirst into total darkness in the **Tactile Dome** (p47).

AFTERNOON

Go gourmet by the bay at SF's local food showcase: the **Ferry Building** (p66; pictured). Explore cutting-edge, multimedia art at **SFMOMA** (p68), or glimpse global art treasures at the **Asian Art Museum** (p73).

EVENING

Get the star-chef treatment with multicourse feasts at **Benu** (p83) or seasonal sensations at **Rich Table** (p170). Cheer for virtuosos at world-renowned **SFJAZZ Center** (p167), **SF Opera** (p76) or **San Francisco Symphony** (p76). Sip rare rum nightcaps at **Smuggler's Cove** – or head to SoMa clubs to see where the night leads.

If You Have More Time

Plot your escape to and from **Alcatraz** (p60) by boat for a spooky night tour of the cell block, with bridge photo-ops on the ferry ride – or plan a romantic sunset cruise across the bay to watch fog tumble over the Golden Gate Bridge's art deco towers. Return for dockside dinner at **Greens** (p56), where you can watch the bridge twinkle across the water.

Picnic on **Presidio Pop Up** (p49) gourmet food-truck fare at **Tunnel Tops** (p48), where picnic benches face your new favorite bridge.

Get up close and personal with San Francisco's icon: the **Golden Gate Bridge** (p46). Hike the span in the early afternoon, when the marine layer lifts to reveal views across the sparkling bay. Between rush hours, you can bike the bridge; during rush hour, head to the roof of **Fort Point** (p49) to see the bridge's International Orange underbelly, and listen to the rhythms of traffic overhead.

Alcatraz (p60)

FILIPPHOTOGRAPHY/SHUTTERSTOCK

A City Day Trip

From the Golden Gate Bridge, it's just a 45-minute detour to idyllic **downtown Sonoma**. There you can lounge on a sun-dappled hilltop with a glass of wine under the ancient oaks of **Bartholomew Park Estate** *(bartholomewestate.com)*, where California's premium winemaking craze began c 1857 – hiking trails offer vineyard overlooks.

Or tour the delightfully sustainable **Hanzell Vineyards** *(hanzell.com)*, where you might spot chickens perched atop snoring pigs in organic vineyards – then head to the stone barn for pinot noir that tastes of morning mists.

Lunch means Portuguese tapas at **Tasca Tasca** *(tascatasca.com)*, pastrami panini at **Salumeria Ovello** *(ovellosonoma.com)* or wild halibut tostadas at **El Molino Central** *(elmolinocentral.com)*.

On a Rainy Day

Heading to **Golden Gate Park** (p178) on a rainy day might sound counterintuitive – but no matter how gloomy it is outside, it's positively tropical inside the **Conservatory of Flowers** (p178; pictured), with rare orchids blooming year-round.

Continue your tropical adventures at the **California Academy of Sciences** (p178), where blue butterflies flutter around you inside the **Osher Rainforest Dome** – or you can escape the rain and the planet at **Planetarium** shows.

Stay dry while you get immersed in art at the **de Young Museum** (p179), and take the elevator up the observation tower to watch the mists roll across the park.

Get Prepared

BOOK AHEAD

Three Months Before
Book accommodations, especially if you're arriving in June or during an SF festival.

One Month Before
SF's top restaurants – including Benu and Three Kings – release reservations exactly 29 days in advance. Have your credit card ready to secure reservations – or join the waitlist.

One Week Before
Snap up show tickets, spa and cocktail bar reservations.

Manners Matter

- **Don't stare**, no matter how little or how much extra a San Franciscan happens to be wearing.
- **Ask before taking a photo** you intend to share – California has strict laws protecting image-usage rights.
- **Put phones away** to enjoy restaurant meals, movies and live shows where video isn't allowed.
- **Calling a person** may be considered intrusive, even if they gave you their number – text first.

San Francisco Nicknames

The City is how Bay Area residents refer to San Francisco (aka SF). '**Frisco**' was legendarily banned by SF's self-appointed 19th-century Emperor Norton – now used by rappers and comedians to get a rise out of local crowds ('What's good, Frisco?!'). '**San Fran**' makes locals shudder, and flags speakers as outsiders. **Karl the Fog** is the affectionate name for SF's marine layer – and its snarky social-media presence.

Things to Know

Coffee is an SF obsession. *Cortados* and Gibraltars are two names for the same SF-favorite drink, with a 1:1 ratio of steamed milk and espresso. Trends shift fast here: pour-overs are almost over but Yemeni coffee is everywhere, from brass pots to iced lattes.

Mocktails and alcohol-free wine appear on many SF drink menus, even at historic saloons and the city's top cocktail bars. SF bartenders know sometimes you want the flavor, company and vibes without the buzz.

Marijuana is legal in California for private use by adults age 18-plus. Places that sell weed are called dispensaries and resemble modern-day spas, with products on display shelves. Dispensaries are strictly regulated by the state and city – you'll need ID to enter. For your safety, never buy from street dealers.

TIPPING

Most SF service-industry workers only make minimum wage and rely on tips to make ends meet. Turnover is high, and many workers are new and/or overworked. Be kind, and only tip less than 15% when service is unforgivably awful.

Bartenders/ baristas per drink (or 15–20%)

Housekeeping staff daily

Restaurant servers

Taxis & rideshares

DAILY BUDGET

Budget: Less than $200

- Hostel bed: **$35–75**
- Mission burrito: **$9–14**
- Mission murals: **free**
- SF Opera standing-room ticket: **$10**

Midrange: $200–350

- Hotel: **$150–200**
- Ferry Building meal: **$30–50**
- Drag-show ticket: **$5–50**
- Muni one-day visitor passport: **$15**

Top End: More than $350

- Boutique hotel: **$200–375**
- Chef's tasting menu: **$90–450**
- Waymo ride: **$20**
- Outside Lands three-day pass: **$539**

Currency
US dollar ($)

Language
Primarily English – though 44% speak another language at home, often Spanish or Chinese.

Time Zone
Pacific Standard Time (GMT/UTC -8 hours)

KIT LEONG/SHUTTERSTOCK

EVERYONE'S WELCOME HERE

Most San Franciscans weren't born in California: we're San Franciscan by choice. SF became the world's first Sanctuary City in 1989 – immigrants, refugees, LGBTQ+ communities and people of all cultures, faiths and identities proudly call SF home. You are most welcome to be our neighbor, for however long you choose.

When to Go

Anytime you're free, San Francisco is ready to show you the time of your life – just throw on a coat, and maybe some glitter.

Whenever you arrive, you're right on time to see San Francisco put on a show. Year-round, there are film festivals, music events, art openings, theater premieres and cultural celebrations. In this multicultural, inter-faith city, festive lights illuminate long nights from Halloween through Lunar New Year, Holi, Nowruz, Ramadan, Passover, Easter and Solstice – some San Franciscans just keep them up year-round, because why not? No matter what you're celebrating, San Franciscans will gladly celebrate with you – and if we get to dress up and eat tasty treats, even better.

Party in the Streets

January/February: Chinatown celebrates Lunar New Year for a month with night markets and events, ending with a bang of fire-works and drums at the **Chinese New Year Parade** (p96).

April: Spring kicks off with Japantown's **Cherry Blossom Festival** (p113), when *taiko* drummers lead parades, fog tastes like teriyaki, and martial artists pound their hearts out with massive mallets at *mochitsuki* (mochi-pounding ceremonies).

June: The month of June is full of **Pride** here in the global hub of LGBTQ+ culture with events galore, especially the glorious final weekend: Friday is the world's largest **Trans March**, Saturday the **Dyke March** rolls into Castro's **Pink Party**, and Sunday is SF's million-strong **Pride Parade**.

September: Sun shines where it usually doesn't at **Folsom Street Fair** (p75), the massive outdoor kink festival in SF's official Leather & LGBTQ District with public spankings for charity.

San Francisco Weather

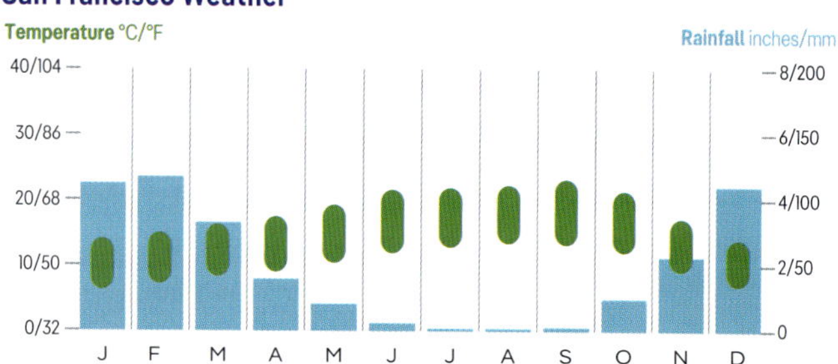

MICHAEL WARWICK/SHUTTERSTOCK

Chinese New Year Parade (p96)

Festivals Galore

April: Catch international award contenders at **SFFILM Fest**, the longest-running film festival in the Americas, with 150-plus films from 50 countries over two weeks – including premieres introduced by directors and stars.

August: Pinch-me-moments keep happening at **Outside Lands** (p180), a top US festival with three days of marquee acts in Golden Gate Park – plus gleeful debauchery at Wine Lands, Beer Lands and Grass Lands.

September: Rock the docks at **Portola Festival** (p133), a weekend rave with EDM and pop legends performing for bouncing, blissed-out crowds at Pier 80.

October: San Francisco scenery is stranger than fiction during **Litquake**, America's largest and wildest literary festival, with over three weeks of spoken word and author events culminating in a night of SF's best untold stories at LitCrawl.

ACCOMMODATIONS LOWDOWN

Pounce on rates under $200/night in summer; hold out for deals in winter. Hotel rates fluctuate wildly from summer peaks (June to July) to low season (January to February) – but you'll find that San Francisco takes a nonconformist approach to the seasons (and everything else).

Getting There

The Bay Area has three international airports: San Francisco (SFO), Oakland (OAK) and San Jose (SJC). Downtown SF is 25 to 60 minutes by car from SFO; BART is cheaper and faster.

From the Airport to the City Center

By BART

Bay Area Rapid Transit (BART; *bart.gov*) trains get you downtown in 30 minutes ($11.15), departing from the station at SFO's International Terminal. Purchase a reloadable physical **Clipper Card** at BART station kiosks, or download the scannable **Clipper app** *(clippercard.com)* for use on SF transit including BART, Muni streetcars and ferries.

By Rideshare

SF-invented rideshare services including **Lyft** and **Uber** serve SFO to get you to your SF destination (30 to 60 minutes; $40 to $60, not including surge pricing or tip). Download the app in advance and ensure you'll have battery power and wi-fi or cell coverage to use it. Rideshares depart from designated areas on Level 5 of the domestic parking garage.

By Taxi

Taxis to downtown San Francisco and other destinations citywide depart from designated zones outside the lower-level baggage-claim area at SFO (30 to 60 minutes; typically $55 to $65, plus tip). To book in advance, download the **Flywheel** app *(flywheel.com)*.

Other Points of Entry

Emeryville Station

Amtrak *(amtrak.com)* serves SF via Emeryville (near Oakland), with Thruway 99 bus connections to SF's Salesforce Transit Center. Amtrak's scenic *Coast Starlight* runs from Los Angeles to Seattle via Emeryville (35 hours; from $292); *California Zephyr* connects Chicago and Emeryville (51 hours; from $302).

Salesforce Transit Center

Daily **Greyhound** *(greyhound.com)* buses connect SF's Salesforce Transit Center with Los Angeles (eight to 12 hours; from $39) and destinations nationwide.

Green Tortoise

Green Tortoise *(greentortoise.com)* organizes trips along California's coast and to national parks via biodiesel-fueled sleeping coach (two to nine days; from $298).

Getting Around

Scenic San Francisco is best seen by cable car, streetcar, bicycle, skateboard and on foot. If you start to flag on uphill climbs, hop Muni or rideshare. Parking is hard to find and not cheap – plus tickets are steep. Given one-ways, slow streets and hills, driving is best avoided until it's time to leave town.

Walking

Limber up: San Francisco has 40-plus hills to summit, with stairway hikes to breathtaking vista points. SF's waterfront is flat and scenic from Dogpatch to Crissy Field, and Golden Gate Park stretches over 50 blocks to Ocean Beach.

Muni Metro & Streetcar

Schedules vary by line and service – vintage F-line streetcars (pictured) are charming but slow – and service is infrequent after 9pm. Muni Metro lines run underground downtown; see sfmta.com for station locations. Fares cost $2.85 with a reloadable **Clipper Card** *(clippercard.com);* included with Muni Visitor Passport (p37).

Cable Car

San Francisco's original steampunk trolley is a total joyride – no seat belts, no automatic brakes. Just grab a wooden bench or leather strap, and hold on for downhill slides. Cable cars are scenic, slow

FROM LEFT: NADIR KEKLIK/SHUTTERSTOCK, IV-OLGA/SHUTTERSTOCK

ESSENTIAL APP

For one-/three-/seven-day passes for cable cars, Muni metro, buses and streetcars, download **MuniMobile** *(sfmta.com/getting-around/muni/fares/munimobile).*

and frequent from 7am to about 11pm. Single rides cost $9; for more than one ride, get a Muni Visitor Passport.

Rideshare & Robotaxis

SF-invented rideshare services **Lyft** and **Uber** are widely used – expect waits and/or premium pricing during peak-use times. Off-peak fares within SF range from $7 to $23 for a direct-to-destination ride. Robotaxi service is also available in SF from **Waymo** *(waymo.com)*, aka Google's self-driving car fleet, via the Waymo One app.

Bus

Muni buses display their route number and final destination. Routes with an X or R are limited-stop or express services; Owl routes run after midnight. Fares cost $3 cash, $2.75 with a reloadable Clipper Card; included with Muni Visitor Passport.

BART

Bay Area Rapid Transit (BART; *bart.gov)* trains link SF to the East Bay and SFO. Within SF, BART is the fastest way to get from downtown to the Mission district – Clipper Card fares run $2.40.

Bicycle

Bike-sharing is available city-wide through Lyft's **Bay Wheels** *(lyft.com/bikes/bay-wheels)*; bring your own helmet. Locate an available bicycle nearby, then use your digital Clipper Card or Lyft app, scan the QR code, and unlock it. Check **San Francisco Bicycle Coalition** *(sfbike.org)* for maps and biking laws.

Public Transportation Essentials

Muni Stops

A detailed **Muni Street & Transit Map** is available free online *(sfmta.com)* and via the MuniMobile app. Some Muni bus and streetcar stops have a sheltered bench; others are indicated by a street sign and/or a yellow-painted stripe on a lamppost with the route number/letter.

Ways to Pay

You can pay digitally with MuniMobile or use a reusable digital or plastic Clipper Card for most San Francisco transit options, including cable cars. Fares can be paid in cash on cable cars, Muni buses and surface Muni streetcars (not underground metro); exact change is required. MuniMobile and Clipper Cards automatically deduct fares and apply transfers – only one Muni fare is deducted per 90-minute period. You can add a digital Clipper Card to your digital wallet to pay with your mobile device, or pay $3 to buy a physical Clipper Card from machines at BART or Muni metro stations. You'll need to tap your Clipper Card on a scanner to enter – and exit – BART and ferries. If your Clipper Card value is less than needed to exit, use a station Addfare machine to pay the remainder.

Muni Visitor Passport

For frequent use of Muni streetcars, metro, buses and cable cars, get a **Muni Visitor Passport** *(sfmta.com; one-/three-/seven-day pass $15/35/47)*. You can add a Muni Passport to your MuniMobile app or digital Clipper Card through the website or at a Clipper Card machine at BART and Muni metro stations. You can also purchase a physical passport at Muni kiosks; see *sfmta.com* for exact locations.

TICKET ZONES

Ticket zones apply only to BART and ferries. When you tap off at your destination, Clipper Cards automatically deduct the appropriate amount. If you forget to tap off, Clipper Card charges the maximum-distance fare.

KEEP YOUR TICKET

Hang onto your ticket – if you're caught without one, it's a $130 fine.

TICKET COSTS

Transportation type	Single ride (cash)	Single ride (Clipper/ MuniMobile)	Muni Visitor Passport
Cable car	$9	$9	included
Muni metro	N/A	$2.85	included
Muni bus & streetcar	$3	$2.85	included
BART	N/A	from $2.40	not included

A Few Surprises

Who knew you could communicate with sea lions, hang with hippies, rock fun fur and pogo like a pro? San Francisco did.

Sea Lions Rule

They were here first: sea lions won squatters' rights over SF's most coveted yacht docks at Pier 39 in 1990, and have been charming crowds with their slapstick antics ever since. You might also spot them body-surfing along Crissy Field's East Beach or frolicking at Aquatic Park, where they've been known to bump swimmers out of their way. Steer clear and don't try to keep up – at ocean swimming speeds up to 25mph, they're faster than Olympians. Even when you don't see them along San Francisco's waterfront, you'll often hear them barking – they're San Francisco's chattiest neighbors.

Any Excuse for a Costume

Time to play SF's favorite street-fashion guessing game: where are they going in that getup? That giant wig might mean a drag star is on her way to werk at **Oasis** (p74) – or a **Cliff's Variety** (p155) customer is rocking a new brunch lewk. Steampunk goggles could be Burning Man–bound gear – or accessories for **Gray Area** (p128) retrofuturist conferences. Leather chaps with fishnet stockings are fit for **Folsom Street Fair** (p75) – or just another night at the **Stud** (p74). Torn Metallica tees might be spotted exiting another surprise **Independent** (p112) show – or heading to another Metallica/**San Francisco Symphony** (p76) concert.

It's Always 4:20

You'll notice that the clock at **Haight & Ashbury** (p161) is stuck at 4:20, better known in the Bay Area since 1971 as International Bong Hit Time. A neighboring watch-repair shop fixed it, but within days it was stuck again at 4:20. Hippie Hill is more funky

OFFBEAT SAN FRANCISCO

Bison have roamed Golden Gate Park's **Buffalo Paddock** (p178) since 1891 – today these shaggy divas coolly ignore their fans.

Ever wanted to invent yoga poses, mock your ex at comedy open-mics or attempt DIY tattoos? **Faight Collective** (p166) is here for you.

Explore sound in 90-minute **Audium** (p112) 'room compositions,' from muscle-car hums to oddly endearing foghorn wheezes.

If you narrowly escaped an alien invasion with survivalist cartoonists, **Noc Noc** (p171) is where you'd all go for a drink afterwards.

NEVSKII DMITRII/SHUTTERSTOCK

Participant at Folsom Street Fair (p75)

and fragrant than usual on April 20, aka **420 Festival** (p180), when bands perform free shows and over-18s sample cannabis goodies to commemorate SF's successful efforts to legalize marijuana. You'll find 50-plus authorized dispensaries citywide, including the best-designed US dispensary according to *Architectural Digest*: the Castro's **Apothecarium** (p155). Check authorized SF dispensary listings and current laws at **California Cannabis** *(californiacannabis.org/city/san-francisco)*.

Punk's Not Dead

Punk explains a lot about SF: if you can learn three chords and start a band, imagine what else you can do. Tidal waves of SF punk from the 1970s and '80s (Dead Kennedys, the Avengers, Operation Ivy) keep rolling today (Green Day, Rancid, La Plebe) – catch the latest and loudest at legendary punk venues **Bottom of the Hill** (p130), **Mabuhay Gardens** (p98), **Savoy Tivoli** (p98) and **The Knockout** (p130). Dead Kennedys frontman Jello Biafra ran for SF mayor in 1979 on a platform scribbled on a bar napkin, requiring businessmen to wear clown shoes – he came in third, and remains a popular write-in candidate. Punk is everywhere lately: cyberpunk festivals at **Gray Area** (p128), Mission underground comics (p134), drag Punk Pride at **Chan National Queer Arts Center** (p128). Go ahead, punk: post a **Thrillhouse Records** (p130) flyer and start a band.

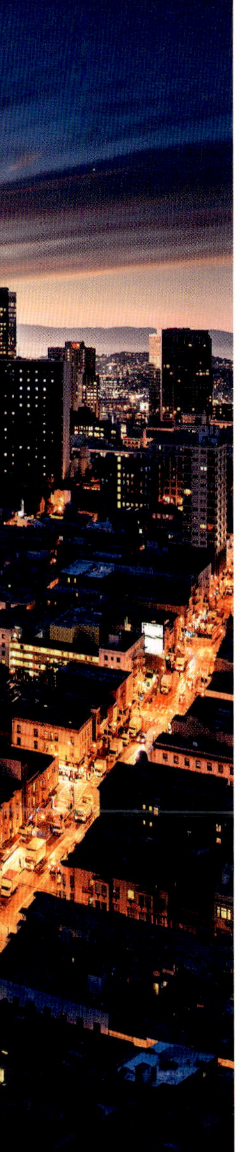

Explore San Francisco

Worth a Trip

San Francisco's Walking Tours

Downtown skyline (p63)
IM_PHOTO/SHUTTERSTOCK

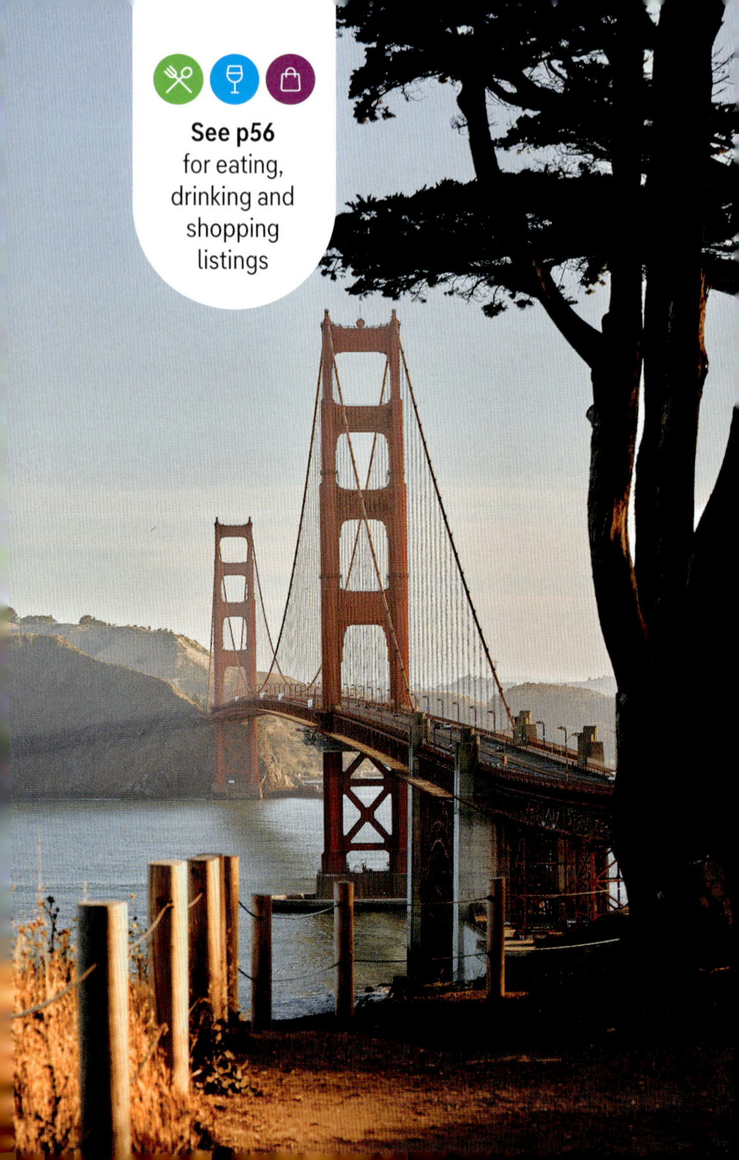

See p56
for eating,
drinking and
shopping
listings

Researched by
Alison Bing

Explore
The Presidio, Marina & Fisherman's Wharf

For centuries, Golden Gate Strait was the main entrance to San Francisco – note the shipwrecks dotting its shores. The Golden Gate Bridge now offers easier entry and spectacular views. Enter the Presidio military base that's now a coastal preserve to spot only-in-SF sights: rare shorebirds on a reclaimed airstrip, priceless sculptures hidden in the woods and goosebumps galore on the clothing-optional end of Baker Beach. The Marina has a waterfront fort overflowing with art, plus bars and chic boutiques in former cow pastures. At Fisherman's Wharf, you'll meet lazy sea lions, legendary cartoonists, pinball wizards, scientific geniuses and salty sailors.

Getting Around

Bus

Muni buses connect the Wharf, Marina and Presidio with points beyond; Golden Gate Transit crosses the bridge; and Presidio GO shuttles cover Presidio parks. Download maps and schedules – cell signal is variable in the Presidio.

Walk

The best way to see Fisherman's Wharf and the Presidio is at your own pace, with frequent stops for fun and photos.

Bicycle

Cover the waterfront on rental bikes with pickups at the Presidio and/or Wharf – but book ahead on weekends.

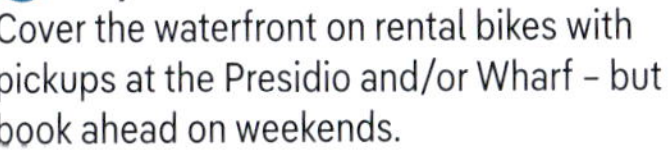

Golden Gate Bridge (p46)

BENJAMIN HEATH FOR LONELY PLANET

THE BEST

PHOTO-OP Golden Gate Bridge (p46)

SUN TRAP Crissy Field (p48)

SCIENTIFIC WONDER Exploratorium (p47)

URBAN WILDLIFE Pier 39 Sea Lions (p54)

PICNIC PERCH Tunnel Tops (p48)

A
B
C
D
1
2
3
4
5
6
Cow Hollow
Francisco St
Chestnut St
Lombard St
Moulton St
Greenwich St
Pixley St
Filbert St
Union St
Divisadero St
Scott St
Pierce St
Steiner St
Fillmore St
COW HOLLOW
0 250 m
0 0.1 miles
16
50
52
18
22
25
21
51
43
20
44
24
40
55
41
53
Golden Gate Bridge
Fort Point
Golden Gate Bridge Welcome Center
Military Intelligence Service Historic Learning Center
Crissy Field
Old Mason St
39
49
Tunnel Tops
Palace of Fine Arts
5
Baker St
Broderick St
Richardson Ave
1
Walt Disney Family Museum
23
MAIN POST
San Francisco National Military Cemetery
Presidio of San Francisco
Presidio Officers' Club
Lyon St
PRESIDIO
Presidio of San Francisco
Presidio Golf Course
Spire
Pacific Ave
Lake St
California St
Park Presidio Blvd
THE RICHMOND
Geary Blvd
0 500 m
0 0.25 miles
San Francisco Bay
Fort Mason Center
Magic Theatre
3
2
26
4
BATS Improv
42
19
Victoria Park
Franklin St
Fort Mason
Macarthur Ave
Marina Blvd
38

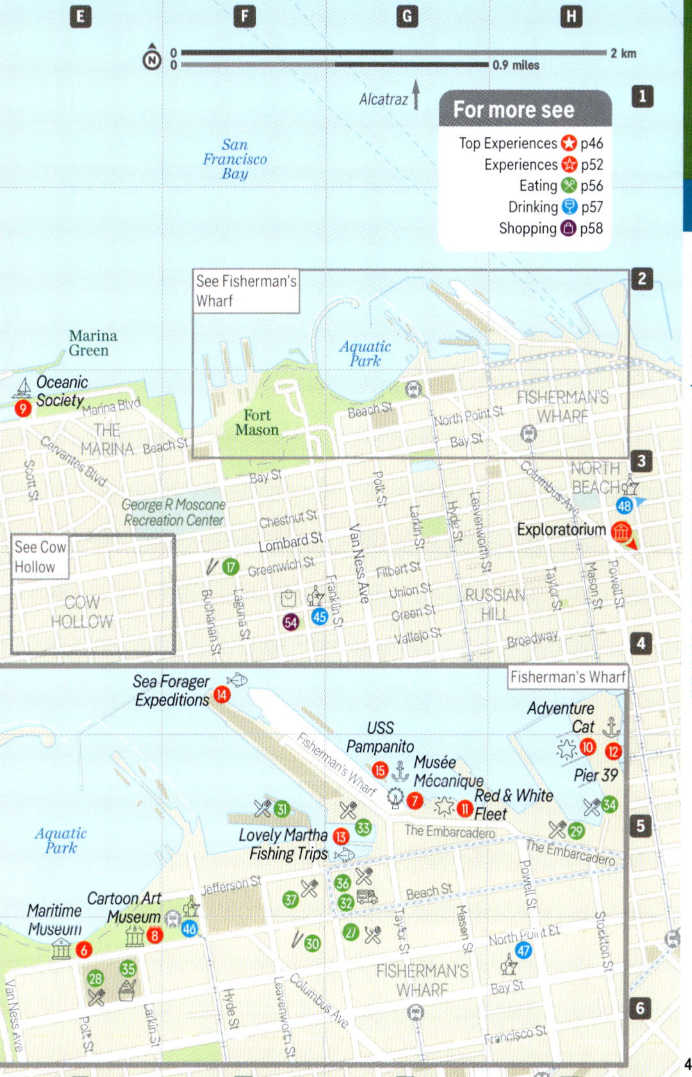
For more see
Top Experiences p46
Experiences p52
Eating p56
Drinking p57
Shopping p58
San Francisco Bay
Alcatraz
0.9 miles
2 km
See Fisherman's Wharf
See Cow Hollow
Marina Green
Oceanic Society
Marina Blvd
THE MARINA
Beach St
Cervantes Blvd
Scott St
Fort Mason
Aquatic Park
Beach St
North Point St
Bay St
FISHERMAN'S WHARF
NORTH BEACH
Columbus Ave
Exploratorium
George R Moscone Recreation Center
Bay St
Chestnut St
Lombard St
Greenwich St
Polk St
Larkin St
Hyde St
Leavenworth St
Van Ness Ave
Franklin St
Filbert St
Union St
Green St
Vallejo St
RUSSIAN HILL
Taylor St
Mason St
Powell St
Broadway
COW HOLLOW
Buchanan St
Laguna St
Fisherman's Wharf
Sea Forager Expeditions
Adventure Cat
USS Pampanito
Musée Mécanique
Pier 39
Red & White Fleet
Fisherman's Wharf
The Embarcadero
Lovely Martha Fishing Trips
Aquatic Park
Jefferson St
Beach St
Cartoon Art Museum
Maritime Museum
Taylor St
Mason St
Powell St
North Point St
Stockton St
FISHERMAN'S WHARF
Bay St
Van Ness Ave
Polk St
Larkin St
Hyde St
Leavenworth St
Columbus Ave
Francisco St

★ TOP EXPERIENCE

Golden Gate Bridge

No other bridge puts on a show like this. Morning mists lift to reveal the Golden Gate Bridge, glowing orange-red against blue skies. Stick around for the late-afternoon grand finale: as fog swallows commuter traffic, art deco towers float above the clouds. Magic.

MAP P44 **A2**

PLANNING TIP
If you get cold or tired walking the 1.7-mile bridge span, catch any Golden Gate Transit bus back from the northern toll plaza.

Scan this QR code for bridge information and free tours.

Iconic Design

Hard to picture San Francisco without its iconic art deco suspension bridge – but the US War Department almost nixed this design in favor of a chunky concrete bridge with caution-yellow stripes. Local architects Gertrude Comfort Morrow and Irving Morrow realized that ships may pass in the night, but San Franciscans would have to live with the bridge every day. Working with engineer Joseph B Strauss, the Morrows submitted a counter-proposal to harmonize with the natural environment: a sleek suspension bridge painted a signature shade known as International Orange. Even though the War Department owned the land on either side, the City of San Francisco gave the ingenious orange bridge design the green light.

Death-Defying Feats

Stop by the **Golden Gate Bridge Welcome Center** to witness precarious construction work in progress, captured in jaw-dropping vintage photos – riveters balanced atop swaying cables 80 stories high, while divers plunged 110ft underwater with only a rubber hose for air. Take a moment to admire the bridge's signature color, still touched up by a daredevil crew of 34 painters suspended from the 764ft suspension towers.

★ TOP EXPERIENCE

Exploratorium

Can you stop time, sculpt fog or make sand sing? At San Francisco's living laboratory of science and human perception, you'll discover superhuman abilities you never knew you had – and emerge from the hands-on exhibits with renewed wonder.

MAP P44 **H3**

Mind-Expanding Experiments

Is there a science to skateboarding? How big is your blind spot? Can plankton make art? You have questions about life's mysteries, and the Exploratorium helps you find answers. MacArthur Genius–winning designers create 700-plus hands-on exhibits to engage all the senses: try static-electricity hairdos, send whispered messages to strangers, and dance with your own rainbow shadows in a light-refraction room.

Tactile Dome

Slip off your shoes and step inside the mysterious geodesic Tactile Dome, and suddenly you're enveloped in total darkness. Rely on your sense of touch to guide you through an elaborate labyrinth – and emerge exhilarated, with hands tingling. Advance reservations, socks and separate ticket required.

Learning Laboratory

The Exploratorium's mind-bending exhibits are inspired by Frank Oppenheimer, a physicist who worked on the atom bomb with his brother Robert, but was blacklisted during the McCarthy era and barred from scientific research. He dedicated the rest of his life to promoting science in the public interest, teaching at public high schools and founding the Exploratorium in 1969. Today the Exploratorium covers Pier 15 – including the mysterious **Fog Bridge** and other free outdoor exhibits.

PLANNING TIP
At **After Dark Thursdays** *(6pm to 10pm; $23)*, 18-plus crowds bond over glow-in the-dark mad-scientist cocktails, technology-assisted sing-alongs, special events and exhibits. Book ahead.

Scan this QR code for hours, tickets and events.

★ TOP EXPERIENCE

The Presidio

Spies, Yoda, Andy Goldsworthy sculptures, Walt Disney drawings: SF's best-kept secrets are revealed along Presidio hiking paths. This retired army base is now a public park packed with attractions – including sweeping Golden Gate Bridge views previously only seen by top brass and passing commuters.

MAP P44 **B4**

PLANNING TIP
Presidio park rangers lead 4pm **Tunnel Tops Campfire Talks** *(free)*, introducing the legendary Indigenous healers, Buffalo Soldiers and Cold War spies whose footsteps you're walking in.

Scan this QR code for park trails, events and self-guided adventures.

Back to Nature

Started in 1776 as a Spanish military post built by conscripted Ohlone people, the Presidio ('fort' in Spanish) retired from military duty in 1996 to become a national park. To allow wildlife to thrive, commuter traffic was rerouted underground – revealing glorious views at **Tunnel Tops** park, plus nature-themed **Outpost Playground**. On hot days, race crowds to **Baker Beach**, the Presidio cove with spectacular Golden Gate views – plus nude sunbathing behind the rocks on the clothing-optional, gay-friendly, no-photography-allowed north end. Picnickers and sand-castle architects stick to the south end.

Happy Trails

Inspirational 1.9-mile **Ecology Trail** leads through redwoods to Inspiration Point, then reaches the Presidio's artistic pinnacle: Andy Goldsworthy's **Spire**, made from reclaimed cypresses. Adventurous hikers take on 2.7-mile **Batteries to Bluffs Trail**, winding above Baker Beach to Golden Gate Bridge vistas. **Crissy Field** is a reclaimed military landing strip where puppies chase kite-fliers, and windsurfers skim bay waters along **East Beach**. Stroll, jog, bike, skate or roll along flat, wheelchair-accessible paths to Fort Point and the Golden Gate Bridge.

Military Secrets, Revealed

For two centuries, the Presidio prepared for invasions that never arrived. Costing $100 million in today's

BRYAN KELLEY/SHUTTERSTOCK

terms, 102 cannons were mounted at **Fort Point** *(free; 10am-5pm Fri-Sun)* for the Civil War – but Confederate ships never made it this far. **Battery Bluff** guns weren't fired in WWI, and Nike nuclear missile operations in **Battery Caulfield** were suspended in 1974. **Presidio Officers' Club** was long off-limits to civilians – now its **Heritage Gallery** *(free; 11am-4pm Fri-Sun)* showcases the Presidio's history as ancestral Ohlone homeland for 10,000-plus years and its military service to Spain, Mexico and the US. At **Military Intelligence Service Historic Learning Center** *(njahs.org/building-640; adult/child $10/free; noon-5pm Sat & Sun)*, see where Japanese American soldiers trained for high-risk WWII spy missions while their families were incarcerated as supposed 'enemy aliens' under Executive Order 9066.

QUICK BREAK
Forgot to pack a picnic? No problem: **Presidio Pop Up** food trucks line the Parade Grounds from 9am to 3pm (to 4:30pm on weekends).

Explore the Wharf's Wild Side

Brace for an action-packed afternoon along SF's wharf. Take selfies with sea lions, stare down sharks, hop a submarine and swap stories with sailors over spiked coffee. Yes, the Wharf can get touristy – its family-friendly attractions draw all-age crowds most weekends – but this quick walk reveals its wild side.

START	END	LENGTH
Pier 39	Buena Vista Cafe	1 mile; one hour

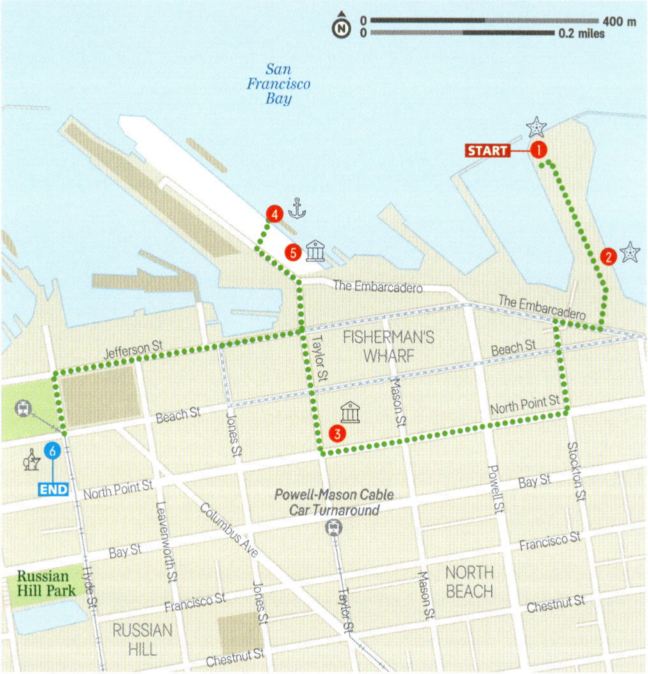

1 Sun with Sea Lions

Take a selfie with SF's favorite sea-lebrity guests. When sea lions took over **Pier 39** (p54) docks in 1990, California recognized their squatters' rights – they were here first, after all – and yacht owners got bumped to accommodate a barking bunch of slapstick comedians as neighbors. Keep a safe distance – they may be adorable, but sea mammals can get territorial.

2 Descend into the Shark Tank

Cross the pier to walk underwater at the **Aquarium of the Bay** (p54). Descend into underwater chambers lined with glowing jellyfish tanks, then step into glass tubes jutting deep into San Francisco Bay. Suddenly you're surrounded by marine life – sharks circle overhead, while manta rays perform underwater ballets.

3 See the Trippiest Spot in SF

Named for SF's 1930s Black union leader, Bill Chester **Longshoremen's Union Hall** works hard and partied hard at the 1966 Trips Festival, when partiers spiked the punch with then-legal LSD. The rest is hippie history: festival promoter Bill Graham launched the Fillmore with festival performers the Grateful Dead. Organizer Stewart Brand hallucinated a military computer shrunk to palm-size – 40 years later, Steve Jobs thanked Brand for the inspiration.

4 Enter Stealth Mode

Take a deep dive into history at Pier 45 inside **USS Pampanito** (p55), a 1943 submarine that survived WWII to tell hair-raising tales of torpedo battles in onboard audio tours. Head below decks to inspect shiny brass knobs and mysterious hydraulic valves that make minimalist modern technology seem boring – these seemingly archaic instruments enabled the *Pampanito* to survive deep dives up to 600ft. Living quarters here seem impossibly close – If you get claustrophobic, surface for commanding deck views.

5 Play the Wildest Games in the West

Cheap thrills await inside the massive Pier 45 boat shed that now houses vintage arcade **Musée Mécanique** (p54). For a buck, start a Wild West saloon brawl, race antique roadsters and save the planet from asteroids.

6 Stop for 'Coffee'

With 175 years of Wharf history and gossip, you're ready to swap stories with sailors over the Wharf's enduring beverage of choice: booze-spiked Irish coffee at **Buena Vista Cafe** (p58), the Wild West saloon where communal tables and creaking floorboards have miraculously survived a century of pounding. Stick around for dessert: sourdough bread pudding doused with whiskey, naturally.

EXPERIENCES

See Presidio Movie Magic

MOVIE MEMORABILIA

MAP: 1 P44 C3

Fans of fairy-tale heroines and Jedi sci-fi legends, the Presidio has hidden gems for you. See how your favorite animated Disney movies were made at the **Walt Disney Family Museum** *(waltdisney.org; adult/student/child $25/20/15)*, featuring early animation cels – courtesy of Walt's daughter Diane Disney Miller – plus major showcases of the trailblazing women designers who made Disney magic. *Star Wars* creator George Lucas transformed the Presidio's former military hospital into Lucasfilm HQ at the Letterman Campus – you'll spot fans taking selfies by the Yoda fountain out front. When the building is open, check out movie memorabilia in the lobby – and consult the **SFFILM** *(sffilm.org)* website for festival screenings in its state-of-the-art Premier Theater.

Make Art, Not War at Fort Mason

ARTS COMPLEX

MAP: 2 P44 C6

During WWII, **Fort Mason Center** *(fortmason.org; free)* shipped out 23 million tons of supplies – now it supplies creative inspiration to 1.4 million visitors annually. Dockside nonprofit **SF Camerawork** *(sfcamerawork.org; free)* has showcased next-wave photographers since 1974, while **Haines Gallery** *(hainesgallery.com; free)* represents leading global contemporary artists like Ai Weiwei, and **Arion Press** *(arionpress.com; free)* showcases letterpress art-book collaborations. On Fort Mason's pier, Herbst Pavilion's arsenal of events includes **FOG Design+Art** *(fogfair.com; admission $35-40)* in winter, **San Francisco Art Fair** *(sanfranciscoartfair.com; admission $35-65)* in spring, and **Renegade Craft Fair** *(renegadecraft.com; free)* and **West Coast Craft Fair** *(westcoastcraft.com; free)* in both summer and fall. Capture inspiration with art and craft supplies from well-stocked **Flax Art & Design** *(flaxart.com)*.

Catch Shows at Fort Mason

PERFORMING ARTS

Pushing boundaries since 1967, **Magic Theatre** (MAP: 3 P44 C6; *magictheatre.org; tickets $35-75)* stages breakthrough works like *Jerry Garcia in the Lower Mission*, plus freeform jazz services for St John Coltrane Church. **Bay Area Theater Sports** *(aka BATS Improv;* MAP: 4 P44 C6; *improv.org; tickets adult/student $25/20)* hosts raucous improvised comedy in a range of styles: madcap musicals, SF rom-coms, B-movie sci-fi. Feeling brave? Book improv workshops online.

Strike Poses at the Palace of Fine Arts

MONUMENT

MAP: 5 P44 **D3**

Like many a fine romance, the **Palace of Fine Arts** *(palaceoffinearts.com; free)* was a folly that wasn't expected to last. The California arts-and-crafts movement's leading architect Bernard Maybeck originally built this Greco-Roman ruin in plaster for the 1915 Panama-Pacific International Expo, but San Francisco decided to keep the Palace as a souvenir after the fair, and eventually recast it in concrete. Join shy prom dates and shivering brides posing for photos under the Rotunda frieze, showing 'art under attack by materialists, with idealists leaping to her rescue' – a timeless sentiment.

Find Underwater Treasure at Aquatic Park Bathhouse

ART LANDMARK

MAP: 6 P44 **E6**

A monumental hint to unwashed sailors, this ship-shaped 1939 Streamline Moderne landmark is decked out with gloriously restored marine-themed masterpieces that upstage rotating **Maritime Museum** *(maritime.org; free)* exhibits. Each floor features original 1930s deco artworks: surreal underwater lobby murals by Ann Sonia Medalie and Hilaire Hiler, Beniamino Bufano's mezzanine seal and toad sculptures, and top-floor tugboat murals and wavy terrazzo floors by Shirley Staschen and Richard Ayer. Black avant-garde sculptor Sargent Johnson created the stunning carved green-slate marquee doorway, plus the veranda's mesmerizing aquatic mosaics with Moroccan mosaic artist Mohammed Zyani. To protest plans to include a private casino in this public facility, Johnson deliberately left unfinished the mosaics on the eastern side. Johnson won: the east wing is now a senior center.

PARTY OF THE CENTURY

San Francisco rebuilt from the ground up after the 1906 earthquake, and to celebrate its comeback and the opening of the Panama Canal, SF invited the world to an epic party: 1915's **Panama-Pacific International Expo**. Minor hitch: SF wasn't big enough to host everyone. Landfill extended the northern shoreline to accommodate fairgrounds covering almost 400 city blocks. PPIE had it all: the 435ft Tower of Jewels glittering with 100,000 cut-glass gems; flashy technology, including a 14-ton Underwood typewriter; eyebrow-raising modern art at the Palace of Fine Arts; and forward-thinking events, including the International Conference of Women Workers to Promote Peace.

BEST WAYS TO SAIL AWAY

When the fog lifts and sun shines on the bay, only one thing tops waterfront strolls: sailing away.

Oceanic Society

MAP: 9 P44 **E3**

Naturalist-led Pacific whale-watching expeditions during migration seasons *(oceanicsociety.org; 7½ hours; $300 per person).*

Adventure Cat

MAP: 10 P44 **H5**

Skim across the bay with the wind in your hair on catamaran trips, including 'Sail and Jail' getaways to/from Alcatraz *(adventurecat.com; 90-mintue cruise adult/child $35/75, Sail and Jail $125).*

Red & White Fleet

MAP: 11 P44 **G5**

Sunset cruises since 1892 – ring boxes just keep popping. Triple-decker boats offer full bars and snacks *(redandwhite.com; one-hour cruise adult/child $39/29, two-hour sunset cruise $58/38).*

Game on at Musée Mécanique

ARCADE

MAP: 7 P44 **G5**

Pier 45's massive boatshed can scarcely contain this collection of 300-plus vintage mechanical amusements. For a buck at **Musée Mécanique** *(museemecanique.com; free)*, you can battle Space Invaders, get your fortune told by robotic wizards, peep at belly dancers through a vintage Mutoscope or get hypnotized by a Ferris wheel made of toothpicks.

Meet Superheroes at the Cartoon Art Museum

MUSEUM

MAP: 8 P44 **E6**

Funded by Bay Area cartoon legend Charles M Schultz of Peanuts fame, the **Cartoon Art Museum** *(cartoonart.org; adult/child $10/4)* showcases cartoon classics, including Batman covers, Calvin & Hobbes strips, Edward Gorey's Goth monsters and Trina Robbins' trailblazing feminist comics. At events, mingle with comic legends and local Pixar animators.

Go for Family Fun on Pier 39

ENTERTAINMENT ZONE

MAP: 12 P44 **H5**

Sea lions took over **Pier 39** *(pier39.com; free)* yacht docks in 1990 and have been making a public display of themselves ever since – up to 2100 of SF's favorite sea-lebrities lounge here daily. Families enjoy Pier 39's amusement-park atmosphere without prohibitive entry fees – antique **San Francisco Carousel** *(10am-8pm; $6 per ride)* twinkles with 1800 lights and hand-painted local landmarks. At not-for-profit, Smithsonian-affiliated **Aquarium of the Bay** *(aquariumofthebay.org; adult/child $28/20)*, visit

ROSIE THE RIVETER & FRIENDS

During WWII, women and men came to the SF Bay to serve as shipbuilders. You may recall the poster of muscle-flaunting Rosie the Riveter proclaiming 'We Can Do It' – the model was Bay Area naval worker Naomi Parker Fraley. Bay Area shipbuilders worked long hours to turn the tides of WWII, building an entire ship every day for the duration of the war – nearly half of all US military cargo ships were built by the bay, plus one in five warships. By the 1950s, Bay Area women were staffing a new local industry: silicon-chip manufacturing.

24,000 aquatic creatures in their underwater habitats – walk through shark tanks, get mesmerized by jellies and join a fish-feeding frenzy.

Fishing at Pier 45 FISHING DOCKS

On Pier 45, behind crab stalls number 8 and 9, you'll spot swinging doors with a mysterious sign: 'Passageway to the Boats.' You've found SF sailors' secret passageway to the Wharf's working fishing docks. For over a century, four generations of the Rescino family have fished these waters on their boat the **Lovely Martha** (MAP: 13 P44 G5; *lovelymartha.com; fishing trips half-/full day $150/200, Bay cruises $15*), so they know how and where to hook halibut, bass and salmon in season. Book half- or full-day trips and get your California fishing license via Lovely Martha's website. For urban fishing adventures on land, James Beard Award–winning Kirk Lombard runs 'from hook to cook' **Sea Forager** (MAP: 14 P44 F4; *expeditions $79-159*) expeditions, where you fish and forage for ingredients around SF to assemble into a sustainable seafood feast.

Enter Stealth Mode Aboard USS Pampanito HISTORIC SUBMARINE

MAP: 15 P44 G5

Explore a restored submarine that did six tours of WWII duty and survived to tell the tale. The award-winning audio tour will have you holding your breath as you hear submariners' stories of sudden attacks and tense moments in underwater stealth mode aboard the **USS Pampanito** (*maritime.org; adult/child $25/10*). Mind your head as you explore tight quarters – blink and you might miss the tiny galley kitchen that fed a crew of 80, complete with built-in ice-cream maker.

LISTINGS

Best Places for...

$ Budget $$ Midrange $$$ Top End

See p44 for map of locations

Eating

Prime Picnics

Lucca Delicatessen $

16 C1

Italian deli classics since 1929 – mighty meatball sandwiches, homemade minestrone soup, spicy-salami Calabrian subs with rustic Chianti. *9am-6pm*

Komeya No Bento $

17 F4

Proper Japanese *bentō* (lunchbox): sustainable salmon or duck breast, sushi rice, dashi broth and side salads. *11am-2:30pm & 5-6:30pm Tue-Sat*

La Fromagerie $

18 B1

Classic French sandwiches: Parisien ham and Gruyère cheese, or Toulouse duck with manchego. *11am-6pm Mon & Tue, from 10am Wed-Sun*

Fort Mason Outdoor Markets $

19 C6

Sunday farmers markets bring readymade food vendors, while Friday nights feature food trucks and local makers. *4-9pm Fri, 9:30am-1:30pm Sun*

Not-So-Fast Food

Blue Barn Gourmet $

20 C1

California-grown salads and sandwiches with gourmet fixings – artisan cheeses, caramelized onions, heirloom tomatoes. *11am-8pm*

Viva Goa $

21 B1

Tangy, warming Goan favorites – prawn *xacuti* (toasted-coconut curry), pillowy naan, made-to-order samosas. *11am-3pm & 5-10pm Tue-Sat, 5-10pm Sun*

Causewell's $$

22 B1

Come for 'fancy-pants burgers' – local beef with pork confit, melted onions and Taleggio cheese. *11am-9pm Tue-Fri, 10am-10:30pm Sat, 10am-9pm Sun*

Date-Night Dining

Dalida $$

23 C4

Top Chef powerhouse Laura Ozylimaz brings sumptuous Mediterranean flavors to the bay – Istanbul stuffed mussels, Aleppo roast chicken, Yemeni lamb stew, mmmm. *11:30am-2pm & 5-9pm Fri-Wed, 11am-2pm Thu*

Atelier Crenn $$$

24 D2

James Beard Award–winning, triple-Michelin-starred Dominique Crenn creates edible art inspired by SF's seafaring legends and her own Sonoma farmstead. *5-9pm Tue-Sat*

A16 $$

25 B1

Romance is ably assisted by James Beard Award–winning wood-fired pizzas, house-cured salami and a deep Italian wine list. *5-9pm Mon-Thu, noon-9:30pm Fri-Sun*

Greens $$

26 C6

Since 1979 Fort Mason's waterfront mess hall has

been commandeered by women star chefs, inventing flavor-bomb vegetarian dishes with organic ingredients. *11:30am-2:30pm & 5-9pm Tue-Sun*

Brunch at the Wharf

Abacá $$

27 G6

Friends become family over Filipino soul food, like fried chicken and pandan waffles. *7-9am & 5-9pm Mon, Tue, Thu & Fri, 8am-1:30pm & 5-9pm Sat & Sun*

Palette Tea House $$

28 E6

Swanky dim sum – Wagyu potstickers, lobster dumplings – with specialty tea or creative cocktails. *11:30am-7:30pm Sun-Thu, to 8pm Fri & Sat*

Eagle Cafe $$

 H5

Brunch with SF perks: crab Benedicts, sourdough French toast and eagle's-eye views over Pier 39. *8am-3pm*

Surisan $

 F6

Warm up with Cal-Korean specials – get savory *pajun* pancakes with shrimp and bacon, plus matcha mojitos. *9am-2pm & 5-9pm*

Ultra-Fresh Seafood

Scoma's $$$

31 F5

Fishing boats docked out front supply ultra-fresh 'pier-to-plate' classics – from decadent Dungeness crab cakes to SF's definitive *cioppino* (seafood stew). *noon-9pm*

Codmother Fish & Chips $

 G5

Crisp, fried-to-order Pacific cod with malt vinegar or tartar sauce plus garlic fries at outdoor picnic tables. *11:30am-6pm Sun-Thu, to 7pm Fri & Sat*

Fisherman's Wharf Crab Stands $

 G5

Steaming cauldrons of Dungeness crab at Pier 45 sidewalk crab-stands are ready for feasts. *11:30am-9pm winter through spring*

Fog Harbor Fish House $$

34 H5

Shimmering Bay views frame sustainable local favorites like petrale sole, Pacific cod and Dungeness crab simply prepared, so flavors shine through. *11am-9pm*

Quick Bites at the Wharf

The Original Ghirardelli Chocolate & Ice Cream Shop $

35 E6

SF's original c 1852 chocolate company. *9am-midnight Wed-Sat, to 11pm Sun-Tue*

Tanguito $

 G5

Hole-in-the-wall serving hearty Argentine fare – steak sandwiches, plump chicken empanadas – at outdoor tables. *1:30am-6:30pm Tue-Fri, noon-7:30pm Sat, noon-6pm Sun*

In-N-Out Burger $

 F5

Follow the '50s bent-arrow logo for prime chuck beef burgers, fries and shakes, with ingredients you can pronounce. *10:30am-1am Sun-Thu, to 1:30am Fri & Sat*

Drinking

Coffee Breaks

Equator Coffee

 C6

Queue for fair-trade espresso at Fort Mason's gatehouse, and catch rays in wind-sheltered outdoor seating. *6:30am-5pm Mon-Fri, from 7am Sat & Sun*

Dynamo Donut & Coffee

 D3

Power hikes with Proyecto Diaz coffee and doughnuts in SF flavors, from berry Pride to May the Fourth chocolate. *8am-1pm Wed-Fri, to 4pm Sat & Sun*

Coffee Bodega

40 D2

Beans grown, roasted and delivered directly from Costa Rican cooperatives make sensational coffee. *8am-4pm Mon-Fri, 9am-5pm Sat, 9am-4pm Sun*

Telve Coffee Shop

41 D2

Coffee breaks become major events over cardamom-spiced Turkish coffee brewed in *cezve* (brass pots). *7am-7pm Sun-Thu, to 9pm Fri & Sat*

Toast-Worthy Bars

The Interval

 C6

Pause for International Orange aged-gin aperitifs at the Long Now Foundation's bar, dedicated to long-term thinking. *5-10pm Mon, 10am-11pm Tue-Fri, 5-11pm Sat, 3-10pm Sun*

California Wine Merchant

 C1

Nonstop block party for 50-plus years, pouring 50 well-chosen wines by the glass/half-glass. *1-10pm Mon-Wed, to 11pm Thu-Sat, 2-7pm Sun*

For the Record

44 D1

Retro dream den with disco balls, DJs spinning vinyl, and EP-style menus of radio-hit-themed cocktails. *5pm-midnight Tue-Thu, to 2am Fri, 3pm-2am Sat*

Better Sunday

 F4

Friendly 'feel-good bottle shop' for alcohol-free brews and zero-proof 'social tonics.' *3-7pm Mon-Thu, from noon Fri-Sun*

Drink Like a Sailor at the Wharf

Buena Vista Cafe

 F6

Century-old saloon slinging Irish coffee to naval officers, cannery workers and Food Network stars alike. *9am-11pm Sun-Thu, to midnight Fri & Sat*

Scoma's Lounge

see 31

Boats dock outside this landmark bar for SF's finest Manhattan, barrel-aged for 1965 nights to honor Scoma's 1965 opening. *noon-9pm*

Sweetie's Art Bar

 H6

Iron chandeliers and jazz combos swing at this pirate's den serving legit navy-strength gin slings, draft Hazy IPA and thin-crust pizza. *4:30-10:30pm*

Pier 23

 H3

Mingle with artists and sailors in the waterfront gallery while you wait your turn for local brews, fish tacos and crab cakes on the bayfront patio. *11:30am-6pm Wed-Mon*

Shopping

Get Equipped in the Marina

Sports Basement

49 C3

The Presidio's former PX (provisions warehouse) stocks gear, bikes and sporting equipment to rent, buy or trade. *10am-8pm Mon-Fri, 9am-7pm Sat & Sun*

MARLEYPUG/SHUTTERSTOCK

Pier 23

Marine Layer

 50 C1

Take the edge off coastal breezes with made-in-California chore coats and that ingenious 'shacket' (heavyweight flannel overshirt) seen on SF surfers. *11am-7pm Mon-Sat, to 6pm Sun*

Books Inc

 51 B1

Independent bookseller supplying Presidio birdwatching books, botany field guides and riveting beach reads by local authors. *10am-10pm Mon-Sat, to 9pm Sun*

Aggregate Supply

52 B1

Look sharp yet casual with California-cool fits – Eat Dust Oakland chinos, breezy Rachel Comey top, Clare V woven bag, done. *11am-6pm Mon-Sat, to 5pm Sun*

Artful Gifts

ATYS

53 D2

Ingenious decor and SF gifts, from SF-woven psychedelic fiber art to steak knives made with reclaimed steel from the Golden Gate Bridge. *noon-6pm Tue-Sun*

Pyarful

 54 F4

Playful South Asian–inspired gifts and stationery, from greeting cards with tea proclaiming 'Chai miss you,' to badges of honor bragging 'Didn't become a doctor.' *noon-6pm Thu-Sun*

Nikoniko Gifts

 55 D2

Japanese and Korean heritage boutique lined with gift suggestions, from goldfish-shaped welcome soap to themed gift bundles wrapped in elegant *furoshiki* cloths. *noon-6pm Thu-Mon*

★ WORTH A TRIP

Alcatraz

Even from afar, the infamous prison island of Alcatraz is more chilling than San Francisco fog. Over 175 years, 'the Rock' witnessed death-defying escape attempts, punishment for gay soldiers, and FBI standoffs with American Indian leaders. Now it's a national park, with gripping audio tours and eye-opening history exhibits.

GETTING THERE
Alcatraz City Cruises *(cityexperiences.com; night/behind the scenes $60/105 per person)* offers popular tours, **Adventure Cat** offers 'Sail and Jail' excursions, and **Red & White Fleet** offers Alcatraz bay cruises.

Scan for events, history, accessibility and visitor information.

Fortress Alcatraz

Visitors arrive by ferry near Building 64, where riveting videos reveal the sunny island's dark history. Alcatraz became the first US fort in 1859, with dungeon cages for Civil War deserters and Native American 'unfriendlies' – including 19 Hopi who refused to send their children to government boarding schools, where Hopi language and religion were forbidden. The cellblocks were expanded to imprison WWI conscientious objectors and gay soldiers awaiting court-martial. Prison reformer Alice Park documented the harsh treatment and extreme conditions – and facing public scrutiny and mounting costs, the military handed Alcatraz to the Federal Bureau of Prisons in 1933.

Life on the Rock

Alcatraz was upgraded to a maximum-security penitentiary for high-profile Prohibition gangsters, from Chicago's Al Capone to Harlem's Bumpy Johnson. First-person accounts of daily life on 'the Rock' are included on the cellhouse audio tour, covering mealtime rules ('Do not exceed the ration. Do not waste food.'), censored library books (war yes, romance no) and 35 escape attempts (one possibly successful). Rule-breakers were subjected to solitary confinements in lightless, cold, 5ft-wide D-block cells. Prisons were routinely segregated, but Black inmate Robert Lipscomb organized protests at Alcatraz demanding desegregation and equal treatment

ONEINCHPUNCH/SHUTTERSTOCK

under US law. Punished with solitary confinement, Lipscomb kept filing appeals until Alcatraz closed, 10 months before the 1964 Civil Rights Act passed.

Red Power on Alcatraz

When the last federal prison on Alcatraz closed in the 1960s, Native Americans claimed sovereignty and occupied the island, standing their ground against FBI raids from 1969 to 1971. Thousands of Native Americans participated in the protest and gained public support, pressuring President Nixon to recognize Native treaties and restore Native territory. As you walk uphill, notice the signs Alcatraz Red Power Movement activists left behind – including 'Home of the Free Indian Land' on the water tower. Every Thanksgiving, the International Indian Treaty Council celebrates Indigenous People's Day with a sunrise ceremony on Alcatraz.

TAKE A BREAK
There's no food for sale on Alcatraz, so bring your own or pick up snacks on board Alcatraz ferries to enjoy dockside. Hot drinks are available from the Building 64 bookstore.

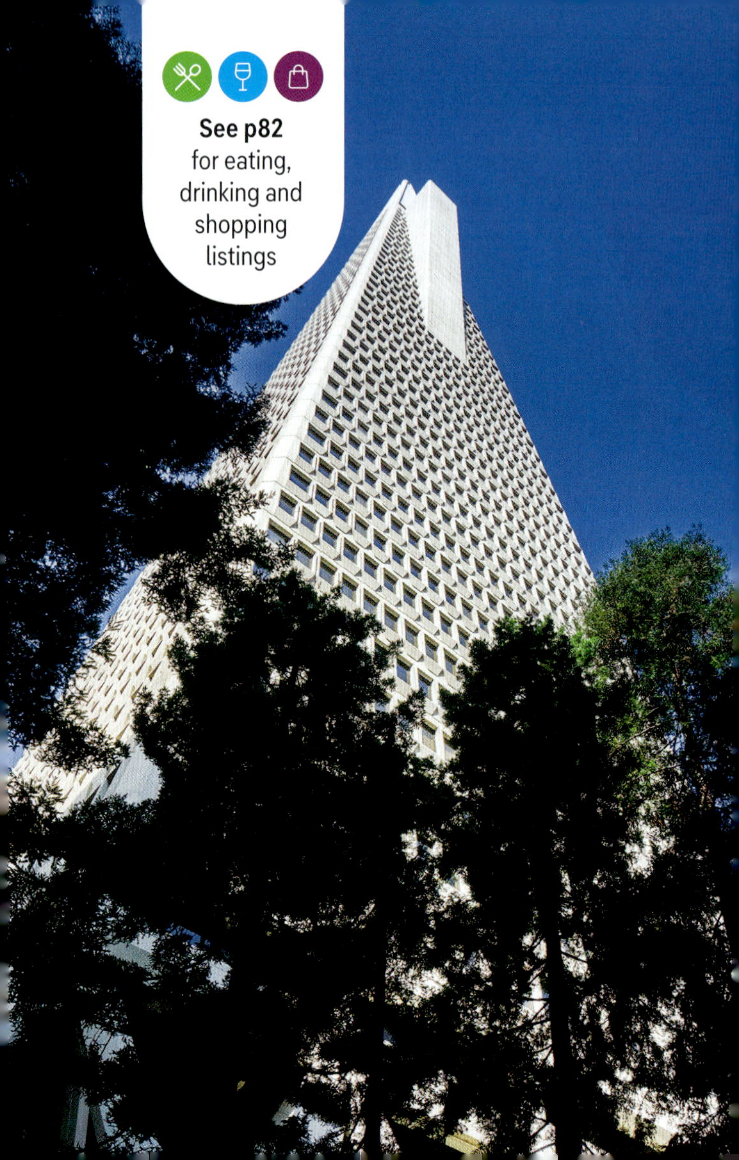
See p82
for eating,
drinking and
shopping
listings

Explore Downtown, Civic Center & SoMa

Researched by Margot Seeto

Downtown is a huge swath of eastern San Francisco that encompasses the neighborhoods of Union Sq, Civic Center and the Tenderloin, South of Market (SoMa), Financial District (FiDi) and parts of Mission Bay. Downtown has all the urban amenities: art galleries, swanky hotels, first-run theaters, malls and entertainment megaplexes. Civic Center is home to great performances and Asian art treasures on one side of City Hall, and dive bars and soup kitchens on the other. SoMa's high-tech landscape is fickle but still present – others like it for high art, but everyone gets down and dirty on the dance floor.

Getting Around

Muni & BART

Muni has buses, metro and streetcars. Multiple buses serve the area. Metro lines J, K, L, M, N and T run under Market St and split to different neighborhoods. F-Market streetcars run above Market St. BART shares Muni downtown stations and connects to the Bay Area.

Cable Car

The Powell-Hyde and Powell-Mason lines link downtown with the Wharf; the California St cable car runs perpendicular, over Nob Hill.

Ferry

From the Ferry Building to: Treasure Island, Angel Island/Tiburon, North Bay and East Bay.

THE BEST

ARTISANAL FOOD Ferry Building (p66)

MODERN ART SFMOMA (p68)

ANCIENT & CONTEMPORARY ART Asian Art Museum (p73)

CLASSY NIGHT OUT San Francisco Opera (p76)

CULTURAL DISTRICT Leather & LGBTQ Cultural District (p74)

Transamerica Pyramid (p79)
SUNDRY PHOTOGRAPHY/SHUTTERSTOCK

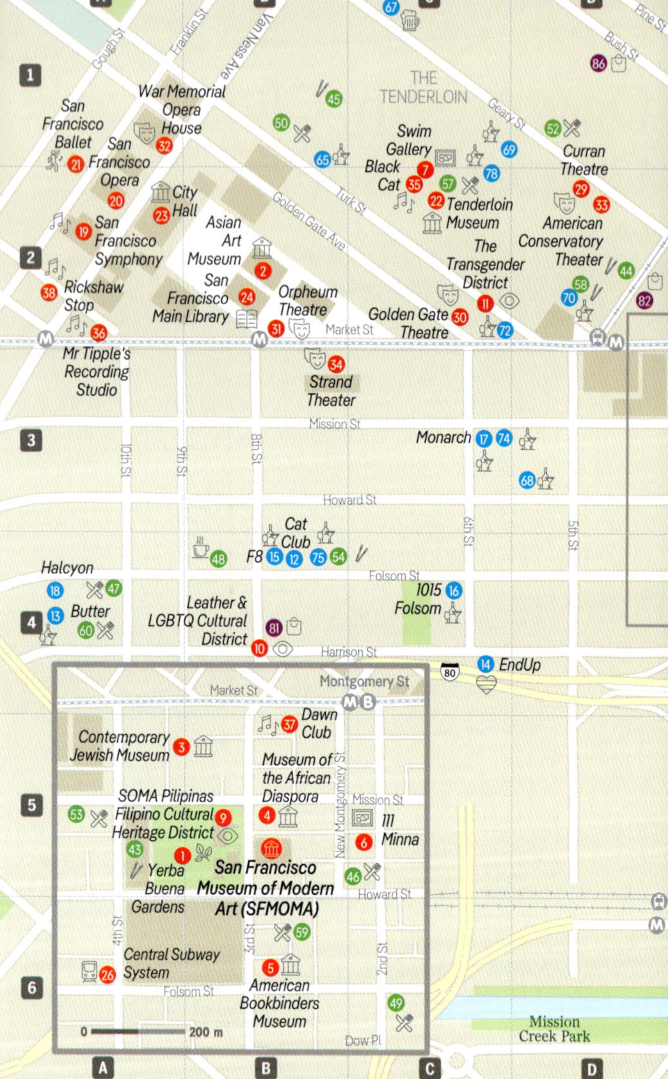
THE TENDERLOIN
Gough St
Franklin St
Van Ness Ave
Pine St
Bush St
Geary St
Turk St
Golden Gate Ave
Market St
Mission St
Howard St
Folsom St
Harrison St
10th St
9th St
8th St
6th St
5th St
4th St
3rd St
2nd St
New Montgomery St
Montgomery St
Dow Pl
San Francisco Ballet
War Memorial Opera House
San Francisco Opera
City Hall
San Francisco Symphony
Asian Art Museum
Rickshaw Stop
San Francisco Main Library
Orpheum Theatre
Mr Tipple's Recording Studio
Strand Theater
Swim Gallery
Black Cat
Tenderloin Museum
Curran Theatre
American Conservatory Theater
The Transgender District
Golden Gate Theatre
Monarch
Cat Club
F8
Halcyon
Butter
Leather & LGBTQ Cultural District
1015 Folsom
EndUp
Dawn Club
Contemporary Jewish Museum
Museum of the African Diaspora
SOMA Pilipinas Filipino Cultural Heritage District
111 Minna
Yerba Buena Gardens
San Francisco Museum of Modern Art (SFMOMA)
Central Subway System
American Bookbinders Museum
Mission Creek Park
0 200 m

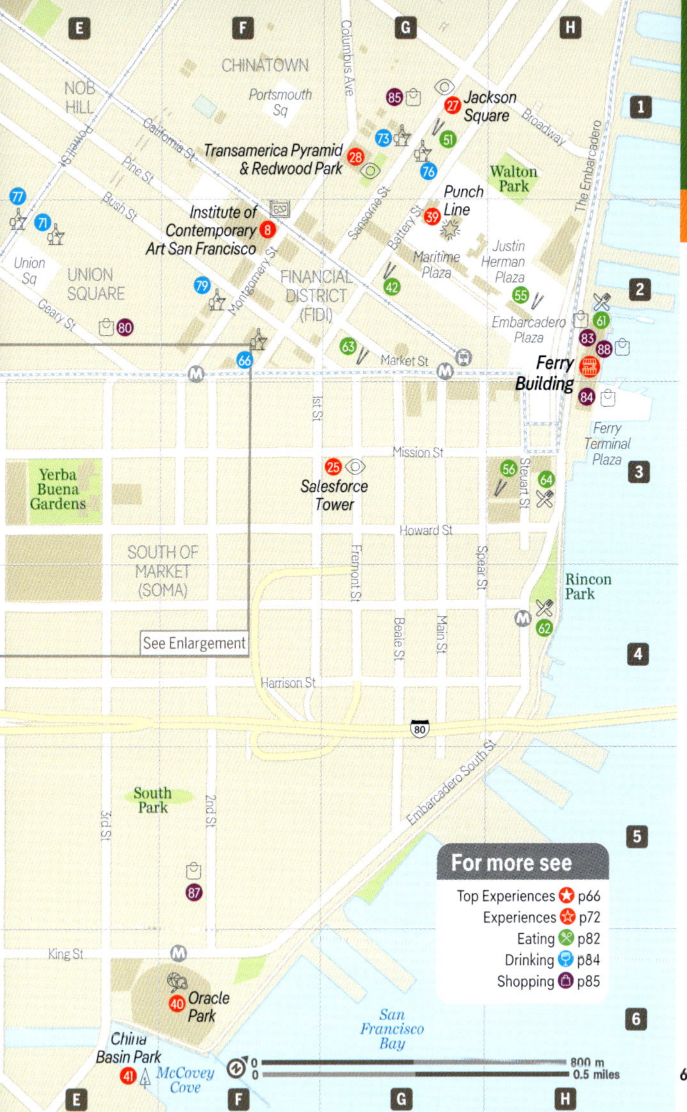

E
F
G
H
CHINATOWN
NOB HILL
Portsmouth Sq
Columbus Ave
85
27
Jackson Square
Broadway
1
73
51
Transamerica Pyramid & Redwood Park
28
76
Walton Park
California St
Powell St
Pine St
Bush St
Sansome St
Punch Line
39
Battery St
The Embarcadero
77
71
Institute of Contemporary Art San Francisco
8
Union Sq
UNION SQUARE
Montgomery St
FINANCIAL DISTRICT (FIDI)
Maritime Plaza
Justin Herman Plaza
2
42
55
79
Geary St
80
Embarcadero Plaza
61
83
88
66
63
Market St
Ferry Building
84
1st St
Ferry Terminal Plaza
Mission St
Yerba Buena Gardens
25
Salesforce Tower
56
Steuart St
64
3
Howard St
SOUTH OF MARKET (SOMA)
Fremont St
Spear St
Rincon Park
See Enlargement
Beale St
Main St
62
4
Harrison St
80
Embarcadero South St
South Park
3rd St
2nd St
5
87
King St
40
Oracle Park
China Basin Park
41
McCovey Cove
San Francisco Bay
6
0
0
800 m
0.5 miles
For more see
Top Experiences p66
Experiences p72
Eating p82
Drinking p84
Shopping p85

★ TOP EXPERIENCE

Ferry Building

Reimagined and reintroduced in 2003 after a four-year restoration, the 1898 Ferry Building is a destination hub for artisanal food-hopping – even better on a Ferry Plaza Farmers Market day.

MAP P64 **H2**

Ferry Building Marketplace

The stately 240ft-tall clock tower of the Ferry Building was overshadowed by a freeway overpass from the 1950s until damage from the 1989 Loma Prieta earthquake necessitated a reimagining of the Embarcadero as a pedestrian hub, accessible by Muni, BART, bicycle and car. The 2003 debut of the **Ferry Building Marketplace** *(ferrybuildingmarketplace.com)* welcomed artisanal food shops in the Grand Hall. While vendors change, staples like Humphry Slocombe ice cream, Hog Island Oyster Company and Far West Fungi have held steady. Currently, marketplace favorites include Hawaii-style *malasadas* (doughnuts) at Ocean Malasada, Red Bay Coffee and Peaches Patties. A La Cocina food entrepreneur incubator alum includes Cambodian eatery Lunette. There are also worthy non-food retailers.

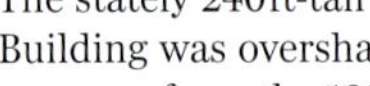

PLANNING TIP
Saturdays are when the farmers market is at its largest, hosting more than 100 vendors that wrap around the building.

Ferry Plaza Farmers Market

In addition to the dizzying array of joy-inducing food inside the Marketplace, the farmers market takes place outside three times a week. About 10 to 15 vendors line the front on Tuesdays and Thursdays. The Saturday market is the beacon of California's bounty, attracting 25,000 visitors weekly. Like the Marketplace, vendors change, but there's never a shortage of super-fresh produce from just

Scan this QR code for a current list of vendors.

BENJAMIN HEATH FOR LONELY PLANET

miles away, plus coffee, baked goods, hot food and pantry staples. Current favorites include Primavera's egg-laden chilaquiles, Dirty Girl Produce, Nusa's pandan-inflected Indonesian sweets, Delightful Foods' creamy bean pies and Hodo's organic tofu.

Ferries

The Ferry Building houses ports for ferries going all over the Bay Area. With the exception of Alcatraz (p60) ferries that launch from Pier 33, 1 mile north, the ferries here are bound for Treasure Island, Angel Island/Tiburon, Sausalito, Larkspur, Vallejo, Oakland and Alameda. Some lines require round-trip tickets purchased in advance. Load your Clipper Card beforehand, consider the SF Bay Ferry app or use paper tickets.

QUICK BREAK

Don't shop 'til you drop. Sit to people-watch on benches and cafe seating behind the building, or cement picnic tables on the north exterior.

★ TOP EXPERIENCE

SFMOMA

The 170,000-sq-ft **San Francisco Museum of Modern Art (SFMOMA)** is one of the largest modern-art museums in the world. After a major expansion in 2016, SFMOMA reopened its doors with a mixture of pioneering pop art and special exhibits from world-renowned artists.

MAP P64 **B5**

PLANNING TIP
Allow two hours up to half a day to visit. There are also 45,000 sq ft of free art areas inside.

Scan this QR code for full opening hours and to book ahead.

Pop Art Masters

From its start in 1935, **SFMOMA** (pictured; *sfmoma.org)* was an early champion of then-emerging art forms. The 5th-floor collection presents some of the greatest hits of pop art from the 1960s, including Andy Warhol's electrically colored prints of celebrities to Ellsworth Kelly's joined canvases of unevenly shaped, bold colors. The pieces push the idea that the consciousness-shifting art movements of the 1960s are still relevant today. The kinetic and whimsical mobiles and metal sculptures of abstract artist Alexander Calder occupy part of the 3rd floor, and include the multicolored *Lone Yellow* and the spellbinding movements of *Quatrro Pendulati.*

1900 to Now: SFMOMA's Collection

Rotating experimental works and masterpieces from its massive collection, SFMOMA encourages viewers to constantly reexamine the contradictions and interpretations of some of the greatest works of our time. Ponder the evolution of Diego Rivera's boldly colored works from Cubist to postimpressionist and beyond, and Georgia O'Keefe's interpretations of nature and the feminine through her genre of combining fine charcoal lines with paint.

Special Exhibits & Art Outside

SFMOMA is a must-stop for both traveling exhibits from internationally renowned artists, and for

CHRIS ALLAN/SHUTTERSTOCK

special exhibits spotlighting local artists. Jump from the head-trippy mirrored infinity rooms of Yayoi Kusama, to Ragnar Kjartansson's immersive instrumental video installation, to Kara Walker's Octavia Butler–inspired sculpture exhibit that combines medieval mechanisms with ideas of transforming trauma. Local spotlights have ranged from the inimitable Ruth Asawa's intricate, curved wire-loop hangings to inclusivity in skateboard culture curated by local skate collective Unity.

On the 3rd floor, outside the Calder exhibit, is the Living Wall – the largest of its kind in the US. It is 30ft high and contains more than 19,000 plants, including wild huckleberry and fragrant pink flowering currant. On the rooftop patio of Cafe 5 on the 5th floor is a sculpture garden.

QUICK BREAK
No outside food or drink is allowed beyond the lobby, but there are three museum cafes at which to refuel on the 1st, 2nd and 5th floors.

WALKING TOUR

Embarcadero Stroll

At the Embarcadero, San Francisco's eastern gateway, stroll along the paved waterfront – part of the San Francisco Bay Trail – to take in the dance between nature and bustling city, historic places and experimental ones. Gaze at the bay and bridge, historic watering holes and public art, with an Oracle Park ending.

START	END	LENGTH
Sue Bierman Park	Oracle Park	1.2 miles; 1½ hrs

1 Starting Green

Start from the small **Sue Bierman Park**, which is especially pretty in spring with pink cherry blossoms bursting from the trees like clouds of cotton candy. A playground with a rope climbing structure is also here if you're with kids. Pass through Embarcadero Plaza, a people-gathering spot that's also popular with skateboarders.

2 Controversial Public Art

The brutalist 40ft-tall **Vaillancourt Fountain**, by Canadian sculptor and painter Armand Vaillancourt, in Embarcadero Plaza has striking concrete angles, which upset some of the public upon its 1971 debut. It may or may not be filled with water, which means you could walk through it for closer art inspection. Pass by pickleball courts, then art vendors lining Market St. A 45ft nude (and also controversial) steel woman sculpture called *R-Evolution*, originally debuted at Burning Man, may or may not still be standing. Artist Marco Cochrane designed it to 'breathe' daily at 5pm, as well as light up at night.

3 The Other Bridge

Turn south at the **Ferry Building** (p66) and stroll along the promenade – sparkling bay waters to your left – weaving past joggers and dog walkers. You may actually appreciate the towering gray Bay Bridge more than the Golden Gate, especially if the Bay Lights turn on.

4 From Legendary Pop Art Sculptors

On the right is the bow and arrow of husband-and-wife Scandinavian sculptors Claes Oldenburg and Coosje van Bruggen. The 70ft-tall **Cupid's Span** sits with its arrow shot into the grass of Rincon Park. The curved bow echoes the shape of the Bay Bridge.

5 Historic Watering Holes

Grab a burger or beer from a trio of historic waterside dive bar shacks – all with patio seating. The first, **Hi Dive**, has a sea-blue exterior and $3 cans of PBR.

6 Sports Shack

Continue to **Red's Java House** where the walls are plastered with sports memorabilia. It's known for the sourdough cheeseburger (order a double patty).

7 Chill Out

Frankie's Java House got a modern facelift – choose your bar vibe accordingly. Red's Java House and Hi Dive have been featured on TV and film – the Goliath series with Billy Bob Thornton and the *Nash Bridges* movie starring Don Johnson, respectively.

8 Play Ball!

The waterfront bar shacks are also walking distance to **Oracle Park** (p81), making for good pre-game options whether for a San Francisco Giants game, concert or other large event at the stadium.

EXPERIENCES

Ride All the Cable-Car Lines

TRANSPORTATION

It won't take as long as you think to ride all three **cable-car lines** *(sfmta.com/getting-around/muni/cable-cars; single/one day $8/13)*. A Muni Visitor Passport is recommended. Go north-south up and down the hills on both the **Powell-Hyde** and **Powell-Mason** lines, which take riders between downtown's skyscrapers, through culture-filled Chinatown (p87), past Nob Hill's Fairmont Hotel and Grace Cathedral, and end at the tourist attractions of Fisherman's Wharf (p50).

Most visitors stick to these lines, but there's a third line that tends to be less crowded – the east-west **California** line that runs between Van Ness Ave in Nob Hill and Davis St in FiDi. It passes many of the same landmarks, with the addition of Polk Gulch and more of FiDi.

Stroll Through Yerba Buena Gardens

GARDENS

MAP: 1 P64 A5

Intended as a downtown green oasis and cultural center, the three-block radius of **Yerba Buena Gardens** *(YGB; yerbabuenagardens.org)* and the connecting **Yerba Buena Center for the Arts** *(YBCA; ybca.org; $10, free Wed & 2nd Sun)* debuted in the 1990s. Across a verdant lawn is the glass-paneled **Martin Luther King, Jr Memorial waterfall**. The **Upper Terrace**, one of SF's first rooftop parks, contains the **Sister City Garden** with 19 types of plants. It also has the Fun Zone with a children's playground and more. YBCA houses a major exhibit plus smaller ones throughout, focusing on local artists, and is home to **Alonzo King LINES Ballet** *(linesballet.org)*, a pioneering majority-Black ballet company, and the annual free **YBG Festival** *(ybgfestival.org)*.

MAYA ANGELOU'S CABLE-CAR CONNECTION

Poet and civil-rights activist Maya Angelou had talents beyond writing, including singing and acting. Then there's the legend of her being the first Black cable-car operator – not entirely true, but Angelou had a pioneering transportation role. As a teen, she and her family moved to the Bay Area in the 1940s. Angelou became one of the first Black female electric-streetcar conductors in SF for Muni's then-competitor, Market Street Railway (think streetcars instead of cable cars), a feat that garnered her a lifetime achievement award from the Conference of Minority Transportation Officials in 2014.

Travel Through Time at the Asian Art Museum MUSEUM

MAP: 2 P64 B2

In a towering beaux-arts-style building in Civic Center, the **Asian Art Museum** *(AAM; asianart.org)* has called this former main public library home since 2003, but originated as a de Young Museum wing in 1966. With more than 18,000 works, AAM bridges the ancient with contemporary across the Asian diaspora in exciting and expansive ways. Highlights include China's oldest dated Buddha, Indonesian rod puppets, the largest outdoor art terrace in the US, and special exhibits like video artist Yuan Goang-Ming's *Everyday War*, a jarring immersive work about the pervasiveness of violence in our culture.

Get Updates on Other Major Downtown Museums MUSEUMS

Post-pandemic effects and unsteady federal funding can be confusing for visitors – so here is a status update for some downtown museums at the time of writing.

North of YBCA, the **Contemporary Jewish Museum** *(CJM;* MAP: 3 P64 A5; *thecjm.org)* is due to reopen at the end of 2025. Past CJM exhibits ranged from singer Amy Winehouse to Muppets master Jim Henson. Next door, the **Museum of the African Diaspora** (MAP: 4 P64 B5; *moadsf.org)* is closed temporarily for remodeling and has a scheduled re-opening for fall 2025, aligning with its 20th anniversary. Before closing, curator Key Jo Lee presented 'Liberatory Living: Protective Interiors and Radical Black Joy,' examining and creating domestic interiors through a feminist framework. The **California Historical Society** *(californiahistoricalsociety.org)* museum closed permanently, but its collection – known for historical documents related to the Gold Rush and statehood – is being moved to Stanford University. The **Mexican Museum** *(mexicanmuseum.org)*, with art ranging from pre-Columbian days to contemporary Latino art, is moving to Yerba Buena Gardens from its previous Fort Mason home, with the goal of opening by the end of 2025. The **California Migration Museum** *(calmigration.org)* HQ is downtown, but is fully virtual. Note its Melting Spots map and podcast of 38 immigrant-owned restaurants.

See Lesser-Known Downtown Art ART GALLERIES

Take time to explore lesser-known art spaces. One is the nonprofit **American Bookbinders Museum** (MAP: 5 P64 B6; *bookbindersmuseum.org; adult/seniors & 10-17s/child $15/12/free)* – the only museum in North America dedicated to preserving and promoting the art and history of Western bookbinding. A banned-book jail debuted as permanent public art on the Folsom St side in 2025. Recorded webinars include the dark and fascinating, like one on books bound by human skin. Quirky art galleries include **111 Minna** (MAP: 6 P64 C5; *111minnagallery.com; free)* and **Swim Gallery** (MAP: 7 P64 C2; *swimgallery.com; free)*. The **Institute of Contemporary Art San Francisco** *(ICASF;* MAP: 8 P64 F2; *icasf.org; free)* funds free, experimental nonpermanent exhibits that start timely conversations, from climate change to reparations, with an on-site maker space.

Explore SOMA Pilipinas

CULTURAL DISTRICTS

MAP: 9 P64 B5

The **SOMA Pilipinas Filipino Cultural Heritage District** formed in 2016 to acknowledge the 100-plus-year-old Filipino community in SF, especially in SoMa. With other community groups, the district throws epic events like the **UNDSCVRD** night market (turned day party), **Yum Yams** *ube* (Filipino purple yam) festival at **Kapwa Gardens** and the annual **Pistahan Festival** at YBG. More than 30 public works splash the district. Black box theater **Bindlestiff Studio** presents genre-bending pieces. **Republika**, a commercial and cultural corridor on the ground floor of Fifth & Mission Garage, will debut in 2026. A 2025–26 exhibit at YBCA, *Makibaka: A Living Legacy,* pays homage to generations that forged the community's *bayanihan* (communal unity) spirit.

Check Out Leather & LGBTQ Cultural District Bars

CULTURAL DISTRICTS

MAP: 10 P64 B4

SoMa's **Leather & LGBTQ Cultural District** *(sfleatherdistrict.org)* is the world's first leather district, and since the 1970s has been home to the largest concentration of queer bars and nightclubs outside of the Castro. **Oasis** *(sfoasis.com; event tickets $10-30)* is drag cabaret's home. **Lone Star Saloon** *(lonestarsf.com)* is the original bear bar. **Hole in the Wall** *(blackwolfmetal.com)* provides a spiritual home to gay bikers. The **Stud** *(studsf.com; event tickets $15),* the US' first worker-owned co-op club, rose from the ashes to host ballroom beats while fundraising for a stage to bring back drag shows. The historic **SF Eagle** *(sf-eagle.com)* has all-you-can-drink Sunday beer busts ($15). Thursdays through Sundays are best at **Powerhouse** *(powerhousebar.com),* a sweaty bar for leathermen.

LEATHER DISTRICT FESTIVALS

Besides Pride (p32), the Leather & LGBTQ Cultural District's signature events include the world's biggest leather street party at **Folsom Street Fair**, where public spankings get the party started. More than 500,000 BDSM enthusiasts converge on the last Sunday of September. Folsom is the culmination of Leather Week, with preceding events like the **Mr SF Eagle Leather Contest**. At summer spinoff **Up Your Alley** fair (aka Dore Alley) – smaller and even more sex-positive than Folsom – sun shines where it usually doesn't in Dore Alley. Both are 18-plus only; request consent and play safe. Also on offer are health services like free HIV testing. Prep sartorially at the renowned Mr S Leather (p85).

Walk the Transgender Cultural District CULTURAL DISTRICTS

MAP: 11 P64 C2

Before the infamous 1969 Stonewall Riots in NYC, SF's Compton's Cafeteria Riot happened on Turk and Taylor in 1966, when queer and trans cafe patrons revolted against escalating police harassment. Today, the sidewalk reads 'Uptown Tenderloin Lost Landmarks, Compton's Cafeteria Riot, 1966.' The Tenderloin, long having been a hub for the trans community, anointed the **Transgender District** in 2017 as the world's first. Pink, blue and white wrap around every lamppost and decorate every crosswalk. Take the monthly 'Valley of the Queens' tour through the district, beginning at the Tenderloin Museum (p77). End at the historic **Aunt Charlie's Lounge** *(auntcharlieslounge.com)* on a Friday or Saturday night for dazzling drag numbers.

Go Clubbing in SoMa NIGHTCLUBS

Aside from SoMa's lively Leather District bars and clubs, most of the city's other nightclubs are also in SoMa. The highest concentration of bars and clubs is around 11th and Folsom Sts. The scene favors EDM and house these days, and pops mostly on weekends.

Cat Club (MAP: 12 P64 B4; *sfcatclub.com; $5-20)* is known for its New Wave and goth/industrial nights, plus a welcoming crowd. **Butter** (MAP: 13 P64 A4; *smoothasbutter.com; $0-5)* is lowbrow and lovely – everyone's wailing to rock anthems and swilling 100% artificially flavored soda-pop cocktails here. Going hard into after hours, Saturday nights at **EndUp** (MAP: 14 P64 C4; *theendupsf.com; $30)* have a way of turning into Sunday mornings. Straight people EndUp here too – but gay Sunday tea dances have been SF staples since 1973. The multi-room, 250-person capacity provides a relatively intimate club experience at **F8** (MAP: 15 P64 B4; *feightsf.com; $0-30)* with music ranging from house to hip-hop to dubstep. Among the city's biggest clubs, **1015 Folsom** (MAP: 16 P64 C4; *1015.com; $10-30)* packs for marquee EDM DJs and hip-hop acts, and has seen performances from the likes of LCD Soundsystem, with five dance floors and bars. **Monarch** (MAP: 17 P64 C3; *monarchsf.com; $0-25)* has a great sound system, multiple rooms with different vibes and DJs, and sometimes aerial dancers. The LED lights in the single-room club **Halcyon** (MAP: 18 P64 A4; *halcyon-sf.com; $12-35)* complement its techno-heavy sets perfectly.

Soothe Yourself with the SF Symphony

ARTS/CULTURE

MAP: 19 P64 A2

The Grammy-winning **San Francisco Symphony** *(sfsymphony.org, $39-329)* carries on the legacy of former conductor Michael Tilson Thomas' 25-year career at the **Louise M Davies Symphony Hall**. Always innovating, see what surprises the symphony presents next, whether it's the classics or screening of *Black Panther* with live orchestra. With the 2025 departure of Thomas' successor, Esa Pekka-Salonen, the symphony pivoted to an interesting interim solution – welcoming two-dozen guest conductors in the 2025 to 2026 season during the search for the next music director. Karina Canellakis, the first female principal guest conductor for several European orchestras, conducted French pianist Alexandre Kantorow's SF Symphony debut with Prokofiev's notoriously difficult Piano Concerto No 3 in C major, Op 26.

Be Enraptured by the San Francisco Opera

ARTS/CULTURE

MAP: 20 P64 A2

While inimitable painter David Hockney no longer actively works for the **San Francisco Opera** *(sfopera.com; $28-426)*, his radical sets and haute-couture costumes are still utilized, and complement Eun Sung Kim's bold musical direction – you can appreciate both with $28 balcony seats (for which you might need $5 rental opera glasses from the north coat check). SF Opera introduces timeless works to new audiences, like Puccini's much-adored *La Bohème*, and newer works like *The Handmaid's Tale*, Grammy-winning *The (R)evolution of Steve Jobs* and Tony Award–winner David Henry Hwang's *The Monkey King*.

Feel Light as Air at the San Francisco Ballet

ARTS/CULTURE

MAP: 21 P64 A2

San Francisco Ballet *(sfballet.org, $35-575),* the USA's oldest ballet company, was founded in 1933 originally to train dancers for opera productions. The repertoire spans the classic *The Nutcracker,* whose US premiere was here in 1944, to modern originals. Performances share the War Memorial Opera House (p80) with the SF Opera, and run December through May. The ballet puts together international collaborations at the intersection of visual art, fashion and music, like Gap Inc Creative Director Zac Posen creating gossamer pink-and-yellow costumes for a revitalized version of Christopher Wheeldon's 2008 *Within the Golden Hour.*

Learn from the Tenderloin Museum

MUSEUM

MAP: 22 P64 C2

The **Tenderloin Museum** *(tenderloinmuseum.org, adult/senior & student/under-12s $10/6/free)* is an essential way to learn about the notorious neighborhood that is rich in history and culture. It takes about 45 minutes to peruse, showing where Muhammad Ali boxed, Billie Holiday sang, and LGBTQ+ activists fought for their right to be served in cafeterias – and established America's first Transgender Cultural District (p75). From housing brothels to becoming an immigrant hub with affordable housing, see how layered the Tenderloin is. Tenderloin Museum historians can also lead intrepid visitors to groundbreaking Tenderloin locales; walking shoes and city smarts essential.

Eat Your Way Through the Tenderloin

RESTAURANTS

The Tenderloin is often a landing point for new immigrants needing affordable housing. That translates to some of the biggest variety of food in the city. The main food drag runs north–south on Larkin

HELGI TOMASSON'S THE NUTCRACKER

The Christmas-season production of the classic *The Nutcracker* is beloved worldwide, but SF Ballet's version is special. Former artistic director Helgi Tomasson, who was at the helm for 37 years, created a San Francisco-specific version in 2004 that the company still performs annually. Taking place in early-20th-century SF, set and costume designers Michael Yeargan and Martin Pakledinaz matched colors and fashions true to the time period – muted grays and blacks suggest city fog, and American circus imagery is apparent. Tomasson's vision includes more than 150 dancers and 150lb of paper snowflakes that fall during a now-iconic scene.

St, from Golden Gate Ave to Post St before turning into Lower Nob Hill ('Tendernob'), and east-west between Polk and Jones Sts. Definitely bring cash. Little Saigon on Larkin is the culinary anchor, where $5.50 banh mi and pho from giant vats of broth are de rigueur. Other prominent cuisines of the Tenderloin include halal and Middle Eastern/North African, Central American, and a growing number of upscale and fine-dining restaurants.

Appreciate Municipal Magic at City Hall & the Main Library

ART GALLERIES

Civic Center is crowned by the gold-accented dome of **City Hall** (MAP: 23 P64 A2), the site of historic happenings like the first same-sex marriages. Inside, the rotunda is favored by wedding photographers. Wander around for vestiges of the past, like a 700lb head of the 'Goddess of Liberty' that once topped the pre-1906 City Hall.

Neighboring City Hall is the **San Francisco Main Library** (MAP: 24 P64 B2), whose Larkin St entrance features a 9ft-tall bronze, book-shaped Maya Angelou sculpture, and *Portrait of a Phenomenal Woman*, by Lava Thomas. Inside, exhibits span all six floors. Outside are the revamped **UN Skate Plaza** and bi-weekly **Heart of the City Farmers Market**.

Rethink Downtown's Urban Spaces

PUBLIC ART

The 2018 opening of the 1070ft-tall **Salesforce Tower** (MAP: 25 P64 G3) forced locals to accept the city's newest tallest building. The art projection atop the tower has 11,000 LED lights, titled *Day for Night* by artist Jim Campbell. Adjacent is the Salesforce Transit Center that houses the 5.4-acre rooftop Salesforce Park, open to the public, including a (short) gondola ride.

Another striking urban space is the **Central Subway** (MAP: 26 P64 A6),

HOMELESSNESS & THE DOOM LOOP

While homeless (houseless, unsheltered) issues are nothing new to SF or any city, it's entwined with the pandemic-spurred 'doom loop' narrative of San Francisco: a combination of empty offices, gentrification, fentanyl crisis and inadequate homeless services creating a crime-ridden city. This view is somewhat exaggerated (SF is a liberal symbol, prone to both attacks and praise) – the streets are cleaner and return-to-office mandates are slowly repopulating downtown – but homelessness is an ongoing issue. Use your gut to decide whether to visit certain neighborhoods, or give money or food. Most folks hanging out are minding their own business.

YHELFMAN/SHUTTERSTOCK

City Hall

debuted in 2023, where the T Muni line runs from 4th and Brannan Sts through Yerba Buena, Union Sq and Chinatown, with 10 works of imposing public art. Outside the Yerba Buena station, *Node* by Roxy Paine is a spindly 102ft-tall sculpture.

Walk Through Urban Redwoods in Jackson Square

ARCHITECTURE

Jackson Square (MAP: 27 P64 G1) has changed since its days as the former coastline of SF. This was a notorious waterfront dock area before the Gold Rush filled in the area with abandoned ships. It's become a post-pandemic refuge for retailers and offices formerly in Union Sq and Mid-Market. **Hotaling Place** is the oldest alleyway in San Francisco, dating to at least 1866.

The signature 1972 **Transamerica Pyramid** (MAP: 28 P64 G1) has a half-acre redwood park with 50 trees, and a slew of eateries have opened. Check out the free exhibit space, which in 2025 featured models of Norman Foster's world-renowned architectural work – Foster led the revitalization of the Transamerica.

Get Cultured in the Theater District LIVE PERFORMANCES

Nestled between Union Sq, the Tenderloin, Mid-Market and Civic Center, SF's **Theater District** is bursting with culture, from majestic old theaters to big-concert venues to hoppin' jazz clubs.

For nationally touring smash-hit musicals like *Wicked* and *Hamilton*, look at the grand old **Curran** (MAP: 29 P64 D2; *sfcurran.com; $40-310)*, **Golden Gate** (MAP: 30 P64 C2; *goldengatetheatresf.com; $75-315)* and **Orpheum** (MAP: 31 P64 B2; *broadwaysf.com; $55-308)* theaters. **Herbst Theatre** *(sfwarmemorial.org/herbst-theatre; $0-105)* is a smaller, 900-seat venue inside the **War Memorial Opera House** (MAP: 32 P64 A1; *sfwarmemorial.org; $28-418)* that hosts performances such as string quartets and solo guitarists.

Go to the **American Conservatory Theater** *(ACT;* MAP: 33 P64 D2; *act-sf.org; $15-109)* for breakthrough shows that launch at this turn-of-the-century landmark. ACT's smaller **Strand Theater** (MAP: 34 P64 B3; *act-sf.org/strand)* presents a wider range of experimental shows like Kristina Wong's Pulitzer Prize-nominated *Sweatshop Overlord*. Smaller or experimental companies downtown also include **San Francisco Playhouse** *(sfplayhouse.org; $40-135)*, **New Conservatory Theatre Center** *(nctcsf.org; $48.50-70.50)*, **CounterPulse** *(counterpulse.org; $0-300)*, **SAFEhouseARTS** *(safehousearts.org; $0-40)* and **Phoenix Theatre** *(phoenixtheatresf.org; $25-30)*.

Several jazz clubs pay tribute to past venues, where Miles Davis, Billie Holiday and Charlie Parker played underground. **Black Cat** (MAP: 35 P64 C2; *blackcatsf.com; free bar entry; shows $9.50-35)* is out to restore the laid-back, lowdown glory of the capital of West Coast cool with both a basement club and street-level bar. **Mr Tipple's Recording Studio** (MAP: 36 P64 A2; *(mrtipplessf.com; $15-30)* hosts top local talent, plus a decent dumpling menu. **Dawn Club** (MAP: 37 P64 B5; *dawnclub.com; free bar entry; shows $15-30)* revives a 1946 jazz venue, with top-rated cocktails.

For other live music, **Rickshaw Stop** (MAP: 38 P64 A2; *rickshawstop.com; $15-25)* is a great small club for indie and underground acts. Larger concert halls like **Great American Music Hall** *(gamh.com; $5-100)*, **Bill Graham Civic Auditorium** *(billgrahamcivic.com; $55-629)*, the **Warfield** *(thewarfieldtheatre.com; $50-250)*, **Regency Ballroom** *(theregencyballroom.com; $44-76)* and **August Hall** *(augusthallsf.com; $49-74)* bring big touring acts like French pop duo Stereolab and American rock band Garbage. Don't forget the longstanding **Punch Line** (MAP: 39 P64 G2;

punchlinecomedyclub.com; $21-49) comedy club in the Embarcadero, which local comedian Ali Wong graced during her rise to fame.

Root, Root, Root for the SF Giants

SPORTS

MAP: 40 P64 F6

Having been a baseball team since 1883 (originally the New York Gothams), the **San Francisco Giants** *(mlb.com/giants/tickets; $15-170)* have called this city home since 1958, and currently call Mission Bay's **Oracle Park** stadium home. Baseball season runs March through September, with other events like major concerts at the stadium year-round.

Preview virtual views from seats when purchasing tickets online. Book parking in advance for about $20 on an app like SpotHero – or pay up to $100! Public transit to 2nd and King Sts is cheap and easy. The park opens 90 to 120 minutes before games. Use one of the multiple stadium entrances, including one through adjoining bar **58 Social** *(mlb.com)*, formerly Public House. Bring sun protection and a jacket. Read stadium rules before going, and carve out three hours for games. The iconic Coca-Cola-bottle sculpture at the Fan Lot has slides for kids.

SEE A GAME FOR FREE

Along the walkway by McCovey Cove behind Oracle Park, look for Triples Alley past the Gotham Club. Enter through metal detectors to a shaded, caged area, which some call the **Viewing Point**, to watch three game innings for free, albeit from a far outfield view. If it's not crowded, stay longer. Those with kayaks can hang out in the cove waters to watch the giant stadium screens. **China Basin Park** across from the cove comes to life 2½ hours before games, with food, drink and plenty of seating to watch the big screens and hear the game action.

MAP: 41 P64 E6

Food-lovers can map out stalls of interest, or do a giant lap around each level. SF institution **Doggie Diner** has locations throughout with staples like hot dogs. Signature park garlic fries are truly vampire repellent. **Crazy Crab'z** crab sandwiches and **Tony's** pizza might sell out. Exciting options include the **Lumpia Company**'s dole whip, chef David Chang's **Fuku** fried-chicken sandwiches, and **Rah Rah Ramen**.

LISTINGS

Best Places for...

See p64 for map of locations

$ Budget $$ Midrange $$$ Top End

Eating

Pho, Ramen & Other Soup Noodles

Turtle Tower $$
42 G2
The first to introduce SF to Northern Vietnamese-style pho with clear broth and wide rice noodles. Gateway dish: *phở gà* (chicken pho). *11am-9pm*

Dabao Singapore $$
43 A5
Fine-dining chef Emily Lim opened a Singapore-style hawker stall serving favorites like seafood laksa. *11am-3:30pm Tue-Thu, to 7pm Fri-Sun*

Hinodeya Ramen $$
44 D2
Inhale whole-grain ramen in a dashi-style broth made with bonito, kombu, scallops, and topped with *chashu* (braised pork belly) and soft egg. *10am-1:30am*

Hải Ký Mì Gia $
45 B1
Tenderloin Chinese-Vietnamese noodle spot famous for its duck-leg noodle soup. *9am-6pm Wed-Sun*

Coffee & Sweet Bites

Sana'a Cafe $
46 C5
A Yemeni coffeehouse whose flaky savory pastries are made in-house. Also fragrant pistachio cakes. *6:30am-10pm Mon-Fri, from 8am Sat & Sun*

Sextant Coffee Roasters $
47 A4
Specializing in Ethiopian coffee, this Black-owned flagship offers signature Wired Ghandi (like spicy dirty chai). *7:30am-4pm Mon-Fri, from 8:30am Sat & Sun*

Cafe Suspiro $
48 B4
Coffee, records, books and art at this Latino-owned joint. *8am-4pm Mon-Thu, to 3pm Fri, 9am-3pm Sat*

Paper Son Coffee $
49 C6
Specialties include the Pandan Aerocano, with Tano's viral Korean salt bread. *8am-2:30pm Tue-Thu, from 8:30am Fri & Mon*

Breakfast & Brunch

Brenda's French Soul Food $$
50 B1
Comforting, rich gumbo and *ube* (Filipino purple yam) beignets by queer Filipina-Creole chef Brenda Buenviaje. Local favorite since 2007. *8am-8pm Wed-Mon, to 3pm Tue*

Cassava Cafe $
51 G1
The dynamic Japanese-Californian courtyard cafe has housemade Spam *onigirazu* (nori-wrapped rice sandwich) and Sonoma duck confit bento boxes. *8am-3:30pm Mon-Fri*

620 Jones $$
 D1
Drag brunches every weekend on the large outdoor patio –

sometimes both days. *9am-2:30pm & 4:30-10pm Tue-Thu, to midnight Fri, 11am-midnight Sat, 11am-3:30pm Sun*

JT Restaurant $$

 A5

Inside Mint Mall, enjoy hearty *silog* plates: garlic rice, eggs and protein like *longanisa* (sweet Filipino sausage). Cash only. *9am-7:30pm Mon-Sat*

Dim Sum

HK Lounge Bistro $$$

 B4

Top-notch, Michelin-recommended dim sum in a small-ish space – make reservations. *11am-2:30pm & 5-8:30pm Wed-Fri, from 10am Sat & Sun*

Harborview Restaurant & Bar $$$

 H2

Upscale dim-sum spot whose outdoor patio overlooks the Ferry Building and water. *11:30am-2pm & 5-9pm Tue-Fri , 10:30am-2:30am Sat & Sun*

Yank Sing $$$

 H3

Pricey dim sum with daily rolling cart service – a rarity these days. Additional location on Stevenson St. *11am-3pm Tue-Fri, from 10am Sat & Sun*

Nice & Fine Dining

Azalina's $$$

 C2

From former Twitter building Malaysian food stall to James Beard–nominated fine-dining in the Tenderloin with an affordable $89 five-course tasting menu. *5-8:30pm Wed-Sat*

Bodega $$$

 D2

Upscale Vietnamese food tribute by chef Matthew Ho to his family's previous Tenderloin restaurant Bodega Bistro. *11am-3pm & 5-9pm Sun-Thu, to 10:30pm Fri & Sat*

Benu $$$

 B6

Chef Corey Lee's three-Michelin-star contemporary Korean cuisine has become synonymous with SF fine dining; $390 fixed menu. *5:30-8:30pm Tue-Sat*

Californios $$$

 A4

Cal-Mexican, two-Michelin-starred fine dining from chef Val M Cantú. Taste wild-caught yellowtail with rhubarb and ceviche-like blood-orange *aguachile*. *5-10pm Tue-Sat*

Seafood

Hog Island Oyster Company $$

 H2

Sustainably grown oysters – Sweetwater to Kumamoto – from just north in Tomales Bay. *11:30am-8pm Mon-Fri, from 11am Sat & Sun*

Waterbar $$$

62 H4

Waterside dining with a notable daily featured oyster at only $1.55 each. *11:30am-2:30pm & 5-9pm Sun-Thu, to 9:30pm Fri & Sat*

Crustacean $$$

 G2

The family gets credit for inventing Vietnamese American garlic noodles, with roast Dungeness crab. *4:45-8:15pm Tue-Thu, to 8:45pm Fri & Sat*

Angler $$$

 H3

Michelin-starred Saison seafood spin-off with live-fire cooking, such as aged black cod with charred snap peas and pickled green garlic. *noon-9pm Mon-Fri, from 5pm Sat & Sun*

Drinking

Dive Bars

Emperor Norton's Boozeland

 B1

This two-floor clean dive has a pool table, back patio, half-pint beers available, and an inclusive culture. *1pm-2am*

Sutter Station Tavern

 F2

FiDi dive open since 1969 with a cable-car parklet. Once a watering hole for stock-exchange traders. *11am-2pm Mon-Sat*

Edinburgh Castle

67 C1

This flag-waving bastion of drink comes equipped with a dartboard and pool tables, plus vinegary fish and chips. *6pm-2am*

Tempest Bar & Box Kitchen

 D3

Cheap shot-and-beers, plus pool table, graffiti and food like pizza pockets. The kitchen is open until midnight. *11am-2am Mon-Fri, from noon Sat & Sun*

Cocktail Bars

Bourbon & Branch

 C1

Prohibition-era speakeasy with deceiving signage; password needed. Reservations are required for its speakeasy-within-a-speakeasy, Wilson & Wilson Detective Agency. *6pm-midnight Sun-Wed, to 2am Thu-Sat*

The Felix

70 D2

Tucked beneath the upscale Bodega, push a framed photo to reveal the 'drinking den' and music venue. *6pm-midnight Thu, 8pm-1am Fri & Sat*

Starlite

 E2

Beacon Grand (formerly Sir Francis Drake) rooftop bar. Reopened with cocktails from the Trick Dog team. *4pm-1am Thu, to 2am Fri & Sat, to midnight Sun*

Dark Bar

 C2

Asian spirits and ingredients focus on seasonality and fermentation. Small bites are also creative. *6-11pm Thu-Sat*

Wine Bars

Verjus

 G1

A hip wine bar and French restaurant reopened with bouillabaisse-like Dungeness crab soup and rare sparkling wines. *4-10pm Tue-Fri, to 11pm Sat & Sun*

Pawn Shop

 C3

Enter the speakeasy-like wine and tapas bar through a pawn shop. Admission: an object to trade. *5-9pm Tue-Sat*

DECANTsf

 B4

Values-driven SoMa wine bar and bottle shop with large tinned-fish menu; queer-, women-, POC-owned. *2-9:30pm Mon-Wed, to 10:30pm Thu-Sat, to 8pm Sun*

SF Wine Society

 G1

Drink hard-to-find international wines in a living-room-like bar, and reserve the bocce ball court. *4-10pm Tue-Sat, to 9pm Mon*

Modern Tiki Bars

Pacific Cocktail Haven

 E2

An ace bar with libations like a Leeward Negroni

– Sipsmith VJOP Gin, coconut-washed Campari, pandan cordial, bitters. *5pm-midnight Mon-Sat*

Zombie Village

 C2

Go on The Vacation with pisco, mango, citrus and baking spices. *5pm-midnight Wed, to 12:30am Thu, to 2am Fri & Sat*

Pagan Idol

 F2

Thoroughly researched shipping-route cocktails, like Hemingway is Dead: rum, bitters and grapefruit. *4:30pm-2am Thu-Sat, to midnight Tue & Wed, 5:30-11pm Mon*

Shopping

Clothing & Gifts

Britex Fabrics

80 E2

Eye-popping silks, hard-to-find international fabrics, or just go for the fabulous window displays. *11am-4pm Mon-Fri & 1st Sat*

Mr S Leather

81 B4

A queer-centric sex shop that is one of the most renowned of its kind on the West Coast. *noon-7pm*

Vacant to Vibrant Pop-Ups

82 D2

Local retail, art, event and food pop-ups in formerly vacant downtown office spaces. Check vibrantsf.org for listings and hours.

SFMOMA Museum Store

see SFOMA B5

A treasure trove of colorful, special gifts ranging from exhibit-inspired jewelry to children's toys. No museum ticket required. *11am-5pm Fri-Tue, noon-8pm Thu*

Crafts & Homewares

Heath Ceramics

 H2

Heath's iconic muted colors and mid-century designs stay true to Edith Heath's originals c 1948. *10am-6pm Mon-Fri, 9am-5pm Sat, 10am to 5pm Sun*

Bernal Cutlery

 H3

Curated international selection of knives, kitchen tools and giftable pantry goods. *11am-5pm*

Bookstores

William Stout Architectural Books

85 G1

SF's design secret, where architects and skateboard makers get inspiration. *12:30-5:30pm Sun-Thu, to 7:30pm Fri, 11:30am-7:30pm Sat*

Argonaut Book Shop

86 D1

Third-generation-run, rare bookshop founded in 1941 focusing on California and Western American history. *Open by appointment*

Chronicle Books

 F5

Local indie publisher HQ with a bookstore on the ground floor offering literary goodies from cookbooks to stationery. *9am-5pm Mon-Fri*

Book Passage

88 H2

Grab a book for the ferry, or stay for one of the many live author events. *10am-5pm Mon-Fri, from 9am Sat, from 11am Sun*

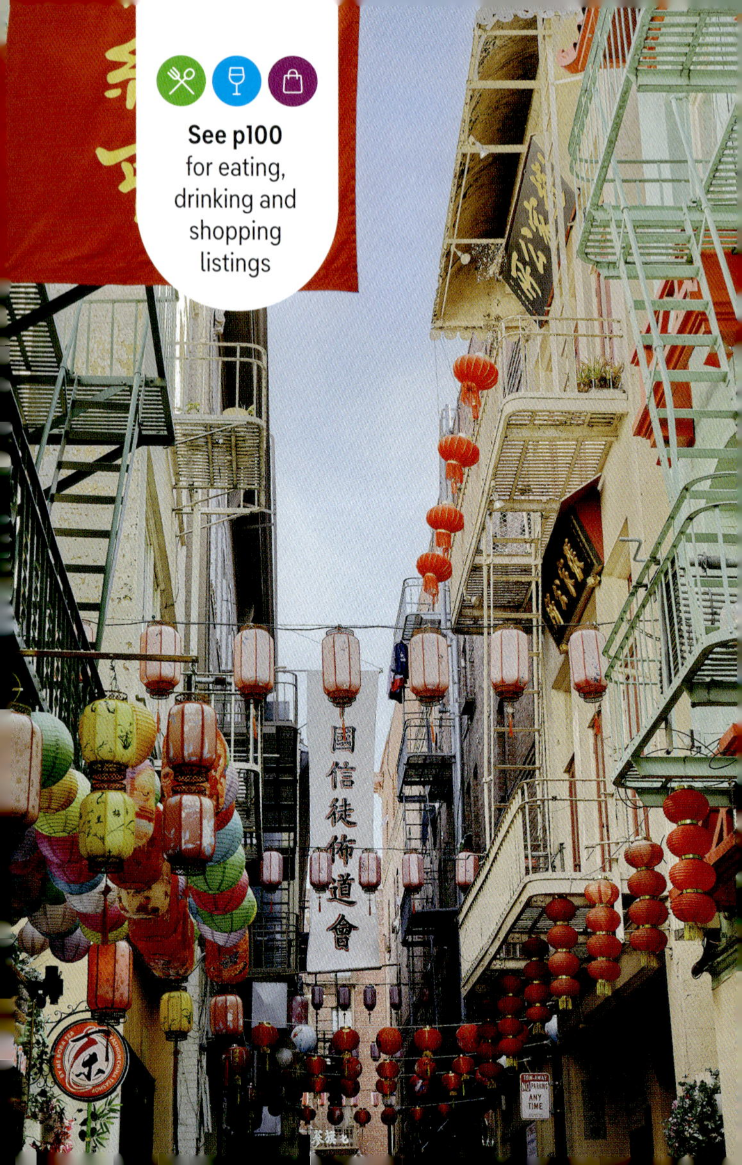

See p100 for eating, drinking and shopping listings

Researched by Alison Bing

Explore Chinatown & North Beach

Grant St connects San Francisco's historic Chinese and Italian neighborhoods, swapping epic stories of immigrant ingenuity, radical ideas, daring art and resilience against all odds. Under Chinatown's pagoda roofs, you'll find noodles, tea and temples, just like in California's Gold Rush days – but you'll also find the future in progress, with cutting-edge contemporary art, trend-setting restaurants and packed event calendars. Wild parrots in North Beach treetops mimic chatter at bohemian bars and Italian cafes, serving enough espresso to fuel the next poetry movement at free-speech landmark City Lights. Whether you're craving Peking duck, pizza or Peking duck pizza, you're in the right place – stick around for breakthrough comedy, raucous punk, Cantonese opera and West Coast jazz.

Getting Around

Cable Car

From downtown or Fisherman's Wharf, take the Powell-Mason or the Powell-Hyde line to Chinatown or North Beach. The California St cable car passes through the southern end of Chinatown.

Streetcar

The extended T-line streetcar service links Chinatown and North Beach to Downtown and Dogpatch.

Bus

Key routes passing through Chinatown and North Beach are 1, 12, 30, 39 and 45.

THE BEST

MONUMENTS TO RESILIENCE Chinatown Alleyways (p90)

FREE-SPEECH LANDMARK City Lights Books (p92)

FORWARD-LOOKING ART Edge on the Square (p96)

SCANDALOUS SCENES Coit Tower (p93)

IMMERSIVE HISTORY Chinese Historical Society of America (p97)

Chinatown alleyways (p90)

BENJAMIN HEATH FOR LONELY PLANET

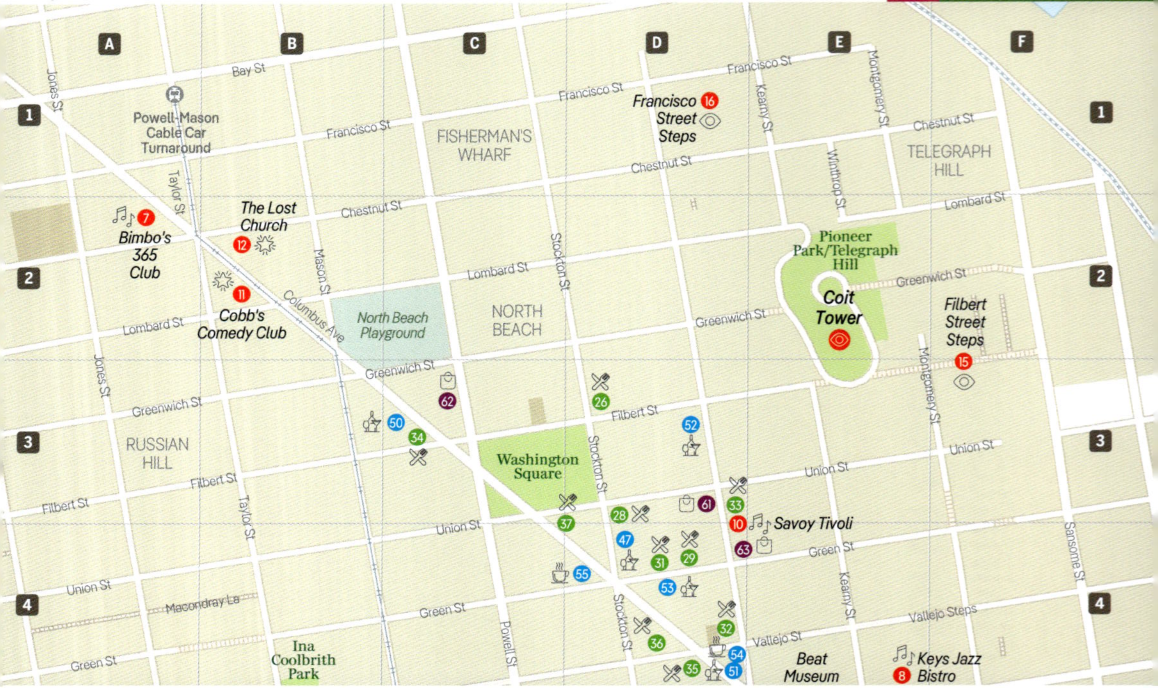

A
B
C
D
E
F
1
2
3
4
Bay St
Francisco St
Chestnut St
Lombard St
Greenwich St
Filbert St
Union St
Green St
Vallejo St
Vallejo Steps
Macondray La
Jones St
Taylor St
Mason St
Stockton St
Powell St
Kearny St
Montgomery St
Winthrop St
Sansome St
Columbus Ave
Powell-Mason Cable Car Turnaround
FISHERMAN'S WHARF
TELEGRAPH HILL
NORTH BEACH
RUSSIAN HILL
North Beach Playground
Washington Square
Pioneer Park/Telegraph Hill
Ina Coolbrith Park
7 Bimbo's 365 Club
12 The Lost Church
11 Cobb's Comedy Club
16 Francisco Street Steps
Coit Tower
15 Filbert Street Steps
10 Savoy Tivoli
8 Keys Jazz Bistro
Beat Museum
62
50
34
26
52
61
33
28
37
47
31
29
63
55
53
32
36
54
35
51

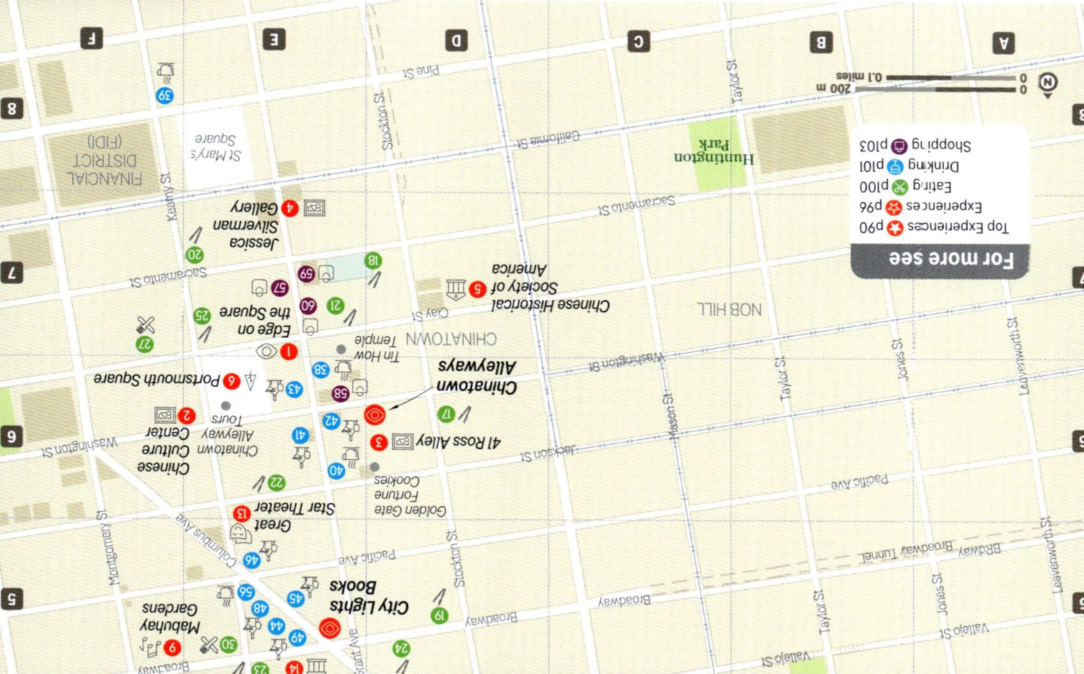
For more see
Top Experiences p90
Experiences p96
Eating p100
Drinking p101
Shopping p103
0 200 m
0 0.1 miles
City Lights Books
Mabuhay Gardens
Great Star Theater
Golden Gate Fortune Cookies
41 Ross Alley
Chinatown Alleyways
Chinese Culture Center
Chinatown Alleyway Tours
Portsmouth Square
Tin How Temple
Edge on the Square
Chinese Historical Society of America
Jessica Silverman Gallery
CHINATOWN
NOB HILL
FINANCIAL DISTRICT (FiDi)
St Mary's Square
Huntington Park
Broadway
Vallejo St
Grant Ave
Columbus Ave
Montgomery St
Pacific Ave
Stockton St
Jackson St
Washington St
Clay St
Sacramento St
Kearny St
California St
Pine St
Mason St
Taylor St
Jones St
Leavenworth St
Broadway Tunnel
BRdway

★ TOP EXPERIENCE

Chinatown Alleyways

Since 1849 Chinatown alleyways have survived gold rushes and revolution, fire and icy receptions. These 41 byways endured exclusion laws restricting Chinese immigration, employment and housing for 73 years – now they're cultural touchstones and places of possibility, through art, mutual aid and shared celebrations.

MAP P88 **D6**

PLANNING TIP
Teenage historians guide two-hour nonprofit **Chinatown Alleyway Tours** *(chinatown alleywaytours.org; adult/student/child $50/20/10)*, from Sun Yat-sen plotting revolution to martial-artist Bruce Lee breaking down racial barriers.

Waverly Place

Through earthquakes, world wars and Prohibition gunfights, Waverly Place changed the culture around it. You'll spot the flag-festooned balcony of **Tin How Temple** *(9:30am-3pm Fri-Wed)*, where prayers have been offered since 1852 – even after the 1906 earthquake and fire, when altars were still smoldering. To pay your respects, follow sandalwood-incense aromas upstairs. Entry is free but offerings customary; no photography inside, please.

Readers may remember Waverly as the namesake of one of the narrators in Amy Tan's novel *The Joy Luck Club* – to find new favorite novels, head to **On Waverly** (p103; *onwaverly.com)*, which showcases Asian American authors and artists.

BENJAMIN HEATH FOR LONELY PLANET

Ross Alley

You might recognize colorful Ross Alley from its cameos in ho-hum Hollywood blockbusters – *The Karate Kid Part II, The Pursuit of Happyness* – and its star turns in indie gems like *Who Is Michael Jang?* and *Chan Is Missing*. Stop by the Chinese Culture Center's contemporary art shows at **41 Ross** (p96; *41ross.org; free)*, then seek your fortune at **Golden Gate Fortune Cookies** *(goldengatefortunecookies.com)*, where cookies are stamped from vintage presses, just as they were in 1909, when fortune cookies were invented in San Francisco.

Scan this QR code for upcoming Ross Alley events and shows.

★ TOP EXPERIENCE

City Lights Books

Free spirits and free speech have found refuge at City Lights since 1957. Words were dangerous business back in the '50s, when library books were often banned, Hollywood screenwriters were blacklisted and comedians got arrested for swearing in North Beach nightclubs – but poet Lawrence Ferlinghetti founded City Lights Books anyway.

MAP P88 **E5**

PLANNING TIP
Don't miss the literary underground nonfiction cellar, unconventionally organized by countercultural themes – including Stolen Continents, Muckraking and Commodity Aesthetics.

Scan this QR code for upcoming readings and events.

'A Kind of Library Where Books Are Sold'

As Ferlinghetti's hand-lettered sign says, idle browsing is highly encouraged at City Lights. Wax poetic in the upstairs Poetry Room, load up on zines on the mezzanine and entertain radical ideas downstairs in the Pedagogies of Resistance section. On the main floor, City Lights publications include titles by Angela Davis, Diane di Prima and Noam Chomsky, proving the point on another of Ferlinghetti's signs: 'Printer's Ink Is the Greater Explosive.'

Poetry Room

City Lights' affordable Pocket Poets series brought poetry to the people, sparking the Beat poetry movement. Number four was Allen Ginsberg's epic *Howl and Other Poems* (1956), an instant sensation that got Ferlinghetti and City Lights manager Shigeyoshi Murao arrested for publishing poetry with homoerotic content. They fought charges of publishing obscenity not on technicalities but on artistic merits, and won a landmark free-speech victory. Celebrate your freedom to read freely in the upstairs Poetry Room overlooking Jack Kerouac Alley, in the designated Poet's Chair with your choice of 60 Pocket Poets books – including *Howl,* available in 24 languages.

★ TOP EXPERIENCE

Coit Tower

The exclamation mark atop Telegraph Hill is Coit Tower, dedicated to first responders by firefighting millionaire Lillie Hitchcock Coit, who raised eyebrows in the 1860s for gambling, drinking and wearing men's gear like other firefighters. The 1930s lobby murals celebrating workers were initially denounced as communist, but are now landmarked.

MAP P88 **E2**

Lobby Murals

Publicly funded 1930s lobby murals show what daily life was like here during the Depression: San Franciscans organized dockworkers' unions, lined up at soup kitchens, partied despite Prohibition and read books – including Marxist manifestos – in Chinese, Italian and English. When they were completed in 1934, the artworks were so controversial that the opening of the tower was delayed by DC censors. Authorities called the 26 artists that painted them communists, and demanded that radical elements be removed. The artists refused, and in a last-minute compromise, park employees painted over a hammer-and-sickle symbol with a union logo. Public opinion overruled the censors: San Franciscans embraced the murals as symbols of the city's openness. In 2012 voters passed a measure to preserve them as historic landmarks, and today the murals are freshly restored – and as bold as ever.

PLANNING TIP
For a parrot's-eye panoramic view of San Francisco, take the creaky 1930s elevator to the tower's open-air **viewing platform** *(adult/student/child $10/7/3)*.

Secret Stairwell Treasures

Book a **tour** *(from $5)* up the narrow 2nd-floor stairwell, where recently revealed murals were hidden for 80 years. The seven murals show San Francisco in the 1930s – the showstopper is Jane Berlandina's strikingly modern egg-tempera mural *Home Life*, showing San Franciscans baking pies and kicking back.

Scan this QR code for mural tours and information.

Beat Walking Tour

Find inspiration in the literary stomping grounds of North Beach, where poets, writers and San Francisco's cast of original characters Kerouac called 'the mad ones' still roam free. In streets named for spoken-word legends, you can get moved to poetry and debate philosophy without missing a Beat.

START	END	LENGTH
City Lights Books	Vesuvio	0.7 miles; 45 min

1 Get Lit at City Lights

At **City Lights Books** (p92), home of Beat poetry and free speech, find a few choice words to inspire your journey into literary North Beach – Ferlinghetti's *San Francisco Poems* make excellent companions.

2 Stop for Opera & Espresso

Head up the block of Vallejo St that Ferlinghetti called 'Poet's Piazza' and duck into **Caffe Trieste** (p103) for opera on the jukebox and potent espresso in the back booth – Francis Ford Coppola drafted *The Godfather* screenplay here.

3 Reflect in an Alley

Observe a moment of silence in **Bob Kaufman Alley**, honoring the legendary Black, Jewish, Buddhist, spoken-word poet and co-founder of *Beatitude* magazine. Frequently jailed for 'resisting arrest' in verse, Kaufman was never at a loss for words – until Kennedy's assassination, when he took a vow of silence that lasted 12 years, until the Vietnam War ended. Then he walked into a North Beach cafe and recited his ode to peace, 'All Those Ships That Never Sailed.'

4 Literary Time Capsules

Rest on the bench dedicated to city founder Juana Briones, whose ranchland became **Washington Square** c 1850. Notice the Ben Franklin statue – a replacement for a statue eccentric dentist Henry Cogswell plunked here of himself. Neighbors toppled Henry, but left the time capsule he buried intact until 1979 – it contained a 19th-century feminist manifesto, SF Chinese-language newspaper and terrifying dental tools. A replacement time capsule is buried here, containing Lawrence Ferlinghetti poetry, Levi's jeans and wine.

5 Sidewalk Poetry

Walk down Columbus past City Lights, and swing into mural-covered, poetry-paved **Jack Kerouac Alley**. Embedded in this alley, you'll spot this ode to the city by the *On the Road* and *Dharma Bums* author: 'The air was soft, the stars so fine, the promise of every cobbled alley so great...' Still true.

6 Epic Toasts at Vesuvio

Jack Kerouac once blew off author Henry Miller to hang at **Vesuvio** (p102) – kick off your own epic night here. Vesuvio's literary-legendary signature cocktail is named for Beat poet Diane di Prima – she published 50 books in her lifetime, including the visionary *Revolutionary Letters*. After today, you'll have enough material to write revolutionary letters of your own.

EXPERIENCES

Look ahead in Chinatown Galleries

GALLERIES

Drop into Chinatown's cutting-edge arts hub **Edge on the Square** (MAP: 1 P88 E7; *edgeonthesquare.org; free)* for fresh takes on current topics with impactful shows like 'All Eyes On Us: Invention & Ingenuity During Artistic Diasporas.' Edge events blend art, community and joy, from Chinatown Pride celebrations to live chef demos exploring Asian American identity through food.

Atop the pedestrian bridge spanning Kearney St, a mosaic sun graces the steps to the **Chinese Culture Center** (MAP: 2 P88 E6; *cccsf.us; free)*, expanding artistic horizons since 1965 with contemporary Chinese artists. Visit the center's satellite gallery at **41 Ross Alley** (MAP: 3 P88 D6; *41ross.org; free)*, and gain deeper understanding of the local art scene on the Center's **Chinatown History and Art Walking Tours** *(1½ to two hours; four-person minimum; $45 per person)*.

Between international art fairs, art stars converge at **Jessica Silverman Gallery** (MAP: 4 P88 E7; *jessicasilvermangallery.com; free)*. Beyond frosted glass doors lie stunning parallel universes, featuring Ruby Tut's cosmic gardeners, Judy Chicago's world-birthing quilts and David Huffman's history-repairing *Traumanauts*.

Celebrate Lunar New Year

FESTIVAL

Chinatown celebrates Lunar New Year for a month, starting with **night markets** *(bechinatown.weebly.com)* along lantern-lit Grant Ave stocked with lucky bamboo, red envelopes and miniature mandarin trees. Chase the 200ft dragon, legions of lion dancers and fierce tiny-tot martial artists at the **Chinese New Year Parade** *(chineseparade.com; free)*. By the end of the night, everyone's happy and hoarse from exchanging best wishes for prosperity: *'Gung hay fat choy!'* (Cantonese) or *'Gōng xǐ fā cái!'* (Mandarin).

Each lunar year is represented by one of 12 Chinese zodiac animal signs and five natural elements – 2026 is the year of the fire horse, 2027 is the fire goat, 2028 is the earth monkey. Every 12 years, the lunar year's sign coincides with your birth year's zodiac sign – which means you have an extra excuse to party. If you don't know your sign, the red-envelope-covered Chinese Zodiac Wall on Jack Kerouac Alley (p95) shows the zodiac signs and character traits associated with birth years.

Time-Travel at the Chinese Historical Society of America MUSEUM

MAP: 5 P88 D7

Picture what it was like to be Chinese in America during California's Gold Rush, the Chinese exclusion era (1870–1943) and SF's hippie heyday at the **Chinese Historical Society of America** *(chsa.org; adult/student/child $12/10/5)*, built as Chinatown's YWCA by Hearst Castle architect Julia Morgan. Exhibits in this 1932 landmark spotlight Chinese American culture, from WWII Chinatown nightclub posters to Bruce Lee's martial-arts costumes and philosophy library.

Play in Portsmouth Square PARK

MAP: 6 P88 E6

Tai chi practitioners greet the dawn, picnickers assemble lunch banquets, toddlers rush the playground and chess players plot moves well into the night. Welcome to Portsmouth Sq, Chinatown's unofficial living room. When California's Gold Rush erupted in 1849, Portsmouth Sq was its center: burlesque Jenny Lind Theater doubled as San Francisco's first City Hall, conveniently located across from Commercial St bordellos, alongside San Francisco's first newspaper offices, public school and vigilante headquarters.

The Victorian madams and vigilantes are long gone, and Portsmouth Sq has mellowed with age – but as you see, this park is still lively and open to ideas. Presiding over the plaza is the **Goddess of Democracy**, a bronze replica of the plaster statue Tiananmen Sq protesters made in 1989. Portsmouth Sq's pedestrian bridge is a magnet for arts and events like **Chinatown Pride**, celebrating the neighborhood's LGBTQ+ community. To glimpse what's ahead for SF and the world, watch this space – and bring a picnic.

GRANT AVENUE'S BRILLIANT NEON

Grant Ave became America's brightest street 100 years ago, as part of Chinatown's brilliant redesign. After the 1906 earthquake, developers schemed to push Chinatown outside SF, on the pretext that this thoroughfare was a red-light strip – never mind that white landlords profited. Savvy Chinatown leaders led by Look Tin Eli lobbied to rename shady DuPont St 'Grant Ave' and consulted architects to design its modern, pagoda-roofed Chinatown deco style. Dim lanterns were replaced with dazzling neon and dragon-wrapped street lamps. The image overhaul worked like a charm: photographers, partiers and celebrities flocked here, establishing neon-lit Li Po (p102) and Buddha Lounge (p102) as signature SF attractions.

THE OTHER BROADWAY

When San Franciscans reminisce about Broadway shows, they're not talking about Disney musicals. North Beach's Broadway strip has seen it all since the 1930s: the nation's first openly lesbian bar (Mona's, 1936), dedicated drag venue (Finocchio's, 1936), uncensored comedy acts (Jazz Workshop, 1961), topless strip club (Condor Club, 1964) and unionized strip club (Lusty Lady, 1997). Some shows here actually changed history: Carol Doda was arrested for going topless but won her case, and Lenny Bruce was arrested and acquitted of obscenity charges. SF Broadway shows continue to push buttons and boundaries, honoring almost a century of fearless performers.

Rock Out in North Beach

LIVE MUSIC

You're right on time for the revival of legendary North Beach clubs. **Bimbo's 365 Club** (MAP: 7 P88 A2; *bimbos365club.com)* is an iconic 1931 speakeasy known for danceable indie bands (Zap Mama, Dandy Warhols) and marquee talent (Adele, Van Morrison, Lizzo). **Keys Jazz Bistro** (MAP: 8 P88 E4; *keysjazzbistro.com)* features rotating residencies by international jazz talents and raucous classics by SF's Jazz Mafia. Punk's not dead at **Mabuhay Gardens** (MAP: 9 P88 F5) – the 1970s Filipino supper club that took a chance on loud local acts, including the Dead Kennedys, the Avengers and an unsigned Metallica, is back. At quaint, mural-lined 1907 **Savoy Tivoli** (MAP: 10 P88 D4; *savoytivoli.com),* the tiny stage that survived earth-shaking shows by the Ramones, Muddy Waters and SF drag phenomenon Beach Blanket Babylon is now reinforced – ready when you are.

Catch Underground Comedy Acts

COMEDY

Comedy acts have packed North Beach clubs since the 1930s – comedian Lenny Bruce got arrested here for cursing in 1961 and won a landmark free-speech victory. Today Bimbo's 365 Club and **Cobb's Comedy Club** (MAP: 11 P88 B2; *18-plus; tickets from $25)* keep launching and relaunching careers – John Oliver, Mo Amer, Michelle Wolf – at cozy showcases with a two-drink minimum. At tiny nonprofit **The Lost Church** (MAP: 12 P88 B2; *thelostchurch.org*) and Chinatown's **Great Star Theater** (MAP: 13 P88 E6; *greatstartheater.org),* comics work up material for **SF Sketchfest** *(sfsketchfest.com)* – you saw it here first.

Dig the Beat Museum MUSEUM

MAP: 14 P88 E5

Dylan jam sessions erupt in the bookshop, Allen Ginsberg spouts poetry nude in documentary footage and stoned visitors grin beatifically at it all. Welcome to the **Beat Museum** *(kerouac.com; adult/student $8/5)*, spiritual home to all 'angelheaded hipsters burning for the ancient heavenly connection' (to quote Ginsberg's *Howl*). The 1000-plus artifacts in the museum's literary ephemera collection include overdue tributes to Diane di Prima and other women Beats, and the writing desk of City Lights (p92) founder and San Francisco Poet Laureate Lawrence Ferlinghetti. Enter the museum through the adjoining museum store, stocked with poetry chapbooks and obscure Beat titles you won't find elsewhere; bookstore entry and poetry readings are free.

Hike Telegraph Hill Stairways URBAN HIKES

In the 19th century, a ruthless entrepreneur began blasting away the side of Telegraph Hill. City Hall eventually stopped the quarrying, but the view of the bay from the **Filbert Street Steps** (MAP: 15 P88 F3) is still (wait for it) dynamite.

Halfway through this steep climb to Coit Tower, you might wonder if it's worth the trouble. Take a breather and notice the scenery: sweeping Bay Bridge vistas, hidden cottages along Napier Lane's wooden boardwalk, and sculpture-dotted gardens blooming year-round. If you need further encouragement, the colorful wild parrots in the trees might interject a few choice words.

For more well-earned views, find the trailhead for **Francisco Street Steps** (MAP: 16 P88 D1) to ascend to Jack Early Park, where you'll find scenic seats for two – a popular spot for marriage proposals, despite the ominous view of Alcatraz from here. Climb higher for bay panoramas, then descend via Grant Ave for pizza.

LISTINGS

Best Places for...

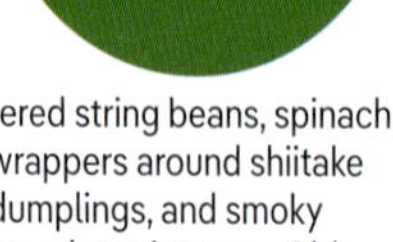

$ Budget $$ Midrange $$$ Top End

Eating

Classic Dim Sum

Good Mong Kok $
17 D6
Join excited eaters waiting at Chinatown's busiest counter, where shrimp dumplings, pork *siu mai* and other classics are whisked from steamers into takeout containers. *7am-6pm*

Hang Ah Tea Room $
18 D7
Chinatown's original dim sum, with century-old menus to prove it – timeless classics include spicy purse dumplings, pillowy pork buns and creamy thousand-year-egg-custard *bao*. *10:30am-8pm*

Dim Sum Bistro $

19 D5
Don't let unconvincing food photos and bargain prices deter you from scoring high-quality takeout, from tender shrimp and chive dumplings to perfectly toasted sesame balls. *8am-3pm*

Today Food $

20 E7
Witness dumpling mastery: dough rolled until translucent, loaded with veggies, shrimp and organic chicken, pinched and pan-fried or steamed to enjoy with aged soy, vinegar, chili and awe. *8am-8pm*

Modern Chinese Feasts

Mister Jiu's $$$
21 E7
Chef/owner Brandon Jew's globally acclaimed, Californian Chinese banquets feature coastal lamb with plum sauce, scallion milk-bread with sustainable caviar, and whole roast Sonoma duck. *5-9pm Tue & Wed, to 10pm Thu-Sat*

Z & Y $$
22 E6
Spicy, sumptuous banquets – Sichuan pork dumplings, flaming cauliflower, and chili-oil-poached fish leave lips buzzing. *11:30am-3pm & 4:30-9pm Wed-Sun*

Osmanthus Dim Sum Lounge $$
23 E5
Gourmet rule-breaker Osmanthus puts XO brandy sauce atop blistered string beans, spinach wrappers around shiitake dumplings, and smoky pu-erh tea into new Old Fashioneds. *10:30am-8pm*

China Live $$
24 D5
Chef/owner George Chen showcases modern regional Chinese dishes with Californian flair – Kurobota pork-soup dumplings, kumquat-glazed Peking duck – plus top-notch tea and cocktails. *4-9pm Sun*

Four Kings $$$
25 E7
Ingeniously remixed Cantonese dishes you'll want to share with someone special – pass the Sichuan peppercorn–spiked *ma-po* spaghetti, please. Reserve 29 days in advance. *6-11pm Tue-Sat*

Pizza & Focaccia

Liguria Bakery $
26 D3
Bleary-eyed rockers and Italian grandmothers queue by 8am for cinnamon-raisin focaccia hot from the 100-year-old oven. Takeout only. *7am-noon Tue-Sat*

Outta Sight Pizza 2 $

 27 F7

North Beach and Chinatown converge for the crossover sensation: Peking duck pizza, with caramelized onions and a dash of hoisin. *11am-8pm Mon-Fri, noon-5pm Sat & Sun*

Tony's Pizza Napoletana $$

28 D3

World-champ pizza-slinger Tony Gemignani ends coastal rivalries with legit Jersey tomato pies. *noon-9:30pm Mon-Thu, to 11pm Fri-Sun*

Golden Boy $

 29 D4

Punks have politely queued since 1978 for the Sodinis' focaccia-crust pizza – try clam-and-garlic slices. Takeout only. *11:30am-9pm Sun-Thu, to 11pm Fri & Sat*

Tommaso's $$

 30 E5

Charming North Beach since 1935 with wood-fired brick-oven Neapolitan pizza, cozy booths and communal tables. *5-10:30pm Tue-Sat, 4-9:30pm Sun*

North Beach Seafood

Sotto Mare $$

 31 D4

From tonight on, the clatter of bowls will make you remember seafood *cioppino* so fresh, it's practically swimming in rich tomato broth. *11:30am-9pm*

Ristorante Ideale $$

32 D4

Roman chef/owner Maurizio Bruschi hand-makes pasta ('of course!'), prepares today's catch simply and curates top-value Italian wines. *5-10pm Tue-Sun*

Cafe Jacqueline $$

 33 D3

Dinner can hardly get more romantic than seafood soufflé floating across your tongue like fog over SF... until you order the chocolate soufflé. *5:30-10pm Tue-Sat*

Da Flora $$

 34 C3

Get cozy in this candle-lit *osteria* over chef/owner Jen McMahon's market-fresh menus – buttery, pan-kissed Pacific halibut, poached in saffron risotto. *5-9pm Wed-Sat*

Panini

Molinari $

 35 D4

Grab a number and sing along to Sinatra while wisecracking staff prepare massive panini to order – get the house-cured salami. *9am-5:30pm Mon-Fri, to 9pm Sat, 11am-3:30pm Sun*

Palermo II Delicatessen $

36 D4

Lucrezia is the 2nd-generation Sicilian deli boss behind *Godfather*-themed panini, crispy arancini (risotto balls), and eggplant parmigiana with her secret-recipe marinara. *10am-5pm Tue-Sun*

Mario's Bohemian Cigar Store Cafe $

37 D4

Mario's switched from smoking to piping-hot panini in the '70s – enjoy onion focaccia with meat-balls, eggplant or grilled chicken, plus Chianti and people-watching. *11am-9pm*

Drinking

Tea

Red Blossom Tea Company

 38 E6

Second-generation tea merchants Alice and Peter Luong feature 100-plus specialty teas at their showroom, where staff share tea-prep tips and recommend samplers. *11am-5pm Wed-Sat*

PlenTea

 39 F8

PlenTea tea-ristas fill mini-milk bottles with

just-brewed, certified-organic bubble tea, classic green or black, seasonal fruit, or original SF flavors like sea-salt cream oolong. *11am-11pm*

Ten Ren Tea

 40 E6

A Chinatown institution since 1953, with specialty teas, iced fruit-tea flavors like kumquat lemon, and classic King's oolong milk boba tea. *10:30am-6pm*

Iconic Bars

Li Po

 41 E6

Enter the 1937 faux-grotto doorway for *baijiu* (rice-liquor) Chinese mai tais under the golden Buddha. Brusque bartenders, cellar bathrooms, random dance-offs: a world-class dive bar. *2pm-1:30am*

Buddha Lounge

 42 E6

The vintage red-neon Buddha sign promises dangerously enlightening nights featuring an eclectic jukebox, cheap well drinks and beer straight from a laughing-Buddha bottle. *1pm-2am*

Empress at Boon Lounge

 43 E6

Chinatown's 1966 landmark is crowned by this swanky octagonal lounge, featuring inventive cocktails and inspired Cantonese bites by chef/owner Ho Chee Boon. *5-10pm Mon-Sat*

Specs

 44 E5

The walls are plastered with merchant-marine memorabilia; you'll be plastered too if you try to keep up with the salty characters holding court over pitchers of beer and navy-strength gin drinks. *4pm-2am*

Historic Cocktails

Vesuvio

 45 E5

The literary-legendary di Prima cocktail (rye/Aperol/bitters) recalls poet Diane di Prima's maxim: 'to remind us all/to celebrate/there is no time too desperate/no season that is not a Season of Song.' *11am-1am Sun-Thu, to 2am Fri & Sat*

Comstock Saloon

 46 E5

SF's martini precursor the Martinez was invented to tide over a Victorian boozehound on the Bay Ferry – it tastes of gin, vermouth, bitters, maraschino liqueur and wild abandon. *4pm-midnight Tue-Sat*

Tony Nik's

 47 D4

North Beach celebrated Prohibition's 1933 end at this tiny 'cafe' – an original deco bar with a vintage dirty martini that's salty and a touch pickled. *4pm-1am Mon-Fri, 2pm-2am Sat, 2pm-1am Sun*

Tosca Cafe

 48 E5

Tosca served its 'cappuccino' (brandy-spiked hot cocoa) through Prohibition, and you can still order their air-quote special at the vintage bar. *5-11pm Tue-Sat*

Devil's Acre

 49 E5

This Victorian apothecary-style bar serves tartly quaffable Lavender 75 (lemon, lavender, gin, bubbly) – a surefire cure for scurvy and/or sobriety. *4:30pm-1am Tue-Sat, 2-8pm Sun*

Wine

Friend of a Friend

 50 C3

Instant friendships form when farmer and winemaker Christopher Renfro pours rare finds from independent wineries and Black winemakers – including his own SF-grown Teroldego. *noon-7pm Wed-Sun*

Golden Sardine

 51 D4

The next Renaissance is underway with Beat poetry readings, winemaker tastings, and free-flowing creativity fed with sardines and cheese. *4-10pm Tue-Fri, 2-11pm Sat, 2-9pm Sun*

Little Vine

 D3

Consult cheesemonger/owner Melissa Gugni to pair California wine with artisan cheese and charcuterie or today's panini – and return for $5 Thursday tastings with winemakers. *11am-7pm Tue-Sun*

Belle Cora

 D4

Join the sidewalk-cafe block party with affordable Italian wines and upbeat live music, from ragtime Parlor Tricks to Danny Herrera's Salsita Brass. *3pm-midnight Sun-Thu, to 2am Fri, 1pm-2am Sat*

Espresso Drinks

Caffe Trieste

 D4

Espresso fuels conversation among artists, writers and filmmakers. Chatting encouraged, phones discouraged, food irrelevant; cash only. *7am-10pm*

Cafe Angolo

 D4

Linger over espresso drinks at sunny bistro tables – this isn't your average American office-cafe, but a true North Beach social hub. *8am-5pm*

Réveille

 E5

Sunny flat-iron storefront, featuring cappuccino with foam-art heart and just-baked chocolate-chip cookies. *7:30am-4pm*

Shopping

Non-Touristy Souvenirs

Wok Shop

57 E7

Get equipped to make five-star meals with expert advice from owner and SF icon Tane Chan, who jokes that she's sold 'woks for all woks of life' since the 1970s. *11am-5pm*

On Waverly

 E6

Delightful locally designed reminders of your time in Chinatown – mah-jongg-tile soap sets, dim-sum plushies, risograph prints of Chinatown neon sign – plus books on Asian American culture. *11am-6pm*

Chinatown Kite Shop

59 E7

Making windy SF days worthwhile since 1971 with colorful kites: fierce 9ft-long flying dragons, pirate-worthy wild parrots (SF's city birds) and flying pandas. *10am-7pm Mon-Fri, to 9pm Sat & Sun*

Kim + Ono

 E7

Chinatown sister-duo designers Renee and Tiffany Tam are bringing silk-robe style back, in soft shades of satin and silk charmeuse, splashed with bodacious blossoms and the occasional peacock. *11am-6pm Mon-Thu, 10:30am-6:30pm Fri-Sun*

Vintage Treasures

Vacation

 D3

Channel your inner SF rocker style with glam-rock metallic platforms, inexplicably well-preserved punk concert tees, mint deadstock denim, psychedelic shifts and Victorian tasseled handbags. *noon-8pm*

San Francisco Rock Posters & Collectibles

 C3

At this trippy temple to rock gods, you'll find psychedelic Fillmore concert posters featuring the Grateful Dead, for a price – plus hand-printed handbills for SF legends like Santana, the Avengers, and Sly and the Family Stone. *11am-6pm Mon-Sat*

101 Music

 D4

Find your own SF anthem here in crates of $10 to $30 vinyl – you might score rare recordings by Nina Simone, Janis Joplin, Alice Coltrane or SF's own Dead Kennedys. *11am-7pm*

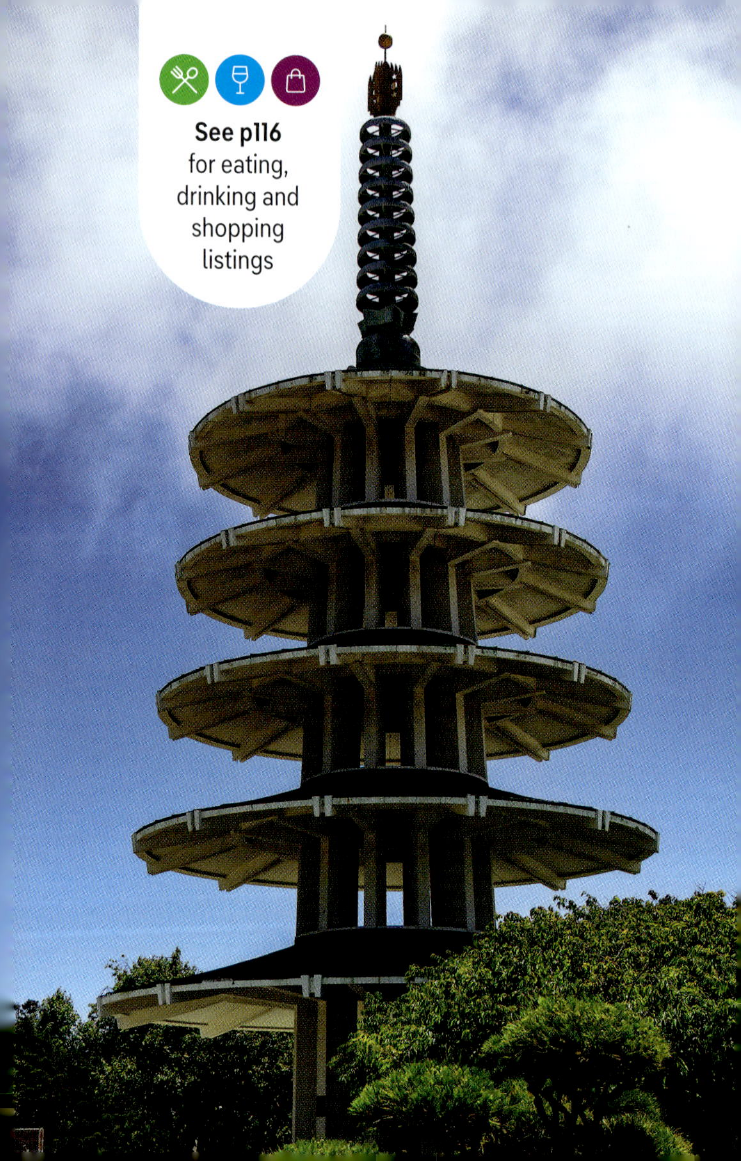
See p116
for eating,
drinking and
shopping
listings

Researched by
Alison Bing

Explore Japantown, Fillmore & Pacific Heights

Don't let the quaint Victorians and upscale boutiques fool you: this neighborhood totally rocks. Japanese Americans have called this area home for over a century, and today Japantown is where J-pop stars and cosplay TikTokkers shoot music videos in Peace Plaza. The Fillmore has been a nightlife hub since the jazzy 1930s and turned totally trippy in the psychedelic '60s – and music legends are still made at live shows here. Hilltop Pacific Heights is ringed with mansions, many owned or once-owned by powerful women – including nude model turned museum founder Alma Spreckles, 19th-century Black billionaire and Underground Railroad pioneer Mary Ellen Pleasant, and former US House Speaker Nancy Pelosi.

Getting Around

Bus

The 38 Geary bus transports you from downtown to Geary and Fillmore. Lines 1, 2 and 22 also serve this area.

Cable Car

Hop the California line west from Market St to Van Ness Ave, then walk to Pacific Heights or Japantown.

Walk

From Van Ness, walk Victorian-lined Sacramento St, then window-shop your way south along Fillmore. At Post St, swing east to reach Japan Center, or west to Pierce St, then south to Alamo Sq.

Peace Pagoda (p114)
UVL/SHUTTERSTOCK

THE BEST

ICONIC VICTORIANS Alamo Sq Park (p109)

ALL-AGES HOTSPOT Japan Center (p108)

ROCK LEGEND Fillmore Auditorium (p112)

ARTS WORKSHOPS JCCCNC (p114)

SPA Kabuki Springs & Spa (p112)

For more see

- Top Experiences p108
- Experiences p112
- Eating p116
- Drinking p118
- Shopping p118

0 — 500 m
0 — 0.2 miles

A B C D E F
1 2 3 4

PACIFIC HEIGHTS
Pacific Ave
Jackson St
Washington St
Clay St
Sacramento St
California St
Pine St
Bush St
Sutter St
Post St
Geary Blvd
Divisadero St
Scott St
Pierce St
Steiner St
Fillmore St
Webster St
Buchanan St
Laguna St
Octavia St
Gough St
Franklin St
Van Ness Ave
Alta Plaza Park
University of the Pacific
Lafayette Park
Haas-Lilienthal House 14
California St Cable Car Turnaround
Audium 4
Konko Church 12
JAPANTOWN
Japan Center
FILLMORE
44
51
49
42
39
37
24
31

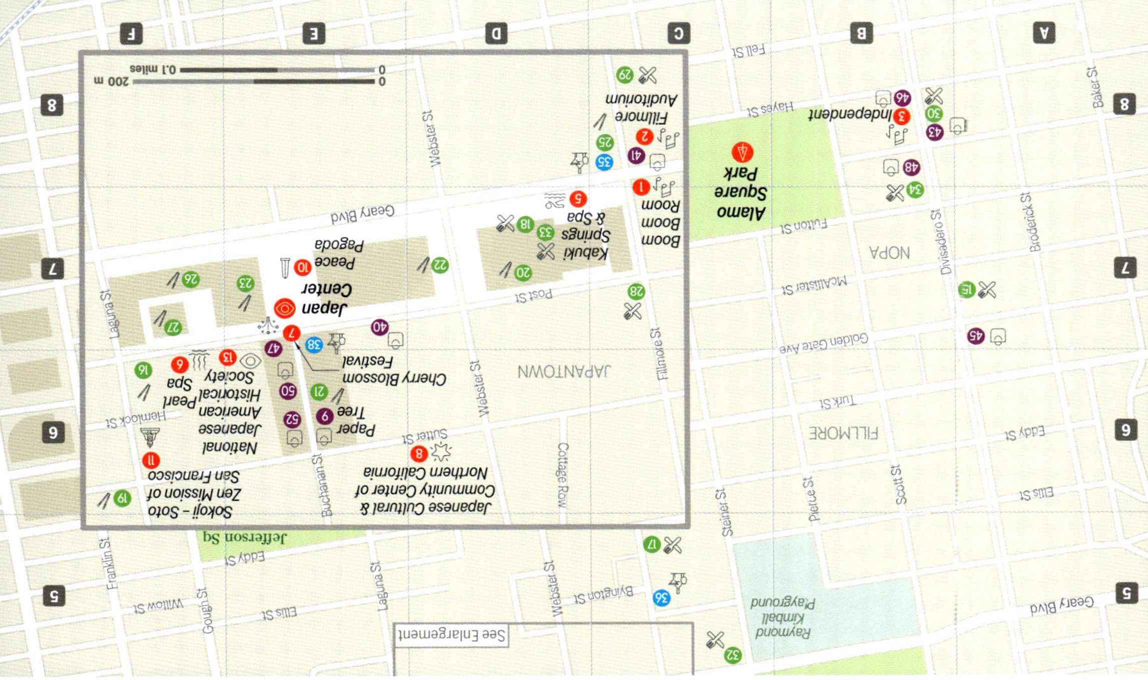
Sokoji – Soto Zen Mission of San Francisco
National Japanese American Historical Society
Pearl Spa
Paper Tree
Cherry Blossom Festival
Japan Center
Peace Pagoda
Japanese Cultural & Community Center of Northern California
JAPANTOWN
Kabuki Springs & Spa
Boom Boom Room
Fillmore Auditorium
Alamo Square Park
Independent
NOPA
FILLMORE
Raymond Kimball Playground
Jefferson Sq
See Enlargement
0.1 miles
200 m
Franklin St
Willow St
Gough St
Ellis St
Eddy St
Laguna St
Hemlock St
Buchanan St
Sutter St
Webster St
Cottage Row
Byington St
Post St
Geary Blvd
Fillmore St
Steiner St
Pierce St
Scott St
Turk St
Golden Gate Ave
McAllister St
Fulton St
Hayes St
Fell St
Divisadero St
Broderick St
Baker St

★ TOP EXPERIENCE

Japan Center

Time-travel to 1968 as you cross Japan Center's indoor wooden bridges, with *maneki-neko* (cat figurines) waving welcomes – yet this *kawaii*-cute mall started with a knock-down fight. After WWII, 1500 Japantown residents were displaced to build a mall. But residents and businesses rallied, converting the mall into a community hub.

MAP P106 **E7**

PLANNING TIP
West Mall has boutiques, arcades and sweet treats. Across Peace Plaza, the **East Mall** has date-night dining and cultural events.

From Manga to Ukiyo-e

Entire afternoons disappear at **Kinokuniya Books**, between stunning art books (Daido Moriyama photography), tempting cookbooks (bento-box lunches) and toys (smiling sushi plushies) – plus manga comics and Tokyo street-fashion mags. Across the hall, Kinokuniya's office and school supplies promise to make work and studying more fun – slow down with sloth-themed to-do lists and reward homework with panda-doughnut stickers. On Japan Center's indoor pedestrian bridge, stop at **Tokaido Arts** *(tokaidoarts.com; free)* to see a major collection of original ukiyo-e (Japanese woodblock prints) in mint condition – including Hokusai's sublime views of Mt Fuji, still vibrant over 200 years later.

All-Ages Entertainment

Vampire kittens and Alice in Wonderland characters occasionally roam the halls of the Japan Center, queuing politely for anime-themed photo booths and arcade games. Cosplay costumes could signal a festival, anime event or pop-up art mart – or just a typical Japan Center Saturday. Follow sounds of familiar tunes into **Festa** *(festalounge.com; age 21-plus)* karaoke lounge, where you too can rock the miniature stage for $2 per song plus liquid courage from *yuzu shochu* cocktails.

Scan this QR code for events, maps, directions and parking.

★ TOP EXPERIENCE

Alamo Square Park

The graceful 'Painted Lady' Victorians lining Alamo Sq have housed bordellos, jazz speakeasies and hippie communes, including east-end Postcard Row and northwest-corner Westerfield House. Earthquakes and fire couldn't destroy Alamo Sq's Victorians, yet redevelopment almost did, until neighbors banded together to save this historic district.

MAP P106 **C8**

Meet the Painted Ladies

When prospectors struck it rich in the Gold Rush, they upgraded from downtown tenements to pastel 'Painted Lady' Victorian flats around Alamo Sq Park, embellished to the eaves with gilded woodwork and look-at-me bay windows. Since the Painted Ladies were built on bedrock, many survived the 1906 earthquake – until 1950s developers began demolishing this diverse neighborhood to clear the way for luxury high-rise condos. Some 38 blocks of affordable Victorian homes and small businesses were destroyed before public outcry stopped the destruction in a landmark win. Today you'll spot fresh 6-10 color schemes inspired by SF's 1970s Colorist Movement, when many Painted Ladies were restored to their full glory.

PLANNING TIP
On sunny days, claim a hilltop picnic table framed by gabled Victorian rooflines and wind-sculpted pines.

Westerfield House

On Alamo Sq's northwestern corner stands Westerfield House, a gilded Stick Italianate Victorian with a spooky watchtower. This 28-room mansion was built by candy baron William Westerfield in 1889, and survived subsequent incarnations as a jazz speakeasy and the legendary 50-person hippie commune described in Tom Wolfe's psychedelic '60s chronicle *The Electric Kool-Aid Acid Test*. Filmmaker Kenneth Anger filmed satanic rituals in the tower with Church of Satan founder Anton LaVey, involving one grumpy lion that was coaxed up four flights of stairs.

Scan this QR code for park information and events.

Victorian Stroll

Every San Franciscan has a favorite iconic Victorian – and you're about to find yours, amid the rows of historic flats and opulent mansions ringing Alamo Sq Park. Multicolor 'Painted Lady' Victorians are irresistible photo-ops – but respect residents' privacy when taking photos.

START	END	LENGTH
Westerfield House	Madrone Art Bar	1 mile; one hour

1 Westerfield House

The stately 1889 Victorian (p109) has survived epic parties by Russian bootleggers, jazz collectives and the Family Dog hippie commune that frequently hosted Janis Joplin and the Grateful Dead – and printed psychedelic posters and handbills for their shows here. Today the mansion has been painstakingly restored to period glory by Jim Siegel, the former Haight teenage runaway turned Burning Man steampunk outfitter – somehow that makes perfect sense here.

2 Bliss Flats

Many historic SF homes were built not as mansions but as affordable flats, including **1347 McAllister**, a 1901 art nouveau landmark built for Annie Bliss and her husband, Czech tailor Charles. Their business was sewing austere uniforms for Presidio soldiers, but self-taught SF architect James Francis Dunn built them an opulent Parisian-style apartment, with Mercury masks above opera-box balconies and winged figures supporting oval windows in the attic ballroom.

3 Chateau Tivoli

The source of neighborhood gossip since 1892, this baroque Queen Anne–style Painted Lady hosted Isadora Duncan, Mark Twain and (rumor has it) the ghost of a Victorian opera diva. Since SF opera owner Ernestine Kraling left the **Chateau Tivoli** in 1930, it's served as a Yiddish school, hippie commune and New Age center – now it's a restored B&B, with a 17-color scheme and 23 karat gold-leaf ornament.

4 Postcard Row

The Painted Ladies of famed **Postcard Row** pale in comparison to other vibrant neighborhood characters – like many SF Victorians, they've been toned down for modern tastes. But with the 1970s Colorist Movement revival, multicolor schemes are returning to Alamo Sq – including 896 Steiner, where 1890 Stick Victorian flats are freshly painted purple with contrasting red and teal tones.

5 Alamo Square Park

Summit **Alamo Square Park** (p109) for downtown views fringed by Victorian rooflines. At the hilltop playground, you'll notice kids climb up and slide down Postcard Row–style playhouses – Victoriana appreciation starts early in SF.

6 Madrone Art Bar

Raise a toast to SF's enduring eccentricity in the 1888 Victorian parlor of **Madrone Art Bar** with a signature Madroni (gin, Campari and Carpano). You'll quickly become part of the local scenery here amid artists' murals and multimedia installations – stick around for live music and dance parties, when everyone bumps into neighbors and/or sculptures.

EXPERIENCES

See Music Legends in the Fillmore

LIVE MUSIC

Music legends keep rocking neighborhood venues here – '30s blues, '50s jazz, '60s rock, '70s punk, '90s hip-hop and current headliners. **Boom Boom Room** (MAP: 1 P106 C8; *boomboomroom.com)* packs its 1930s checkered-linoleum floor with R&B and funk. Lines down the block signal showtime at legendary **Fillmore Auditorium** (MAP: 2 P106 C8; *thefillmore.com),* where Jimi Hendrix, Janis Joplin, Aretha Franklin and the Grateful Dead rocked, with '60s psychedelic posters to prove it – free posters are still distributed after sold-out shows. Bragging rights are earned at small yet mighty **Independent** (MAP: 3 P106 B8; *theindependentsf.com),* featuring indie dreamers (Magnetic Fields, Death Cab for Cutie), music legends (George Clinton, Metallica) and alterna-stars (Superchunk, Tokimonsta). Dig the vibes at **Audium** (MAP: 4 P106 F3; *audium.org; tickets adult/student $30/20),* a 1967 sound sculpture emitting meditative, 90-minute 'room compositions.'

Relax in Japantown Spas

SPAS

Salt-scrub in the steam room, soak in the hot pool, cold plunge, reheat in the sauna, rinse and repeat at **Kabuki Springs & Spa** (MAP: 5 P106 D7), Japantown's communal bathhouse. Men and women alternate days (cisgender and transgender alike), and bathing suits are required on all-gender Mondays and Tuesdays. Bath access is $49, or $20 with **shiatsu massage** *(from $135).* For a skincare glow-up, head to women-only, clothing-free Korean **Pearl Spa** (MAP: 6 P106 F6). Recover from jet lag and late Fillmore nights in the cedar sauna, hot tub, cool pool, warming clay-ball pit and Himalayan-pink-salt room. Gain access with appointment-only treatments, including deliciously slurpy **seaweed massages** *($200, 90 minutes).*

FILLMORE POSTERS

When San Francisco's hippie scene exploded, Fillmore Auditorium launched era-defining acts – including Sly and the Family Stone, Jefferson Airplane and the Grateful Dead, who played the Fillmore 51 times from 1965 to 1969. SF psychedelic artists like Wes Wilson, Bonnie MacLean, Stanley 'Mouse' Miller and Victor Moscoso silkscreened promotional posters in Day-Glo colors and fonts so trippy, they were nearly impossible to read. Soon every rock star wanted their illegible name on a Fillmore poster. Today the Fillmore's hallways and bars are lined with iconic posters, while artists from Snoop Dogg to Green Day play the intimate hall for street cred – and for collectible posters.

NIHONMACHI, THEN & NOW

Nihonmachi (Japantown) started in the 1880s, when Japanese American farmers settled Cottage Row. Savvy builders applied swanky Pacific Heights style, attracting middle-class Filipino, Jewish and Black entrepreneurs to Japantown. WWII changed everything. In 1942 President Roosevelt issued Executive Order 9066, imprisoning Japanese Americans in camps as 'enemy aliens.' Meanwhile, thousands of Black workers were settled in areas where Japanese Americans had been forced out. After WWII, many Japanese Americans returned, only to discover that real-estate speculators had earmarked 60 blocks in and around Japantown for demolition. Japanese American and Black neighbors worked together to demand fair housing – sparking SF's Civil Rights movement.

Join Japantown Festivities FESTIVALS

Spring hasn't officially begun in SF until parades and *taiko* drums welcome it at the **Cherry Blossom Festival** (MAP: 7 P106 E7), Japantown's biggest annual event. For 50 years, **Nihonmachi Street Fair** *(nihonmachistreetfair.org)* has celebrated Japantown's endurance and its multicultural Japanese, Pacific Islander and native Hawaiian heritage. Other cities celebrate Japan Day, but in SF it's expanded to **Japan Week** *(japanweeksf.com)*, packed with cultural events and festivities. Between Japantown's major festivals, **GenRyu Arts** *(genryuarts.org)* also organizes art programs to celebrate Hina Matsuri (Girls' Day), Keiro no Hi (Respect for the Aged) and Midori no Hi (Greenery Day).

Self-Guided Japantown Walking Tour WALKING TOUR

'What happened here?' asks an intriguing sign in Peace Pagoda Plaza, on the outside wall of **Japan Center** (p108). This sign marks the start of a self-guided 10-block **Japantown History Walk** *(jcccnc.org/community/cultural-preservation/jhw; free)*, following the footsteps of Japantown trailblazers. Along the way, you'll discover how the US imprisoned Japanese Americans during WWII – and how Japantown leaders fought this civil-rights violation, winning reparations and an official apology in 1988. Take a picture of this sign as a map reference and handy timeline of 150 years of Japantown history – then follow signs to explore the origins of San Francisco sushi, Japanese baseball, civil-rights movements, psychedelic music and Japantown's enduring community.

Learn New Skills in Japantown

CULTURE CENTER

Japantown has inspiration to spare – so nonprofit **Japanese Cultural & Community Center of Northern California** (JCCCNC; MAP: 8 P106 D6) generously offers affordable workshops with acclaimed local artisans, chefs, artists and performers. Get hands-on experience in person and online with *kaiseki* (seasonal meal) cooking, ikebana flower-arranging, *washi ningyo* (paper dolls), *doburoku* (home-brew sake) and *magawappa* bento-box woodcraft. Check the calendar for upcoming events, including dance and *taiko*-drumming workshops from **GenRyu Arts** *(genryuarts.org)*. Around the corner, endless possibilities have unfolded since 1968 at **Paper Tree** MAP: 9 P106 E6; *paper-tree.com)*, the paper-craft emporium that showcases astounding origami creations: cocoon dresses, minuscule frogs and vast coral reefs made entirely of paper. Beginners can fold their own Death Star with *Star Wars* kits, while decoupage pros get creative with handmade *washi* paper.

Meditate in Japantown

MEDITATION CENTER

When travel schedules or news headlines get you stressed, take a breather in Japantown. Yoshiro Taniguchi's **Peace Pagoda** (MAP: 10 P106 E7) is a striking modernist landmark donated by SF's sister city of Osaka, Japan, in 1968. Sit on boulder benches in the renovated Peace Plaza, and notice how the concrete stupa provides a focal point for life unfolding around it: cherry trees bloom, kids chase seagulls, Tiktokkers shoot dance videos. For a more secluded meditation spot, detour to Cottage Row, where early Nihonmachi 1860–70s clapboard cottages line a blooming mini-park.

Two of Japantown's longest-established spiritual centers graciously open their doors for meditation practice. Founded in 1934, **Sokoji – Soto Zen Mission of San Francisco** (MAP: 11 P106 F6; *sokoji.org)* welcomes newcomers to Wednesday-evening zazen sitting meditation – if you're new, Reverend Kurotaki offers helpful introductions. **Konko Church** (MAP: 12 P106 D3; *konkofaith.org)* has welcomed all faiths since 1931. On weekdays, Reverend Joanne Tolosa kindly answers questions about spirituality and Konko's Shinto-inspired beliefs, then leaves you to quiet contemplation in the serene sanctuary.

Look Deeper into Japanese American History

HISTORY CENTER

MAP: 13 P106 E6

The **National Japanese American Historical Society** (NJAHS) shares insider perspectives on historic events that unfolded here over eight generations, with compelling

Peace Gallery exhibits covering marathon baseball games, art in desert incarceration camps, and origami to promote world peace. NJAHS also organizes insightful, docent-led walking **tours of Japantown** *(adult/student $20/15 by prior booking; 10am-5pm Mon-Fri)* and tours of the Presidio's **Military Intelligence Service Historic Learning Center** *(p49; $20 by prior booking; 10am-5pm Wed-Fri)*, where Japanese American soldiers were trained for top-secret missions in WWII and for postwar US occupation of Japan.

Ascend Pacific Heights Hilltops

HISTORIC SITES

To see how the city looks from above – and glimpse how SF's leisure class lives – hit Pacific Heights, nicknamed 'Specific Whites' for its target demographic. Head to **Alta Plaza Park** for hilltop picnics surrounded by puppies in sweaters, kids racing around immaculate playgrounds, and parents day-trading on smartphones.

At hilltop **Lafayette Park**, sprawling mansions vie for attention like socialites at a ball. Off the parks' northeast corner is a Victorian showstopper: **Haas-Lilienthal House** (MAP: 14 P106 E1; *haas-lilienthalhouse.org; one-hour house tour $10)*, a swaggering 1886 Queen Anne–style mansion. Docents from architectural conservation nonprofit SF Heritage usher you from the parlor to the ballroom like an honored guest of SF's prominent Jewish refugee Haas family – then take you behind the scenes to reveal how staff kept the household going. If these red-velvet walls could talk, they'd cover earthquakes, booms, busts and untimely deaths – check the website for upcoming fancy-dress Victorian balls and eerie haunted-house tours.

WHERE DID THE VICTORIANS GO?

If you're wondering why there are no Victorian homes around Geary Blvd, that's the result of 1950s US redevelopment policies targeting Black and brown communities. Declaring this multiethnic, interfaith, middle-class neighborhood to be 'urban blight,' developers demolished 38 square blocks of affordable Victorian flats and family businesses for high-rise condos. With wrecking balls swinging around Alamo Sq (p109), Japanese American, Filipino, Latino, Black and white neighbors banded together to stop the luxury-condo takeover. On Fillmore St sidewalks, bricks mark spots where local luminaries once lived and worked – from jazz greats to civil-rights-movement leaders. Today, this neighborhood remains a vibrant patchwork of eclectic architecture, resilient small businesses and welcoming cultural venues.

LISTINGS

Best Places for...

$ Budget $$ Midrange $$$ Top End

Eating

Cross-Cultural Comfort Food

Brenda's Meat & Three $
15 A7
Only superheroes can finish chef Brenda Buenviaje's shrimp and grits, let alone the fluffy biscuits – but it's fun trying. *8am-9pm*

Daeho Kalbijjim $$
16 F6
Go early or late for sizzling platters of *kalbijjim* beef topped with cheese and torched tableside. *11am-2:30pm & 4:30-9pm Mon-Fri, 10:30am-9pm Sat & Sun*

Minnie Bell's Soul Movement $
17 C5
Sip bubbly with chef/owner Fernay McPherson's rosemary-infused fried chicken and gooey mac-n-cheese. *4-9pm Tue-Thu, 11am-2pm & 4-10pm Fri & Sat*

Yakitori Edomasa $
18 D7
Grilling since 1924, Edomasa makes yakitori skewers to order, from flavor-bomb chicken thighs and *harami* skirt steak to shiitake mushrooms. *11am-2:30pm & 5-9:30pm Tue-Sun*

Noodles

Sobakatsu $
19 F6
Few seats, no reservations or takeout, soba only: with organic, handmade soba noodles this tasty, Sobakatsu sets the rules. Come around 2pm to dodge rushes. *noon-7pm*

Marufuku Ramen $
20 D7
No Silicon Valley technology excites as much local geekery as Marufuku's slurp-worthy ramen: 20-hour *tonkotsu* broth, handcut ultra-thin noodles, creamy seasoned egg. *11am-10pm*

Hinodeya Ramen Bar $
21 E6
Dashi broth perfected since 1885 graced with toothsome ramen, Kurobota pork, black garlic and jammy eggs. *10am-10pm Sun-Thu, to midnight Fri & Sat*

On the Bridge $
22 D7
Expand dinner horizons with Nakamura family specialties, since 1979: curries made from scratch, vast Japanese beer menus, and *mentaiko* spaghetti with cured cod roe. *12:30-8pm*

Sushi

Sasa $$$
23 E7
Enjoy *kaiseki* (a seasonally inspired menu) or order gently packed *kanpachi nigiri* and creamy scallop-salmon 49er rolls. *5:30-9pm Mon, noon-2pm & 5:30-9pm Tue-Sun*

Tataki $$

 A3

Satiny, sustainable seafood cut with gem-like precision lures sushi savants to this cozy spot for neighborly happy hours (4:30pm to 6:30pm). *4:30-8:30pm*

Aji Kiji $$

25 C8

Impress picnic dates by preordering Aji's jewel-box bento – sashimi, *nigiri* and *maki* meticulously presented, with a fish-shaped container of soy sauce. *11am-4pm Tue-Sat*

An Japanese Restaurant $$$

26 F7

Reserve via text to enter this sushi speakeasy, serving 20 lucky diners eight-course *omakase ($135)* or pristine Pacific seafood à la carte. *5:30-9:30pm Tue-Sat*

Date-Worthy Shared Plates

Nari $$

 F7

Day-Glo bright flavors and lush textures make chef/owner Pim Techamuanvivit's Thai-California dishes as mind-blowing as Fillmore shows – including seasonal specials like cured *kampachi* (yellowtail) with pear and chili jam. *5:30-9pm*

Copra $$

 C7

Feast on edible art with regional Indian flavors and SF flair: Kerala shrimp mango curry, puffy passion-fruit poori, an artist's palette of chutneys, and decolonized cocktails featuring top-shelf Indian rum. *5-10pm daily, brunch 11:30am-2pm Sat & Sun*

State Bird Provisions $$

 C8

Mini-plates pack mega-flavors in award-winning, California-inspired signature dishes: savory ricotta-sourdough pancakes, pickled-lime albacore toast, and California's state bird (quail) nested in slow-cooked onions. *5:30-10pm*

Bar Crudo $$

30 B8

Pair craft beer with local oysters and seasonal surprises – snapper crudo with Buddha-hand citrus, porcini-crusted black cod – plus happy-hour *(5pm to 6:30pm)* fish tacos and seafood chowder. *5-9pm Mon-Sat*

Baked Goods

b patisserie $

 A3

James Beard–winning pastry chef Belinda Leong bakes *kouign-amann* in sensational flavors – get the black sesame – plus tartines for lunch and pistachio-raspberry cake anytime. *8am-4pm Wed-Sun*

Jane the Bakery $

 C5

Spa treatments can't compare to the serotonin glow from Jane's chocolate hazelnut babka, hearty California multigrain bread, and cookies big enough to share...maybe. *7am-5pm*

Jina Bakes $

 D7

Melt-in-your-mouth matcha butter mochi, *hojicha* cream puffs, and croissants filled with Daeho's *kalbijjim* beef – don't miss pastry chef Jina Kim's latest crossover sensation. *10am-4pm Wed-Mon*

The Mill $

 B7

Baked with organic whole-grain stone-ground on-site, Josey Baker bread becomes brunch with California-grown almond butter, or lunch with smoked trout and crème fraîche. *7am-5pm*

Drinking

Bars with Beats

Social Study

 C8

Observe San Franciscan dating rituals, while DJs spin soul and bartenders pair local wine and beer with gourmet 'study snacks.' *5-10pm Mon, from 1pm Tue-Sun*

Sheba Piano Lounge

 C5

The Alamayehu sisters host Fillmore's jazz supper club with spicy Ethiopian platters, NorCal wines and beer, plus *tej* (honey wine) cocktails. *5-11pm Wed-Sun*

Scopo Divino

 A3

Wine, music and conversation blend brunch into happy hour (3pm to 6pm) – and jazz combos regularly swing 5pm to 8pm. *3-8:30pm Sun-Tue, to 11pm Wed-Sat, brunch 11am-2:30pm Sat & Sun*

Fermentation Lab

 E7

Sip successful experiments – yuzu margaritas with fermented-chili bitters, or the Nihonmachi (Toki whiskey with cherry-infused vermouth) – with fun, unpredictable playlists. *3:30-11pm Tue-Thu, from 9am Fri-Sun*

Shopping

Signature SF Style

Zuri

 C3

Upgrade travel wardrobes with colorful tunics and dresses from Zuri design collective, ethically made in Kenya by women entrepreneurs in all sizes, with joyous prints: chickens, pretzels, fireworks. *11am-6pm*

New People

 E7

Tokyo style hits SF streets, with Lolita Goth mini-pinafores from Baby the Stars Shine Bright and Sou Sou's mod graphic shifts inspired by *kantoui* (tunics) worn circa 500 BCE. *noon-5pm Wed-Mon*

In the Black

 C8

Complete SF fits at Fillmore's Black design showcase – bucket hats for sunny days, 'The City' hoodies for fog, hand fans for hot shows at the Fillmore. *10am-9pm Mon-Fri, from 11am Sat, 11am-5pm Sun*

Crossroads Trading

 C3

Pro tip: score gently worn, high-end designer looks for less at Crossroads, thanks to PacHeights socialites who ditch last season's wardrobe here. *11am-8pm Mon-Sat, to 7pm Sun*

Fibers of Being

43 B8

Modern one-stop shopping for all genders, with SF rodeo tees, suede bomber jackets and black denim long shorts – plus nonbinary bling, from chainmail earrings to turquoise beads. *noon-6pm Tue-Sat, to 5pm Sun*

Freda Salvador

44 C2

For SF hills, you'll need sturdy yet stylish shoes – and Freda Salvador's sleek, comfortable low-stacked heels are designed in the Bay Area and handcrafted in Spain to last. *11am-6pm Mon-Sat, noon-5pm Sun*

Westside Cuts & Style

45 **A7**

Complete your look with sharp cuts and clean fades from second-generation barber Nate Thorner, who takes time to make it right and tight. *10:30am-7pm Mon-Sat*

SF-Inspired Decor

Rare Device

46 **B8**

Rainbows of colorfully glazed cups and vases brighten even the foggiest days at Rare Device, a showcase for local artists and clever designers downhill from Alamo Sq. *11am-7pm Mon-Sat, to 6pm Sun*

Soko Hardware

47 **E7**

Since 1925 four generations of the Ashizawa family have made it their mission to source ikebana, bonsai, tea-ceremony and Zen rock-garden supplies, so you can take Japantown's creative inspiration home. *9am-5:30pm Tue-Sun*

Perish Trust

48 **B8**

Fingertips tingle with these earthy textures: sleek brass barware, raw terra-cotta candelabras, creamy SF-made Heavenly sake soaps, wind-sculpted driftwood brushes by SF's Erin Irber. *noon-6pm Wed-Sun*

Jonathan Adler

49 **C3**

Mirrored Lucite bar carts and psychedelic cookie jars labeled 'LSD' bring swinging SF '70s vibes to any home – as California's pop-art potter and designer Jonathan Adler says, 'Minimalism is a bummer.' *10am-6pm*

SF76

50 **E6**

Upgrade ho-hum housewares to joyous modern Japanese designs, creating stunning tablescapes with hand-forged knives and stoneware bowls by San Francisco potters. *noon-6pm*

Nest

51 **C2**

An installation artwork that doubles as a store, where bird baths overflow with hand-dyed textiles, ladders are laden with dessert plates, and toys peek from antique French millinery cabinets. *11:30am-6pm Mon-Sat, noon-5pm Sun*

Forest Books

52 **E6**

When a change of scenery isn't enough, find fresh perspectives in well-curated new and used poetry, culture and art books – as the storefront sign says: 'Work quietly and diligently for peace. Begin within.' *noon-8pm Mon-Fri, to 9pm Sat, 11am-7pm Sun*

See p135
for eating, drinking and shopping listings

Researched by
Alison Bing

Explore
The Mission, Dogpatch & Potrero

Enjoy sunshine, burritos and books among neighborhood filmmakers, grocers, techies, skaters and novelists. Calle 24 (24th St) is SF's designated Latino Cultural District, and the Mission is also a magnet for lesbians, Asian Americans and Arab Americans – everyone's welcome and celebrated in multicultural Mission arts, food and festivals. Valencia St is hipster central, but you'll be won over by their excellent coffee, baked goods, vintage shops and maker spaces. Waterfront Dogpatch is creatively repurposing rusty industrial docks into parks, arts and music venues, and Potrero throws down at punk shows and art openings.

Getting Around

BART

Hop off at 24th St Mission for Calle 24. The 16th St Mission station is sketchy, but near the bustling Valencia/16th hub.

Bus

Lines 12, 14, 48 and 49 drop off near mural-lined Calle 24. The 48 runs east–west from Dogpatch to Ocean Beach, 14 connects Mission to downtown, and 49 travels to the Wharf. Bus 22 connects Dogpatch, the Mission, Haight, Fillmore and Marina.

Walk

The Mission is flat and walkable; hop buses to/from Potrero or Dogpatch.

THE BEST

LANDMARK ART Mission murals (p125)

INSTANT CULTURE Calle 24 Latino Cultural District (p126)

SUNNY HANGOUT Dolores Park (p128)

EYE-OPENING ART OPENINGS Minnesota Street Project (p131)

CUTTING-EDGE CINEMA Roxie Cinema (p128)

Dolores Park (p128)
PHOTRAVEL_RU/SHUTTERSTOCK

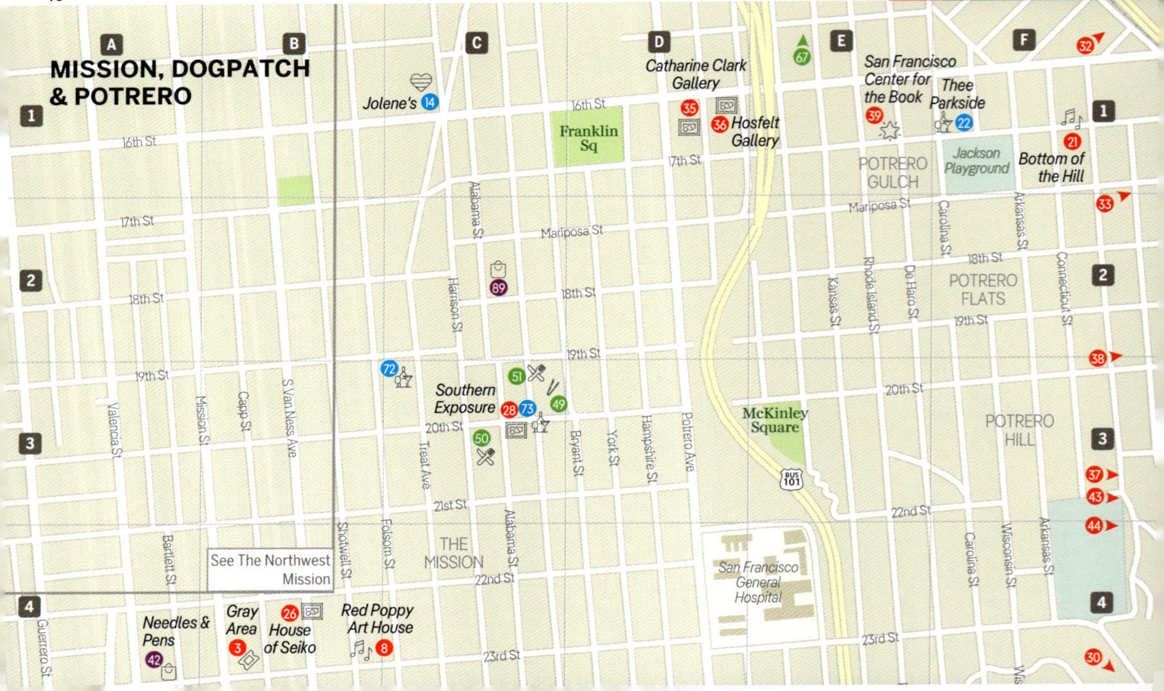
MISSION, DOGPATCH & POTRERO
A
B
C
D
E
F
1
2
3
4
Jolene's 14
Catharine Clark Gallery
35
Hosfelt Gallery 36
67
San Francisco Center for the Book 39
Thee Parkside 22
Bottom of the Hill 21
32
33
38
37
43
44
30
Franklin Sq
Jackson Playground
POTRERO GULCH
POTRERO FLATS
POTRERO HILL
THE MISSION
McKinley Square
San Francisco General Hospital
Southern Exposure 28
73
51
49
50
72
89
Needles & Pens 42
Gray Area 3
House of Seiko 26
Red Poppy Art House 8
See The Northwest Mission
16th St
17th St
18th St
19th St
20th St
21st St
22nd St
23rd St
Mariposa St
Valencia St
Mission St
Capp St
S Van Ness Ave
Bartlett St
Guerrero St
Shotwell St
Folsom St
Treat Ave
Harrison St
Alabama St
Bryant St
York St
Hampshire St
Potrero Ave
Kansas St
Rhode Island St
De Haro St
Carolina St
Arkansas St
Connecticut St
Wisconsin St
Wis
BUS 101

For more see
Top Experiences p125
Experiences p128
Eating p135
Drinking p137
Shopping p139

A
B
C
D
E
F
5
6
7
8
0 0.2 miles
0 800 m

Bernal Heights Park
BERNAL HEIGHTS
Precita Park
Garfield Sq
Potrero del Sol/La Raza Skatepark
Precita Eyes Mission Mural Tours
Mission Skateboards
Mission Cultural Center for Latino Arts
El Rio
The Knockout
Thrillhouse Records

Cesar Chavez (Army) St
Cesar Chavez St
Bay Shore Blvd
Holladay Ave
Montcalm St
Brewster St
Franconia St
Powhattan Ave
Prentiss St
Gates St
Moultrie St
Eugenia Ave
Kingston St
Virginia Ave
Esmeralda Ave
Bernal Heights Blvd
Ripley St
Elsie St
Winfield St
Coso Ave
Montezuma St
Mirabel Ave
Precita Ave
Peralta Ave
Alabama St
Harrison St
Treat Ave
Folsom St
Manchester St
Shotwell St
Tiffany Ave
San Jose Ave
Duncan St
27th St
29th St
26th St
25th St
Lucky St
Florida St
Bryant St
York St
Hampshire St
Potrero Ave
Kansas St
Rhode Island St
Dc Haro St
consin St
S Van Ness Ave
Capp St
Mission St
Bartlett St
Valencia St
Guerrero St
Jerrold Ave
Upton St
Toland St
McKinnon Ave
Newcomb Ave
Oakdale Ave
BUS 101

NORTHWEST MISSION
A
B
C
D
1
2
3
4
5
6
SoMa West Skatepark
Chan National Queer Arts Center
Duboce Ave
Market St
Valencia St
Brick & Mortar
14th St
Double Down
Guerrero St
15th St
16th St
Creativity Explored
Sour Cherry Comics
Roxie Cinema
Mission St
THE MISSION
Shotwell St
Dolores St
Clarion Alley
17th St
ODC Theater
Dearborn St
Sycamore Al
Dorland St
Women's Building
18th St
Mission Comics & Art
Capp St
S Van Ness Ave
Incline Gallery
Chapel
Dolores Park
19th St
Linda St
Lexington St
San Carlos St
Casements Bar
Cumberland St
20th St
500 Capp Street
Liberty St
Artists' Television Access
Alamo Drafthouse Cinema
21st St
Foreign Cinema
the Marsh
0 300 m
0 0.15 miles
For more see
Top Experiences p125
Experiences p128
Eating p135
Drinking p137
Shopping p139

★ TOP EXPERIENCE

Mission Murals

Frida Kahlo and Diego Rivera came to SF for a working honeymoon in the 1930s, and permanently changed the landscape. Mexico's superstar painters inspired generations of muralists to create 500-plus Mission murals – a splendid show of political dissent, community pride and street-art bravado.

MAP P122 **C5**, P124 **C4** & **B4**

Balmy Alley

Inspired by Mexican mega-artists Frida Kahlo and Diego Rivera, Mujeres Muralistas ('Women Muralists') began painting garage doors here in 1973, turning a neglected backstreet into a neighborhood landmark. Today Balmy Alley murals are maintained by nonprofit **Precita Eyes**, including early Frida Kahlo homages, Placa artists' 1985 memorial for El Salvador activist Archbishop Óscar Romero, and Lucía González Ippolito's homage to 'Women of the Resistance.'

Clarion Alley

Most graffiti artists shun broad daylight – but not in Clarion Alley, SF's street-art showcase maintained by neighbors and the Clarion Alley Collective. Over 900 murals have been created by Clarion artists since 1992, but few survive the tests of time and tagging – survivors include Megan Wilson's daisy-covered 'Tax the Rich' and Jet Martinez' glimpse of Clarion Alley inside a forest spirit.

Women's Building

America's first women-owned-and-operated community center has housed 150 women's organizations since 1979 – and the 1994 *Maestrapeace* mural celebrates the Women's Building as a herstory landmark. Mission *muralistas* worked with 100 volunteers to cover the building with goddesses and women trailblazers, including poet Audre Lorde, artist Georgia O'Keeffe, Palestinian human-rights leader Hanan Ashrawi and Nobel Prize–winner Rigoberta Menchú.

PLANNING TIP
Muralists lead weekend **Precita Eyes** walking tours that last just under two hours; proceeds fund mural upkeep and new commissions. When posting photos, kindly credit muralists.

Scan this QR code for mural tours and information.

Calle 24 Culture Stroll

Monumental murals unfold around you on Calle 24 (24th St). Mosaic adorns doorways and parks; windows fringed with *papel picado* (cut-paper streamers) set a fiesta mood year-round; and the smell of fresh coffee and steaming tamales beckons. Now you understand why 4000-plus people stroll here every day.

START	END	LENGTH
Medicine for Nightmares	La Palma Mexicatessen	0.5 miles, 45 min

1 Medicine for Nightmares

Before there were street signs here, indigenous Ohlone, Spanish friars and Mexican ranchers found their way by memory and shared stories. Calle 24's bookstores keep those memories alive, and find new words to point the way forward. When bookstores began losing business to online megastores, Mission readers rallied, turning this bilingual bookstore into a community-supported collective: **Medicine for Nightmares** (Medicina para Pesadillas; p139).

2 Balmy Alley

To see where the Mission mural movement took off, duck into **Balmy Alley** (p125), where Mujeres Muralistas (Women Muralists) began transforming garage doors into artistic statements in 1973. You may recognize beatified activist Archbishop Romero and surrealist painter Frida Kahlo among the colorful characters illuminating this mural-covered backstreet.

3 Precita Eyes

Calle 24 murals always look fresh thanks to **Precita Eyes** (p125), the mural arts nonprofit that restores historic murals, organizes new commissions and leads Balmy Alley mural walking tours. You can't miss Precita Eyes' Calle 24 storefront, graced by a stunning mosaic of flower goddess Xochiquetzal by muralist and founder Susan Cervantes.

4 Brava Theater

Under the marquee, a glorious mural of two women breathes life into this 1926 deco theater. **Brava Theater** (*brava.org*) has been staging new works by women and queer playwrights here for 40-plus years, from V-day monologist Eve Ensler to Culture Clash comedy. The wraparound mural by Agana and her crew includes a gentle reminder to 'smash the patriarchy' over the ticket booth.

5 24th & York Mini Park

Across the street, serpent-god Quetzalcoatl raises his fierce head from the rubberized ground of idyllic **24th & York Mini Park**. Quetzalcoatl first appeared in murals here in 1972, when neighbors rallied to transform a derelict lot into a point of Mission pride. Today his dazzling mosaic sculpture is irresistible to toddlers, and his transformative powers are irrefutable – since Quetzalcoatl first appeared here, San Franciscans have created 40 more mini parks citywide.

6 La Palma Mexicatessen

Follow the sound of applause to **La Palma Mexicatessen** (p136), where that clapping means *tortilleras* are busy making organic tortillas by hand. Enjoy tacos, tamales and *huaraches* (stuffed masa) made to order at a sunny sidewalk table under the mural honoring Centeōtl, the Aztec god of corn.

EXPERIENCES

Hang out in Dolores Park
PARK

MAP: 1 P124 A5

Welcome to San Francisco's sunny side, home to street ball and Mayan-pyramid playgrounds, taco picnics and semi-professional tanning. At **Dolores Park** *(sfrecpark.org; free)*, grassy slopes are dedicated to lolling, while lowlands host soccer, Frisbee, political protests and other local sports. Good weather brings major events, including Easter's **Hunky Jesus** *(thesisters.org; free)* drag contest, free summer movie nights and fall performances by the **San Francisco Mime Troupe** *(sfmt.org; free)*.

Catch Breakthrough Performances
PERFORMING ARTS

Brace for impact: at Mission entertainment spaces like **ODC Theater** (MAP: 2 P124 D3), risky, raw dance performances leave audiences gasping. **Gray Area** (MAP: 3 P122 B4; *grayarea.org; events $0-50)* blurs boundaries between art and science, and culture and technology with mind-expanding programs – immersive electronica shows, workshops on 3D art, psychedelic cyberpunk festivals – in the historic Grand Theater. **Chan National Queer Arts Center** (MAP: 4 P124 B1; *sfgmc.org)* hosts SF's crowd-pleasing Gay Men's Chorus – as seen in the award-winning documentary *Gay Chorus Deep South* – plus boundary-pushing Q-lab theater and raucous drag punk Pride events. **Brava Theater** (p127) has produced original works by women of color and LGBTQ+ playwrights for over 40 years, hosting more than 200 events annually in a mural-covered 1926 theater. One-acts at **The Marsh** (MAP: 5 P124 C6; *themarsh.org; tickets $10-50)* involve the audience in original works, from comedian Marga Gomez' *Swimming with Lesbians* to Monday local storyteller showcases – with sliding-scale pricing, so everyone can participate.

Mission Movies
CINEMAS

When you're bored of standard streaming options, watch something completely new in historic, independent Mission cinemas – with zero ads and personal introductions to many films. If artists programmed TV instead of profiteers, the result would be nonprofit **Artists' Television Access** (MAP: 9 P124 C6; *atasite.org)*, showing mesmerizing art video, local filmmaker showcases and global underground films since 1984. The Mission's 1909 **Roxie Cinema** (MAP: 10 P124 B3; *roxie.com)* is a neighborhood nonprofit with an international reputation for year-round film festivals, including Center for Asian American Media's **CAAMFest** *(caamfest.com; May)*, LGBTQ+

Frameline Film Fest *(frameline.org; June)*, **Jewish Film Festival** *(jfi.org; July)* and **Arab Film Festival** *(arabfilminstitute.org; November)*. **Alamo Drafthouse Cinema** (MAP: 11 P124 C6; *drafthouse.com)* screens blockbusters and cult revivals in a 1932 movie palace, while serving movie-themed cocktails, mocktails, beer, burgers and all-day brunch. At **Foreign Cinema** (MAP: 12 P124 C6; *foreigncinema.com)*, timeless films accompany chef/owner Gayle Pirie's seasonal, sustainable California cuisine.

Toast Herstory at Lesbian Landmarks LESBIAN VENUES

Women keep making herstory in the Mission, running nonprofits at the Women's Building (p125), staging Brava shows, organizing SF's **Dyke March** *(thedykemarch.org)*, and providing healthcare at Lyon-Martin Community Health Clinic – this calls for a toast. Since 1962 **Wild Side West** (MAP: 13 P122 B8; *wildsidewest.com)* patrons have made herstory in the beer garden and made out on the pool table (Janis Joplin started it). **Mother** *(mothersf.com)* is a femme-forward, cash-only joint known for the Ex – a gingery gin cocktail that's slightly bitter – and nonalcoholic BFF – like the Ex, 'but without the drama.' Join scenes in progress for 12-plus years at **Jolene's** (MAP: 14 P122 C1; *jolenessf.com; $0-15)* with lesbian UHaul parties, power-suit contests and 'queer speed-friending' marathons. Swing by lesbian-owned **El Rio** (MAP: 15 P122 B6; *elriosf.com)* for knockout margaritas and shameless flirting on a patio that's seen it all since

MISSION LIVE-MUSIC VENUES

Chapel

MAP: 6 P124 C4

Musical prayers are answered in a 1914 California arts-and-crafts landmark with heavenly acoustics for folkYEAH! indie artists and performance-art mayhem by the likes of Robyn Hitchcock and the Residents *(5-10pm Mon-Wed, to midnight Thu & Fri, 10am-2am Sat, 10am-10pm Sun).*

Brick & Mortar

MAP: 7 P124 C1

Break out of radio ruts and playlist loops with outlandish bands rocking the mortar loose, from breakthrough Popscene shows to NPR Tiny Desk artist showcases *(5pm-1:30am).*

Red Poppy Art House

MAP: 8 P122 C4

A snug Mission storefront doubles as a concert hall for international artists-in-residence, from Armenian *duduk* virtuosos to Argentine tango quartets – plus roving local artists at Mission Stoop Fest *(7-10pm Thu-Sun).*

1978, including Saturday mango lesbian parties, salsa Sundays and free-oyster Fridays. Mission Irish pubs and lesbian bars have historically attracted different clienteles – but Irish lesbian-owned **Casements Bar** (MAP: 16 P124 C5; *casementsbar.com)* brings everyone to the mural-lined patio for Guinness, 50-plus Irish whiskeys and California-fresh pub grub.

Skate the Mission SKATEBOARDING

Street skating is the chosen sport, art and commuting method of Mission cool kids – and their parents. Women and nonbinary street skaters get their due at **Double Down** (MAP: 17 P124 B2; *doubledownzine.com),* SF's women and nonbinary street-skater zine/scene – its eye-popping Valencia storefront offers back issues, merch, free stickers and general mayhem. SF street-skate legend Scot Thompson owns **Mission Skateboards** (MAP: 18 P122 C5; *missionsk8shop.com),* which supplies instant street cred with locally designed Mission decks, custom tees, skate shoes and stacks of SF's own *Thrasher* magazine. Around the corner at **Potrero del Sol/La Raza Skatepark** (MAP: 19 P122 E5; *sfrecpark.org),* you can grab air with pro skaters blasting ollies off SF's best concrete bowls – though graffiti can make for slippery rides. Wait for a clean area of the bowl to bust big moves, and make room for kiddos in kneepads. Shredders brave **SoMa West Skatepark** (MAP: 20 P124 B1; *sfrecpark.org),* the urban-legendary skatepark under SF's freeway – regulars can get territorial and nighttime scenes get sketchy, but there's no place better to earn respect with big, bold moves.

Pogo to Punk MUSIC VENUES

'Go ahead, punk: make my day,' snarled Clint Eastwood as a San Francisco cop in *Dirty Harry* – but SF punks kept rocking anyway. **Bottom of the Hill** (MAP: 21 P122 F1; *bottomofthehill.com)* still tops the list for featuring punk legends like the Avengers, Pansy Division and Dead Boys, plus newcomers worth checking out for their names alone (Junior Painkillers, The Hot Takes, Buzzed Lightbeer). Punk-band stickers plastering courtyard walls may actually be holding up **Thee Parkside** (MAP: 22 P122 F1; *theeparkside.com; cover $0-15)* – local bands have rocked hard here every weekend for decades. Volunteer-run, nonprofit **Thrillhouse Records** (MAP: 23 P122 A8; *thrillhouserecords.com)* stocks punk on vinyl and throws free weekend shows – its outdoor billboard is a snapshot of SF's punk scene. **The Knockout** (MAP: 24 P122 A7; *theknockoutsf.com)* books fun, loud bands – plus chill reggae, danceable darkwave, and punk drag shows – and serves craft beer, PBR with JD shots, and a cocktail called the Off-Kilter: St George

Botanist gin, St Germain and tonic, stirred with rosemary and attitude. Go ahead, punk: enjoy your night.

Explore the Mission's Alternative Art Spaces GALLERIES

Be the first to glimpse artworks destined for museum retrospectives, international art fairs and Marc Jacobs handbags, all by local artists with developmental disabilities at nonprofit **Creativity Explored** (MAP: 25 P124 B3; *creativityexplored.org*), and join the creative fray at **Imaginate Saturdays** *(noon-3pm; free; all ages)*. Lose track of time in the repurposed watch-repair shop that's now **House of Seiko** (MAP: 26 P122 B4; *houseofseiko.info; free*) gallery, and ramp up your art collection at **Incline Gallery** (MAP: 27 P124 B4; *inclinegallerysf.com; free*), an ex-mortuary ramp where bodies were once transported. Art ties the room together at nonprofit **Southern Exposure** (MAP: 28 P122 C3; *soex.org; donations welcome*), from fundraising drawing rallies to Resist and Rejoice art parties. At nonprofit **500 Capp Street** (MAP: 29 P124 C5; *500cappstreet.org; free Saturday visits*), the Mission home of late sculptor David Ireland overflows with experimental installations.

Look Ahead at Minnesota Street Project ART CENTER

MAP: 30 P122 F4

An old factory showcases new talents at nonprofit **Minnesota Street Project** *(minnesotastreetproject.com)*. Shows here are free and fearless, from meticulously crafted dreamscapes at **Eleanor Harwood Gallery** *(eleanorharwood.com)* to **Jack Fischer Gallery** *(jackfischergallery.com)* multimedia think-pieces. **Casemore Gallery** *(casemoregallery.com)* features renowned photographers – Jim Jocoy's club-kid portraits, Todd Hido's eerie suburban subdivisions – and **Anglim/Trimble Gallery**

MISSION SCHOOL COOL

In the '90s, skate culture, underground comics and graffiti met in Mission alleys – and the art world hasn't been the same since. Art critic Glen Helfand dubbed the movement 'Mission School,' including artists who drew outside the lines of MFA programs like SF graffiti/mural/zine/skate artists Margaret Kilgallen, Barry McGee, Ruby Neri and Chris Johanson. SF's indie art spaces invited Mission School artists indoors, launching the 'Beautiful Losers' group show – outsider slang from Leonard Cohen's 1966 counterculture novel – with a 2008 documentary that made Mission School artists mainstays at museum shows and art fairs. What's next? Find out in Mission alleys.

(anglimtrimble.com) launches Bay Area art movements, from Beat assemblage to Bay Area conceptualists. Galleries stay open until 8pm for First Saturday artist talks and free workshops.

Join Mission Cultural Festivals FESTIVALS

No place celebrates life quite like the Mission. SF is far from Rio, but you'd never know it during **Carnaval** *(carnavalsanfrancisco.org; free)*, when everyone shakes their tail feathers in Mission streets. For **Día de los Muertos** *(dayofthedeadsf.org; free)*, brass bands, lowriders and dancing skeletons honor the dead along Calle 24, community altars line Potrero del Sol/La Raza Skatepark (p130) and **Mission Cultural Center for Latino Arts** (MAP: 31 P122 **B5**; *missionculturalcenter.org)* hosts art shows and epic mole tastings. The nation's biggest and most outlandish literary festival is SF's Litquake (p33), and the highlight is LitCrawl, when writers spill secrets along Valencia St. **Flor y Canto** (Flower and Song) and **Paseo Poetico** fill Mission streets with poetry and the limitless joy of living.

Catch a Warriors Game BASKETBALL

MAP: 32 P122 **F1**

The sing-song chant 'Warr-i-ors!' is both a San Francisco game-day greeting and a taunt to fans of visiting teams, taking on the Bay Area's repeat NBA champions (four times since 2014) with a home-court advantage. Single-game tickets are sold via the **Chase Center** *(nba.com)* website, with prices ranging from $40 nosebleed bleachers to high triple digits for LA Lakers grudge matches. Between the October and May seasons, Chase Center hosts headliners from pop (Paramore, Drake) to comedy (Jerry Seinfeld–Jim Gaffigan double bill).

Ditch Work at Crane Cove Park BEACH

MAP: 33 P122 **F2**

Dogpatch piers are dotted with rusted equipment left over from San Francisco's industrial past and WWII shipbuilding era – poignant reminders that every boom/bust cycle is bound to pass. San Franciscans look fondly on the massive industrial cranes – nicknamed Nick and Nora – framing SF's bay port for more than a century, and insisted on preserving them as features of **Crane Cove Park** *(sfport.com; free)*. Nora overlooks bayside picnic tables, while Nick watches over paddleboarders braving chilly bay waters and kiddos playing on the rocky beach (there's no lifeguard). From here, you can follow the Bay Trail all the way to the Embarcadero.

Feel the Beat at Pier 80

MUSIC EVENTS

MAP: 34 P122 F6

Once Dogpatch was a working port, but now these docks are ready to party. Down by Pier 80, the **Midway** *(themidwaysf.com)* comes roaring to life with indoor and outdoor events, including DJ day parties and mega-raves like the '90s never ended. Deep inside the Midway is **Envelop**, a nonprofit immersive audio venue lined with 32 speakers and interactive lights where you take off your shoes to feel, hear and see epic albums played in their entirety – *Purple Rain, Dark Side of the Moon, Sgt Pepper, Kid A*. Crowds thoroughly pound Pier 80 during the **Portola Festival** *(portolamusicfestival.com)*, squeezing three decades of EDM and power-pop mayhem into two days – headliners have included the Chemical Brothers, The Prodigy, Christina Aguilera and LCD Soundsystem. Go wild and wear sunscreen.

Visit Letterpress Landmarks

ART CENTERS

Texts disappear into the ether, but print leaves a lasting impression at SF book arts centers. Punk zine publishers and app designers converge at nonprofit **Letterform Archive** (MAP: 38 P122 F3; *letterformarchive.org; adult/student $10/5*) to see iconic, wordy works on paper, from 1960s Black Panther newspapers to 1980s AIDS-awareness posters. Hitting the books takes on another meaning entirely at **San Francisco Center for the Book** (MAP: 39 P122 E1; *sfcb.org*), San Francisco's nonprofit community press – a booklover's dream for

POTRERO GALLERIES

Catharine Clark Gallery

MAP: 35 P122 D1

Art revolutions are instigated here with gorgeous provocations, from Masami Teraoka's paintings of samurai battling the AIDS epidemic to Zeina Barakeh's videos of ancient Egyptian guardians defending cyberspace *(11am-6pm Tue-Sat)*.

Hosfelt Gallery

MAP: 36 P122 D1

Trancelike states are induced by ultra-slow, extra-pixelated images artistically engineered by Jim Campbell (of Salesforce Tower fame) and Marco Maggi's tiny paper curls covering vast surfaces *(10am-5:30pm Tue-Sat)*.

Romer Young Gallery

MAP: 37 P122 F3

Witness artists performing mysterious alchemy: Erik Scollon weaves all-seeing eyes and erotica into talismanic textiles, and Leah Rosenberg evokes cake and community in vast, vivid dot paintings *(noon-5pm Thu-Sun)*.

classic binding and letterpress workshops, plus exhibits of unique art books that fit into matchboxes, pop up into theaters and contain secret treasures.

Collect Comics & Zines in the Mission

COMICS

Book-club selections seem tame compared to the indie comics and freshly photocopied zines lining Mission shelves. Heads will roll, fists will fly and furious vengeance will be wreaked inside **Mission Comics & Art** (MAP: 40 P124 **C4**; *missioncomicsandart.com),* with shelves of indie comics *(Snotgirl, Head Lopper)* alongside new and used marquee titles *(Walking Dead, Star Wars).* Signings and events showcase local comic-book heroes, from *Poison Ivy* cover artist Jessica Fong to *Raised by Ghosts* graphic novelist Briana Loewinsohn – and comics fans come correct at trivia nights and dog-costume contests. **Sour Cherry Comics** (MAP: 41 P124 **B3**; *sourcherrycomics.com)* earns dedicated fan followings for its vast selection of queer comics, monthly manga club, regular community fundraisers, and DIY zines covering top-of-mind topics from affordable housing to how to say no to working overtime. Find fresh ideas at zine newsstand **Needles & Pens** (MAP: 42 P122 **A4**; *needles-pens.com),* including Finn Cunningham's *Mental Health Cookbook* – and make your own zine with collage clip art from *Crap Hound* zine.

Go Handmade in Dogpatch

CRAFTS

High craft meets high tech in Dogpatch, where artists and self-driving cars roam waterfront streets. Offset screen time with sensory delights at **hugomento** (MAP: 43 P122 **F3**; *hugomento.com; free),* a showcase for lushly textured, handmade, 'storied art and objects.' Meticulously crafted, mesmerizing abstract works bring SF innovation to NorCal crafts – from Carrie Crawford's delicate hand-dyed textiles to George William Bell's sand-carved glass burl sculptures.

Around the corner, one-off works not meant for mass production reignite wonder at the **Museum of Craft & Design** (MAP: 44 P122 **F4**; *sfmcd.org; adult/student $10/8).* Traditional crafts find fresh purpose here: carpets capture the topography of climate-changed wetlands, an entire cosmos is formed from fossils, and durags completely covered in buttons become contemporary crowns. Shows include a hands-on maker space, equipped with supplies so that you can capture inspiration while it's fresh.

Best Places for...

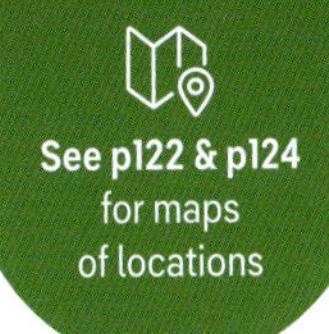

$ Budget $$ Midrange $$$ Top End

Eating

Mission Burritos

La Taqueria $

45 P122 **B5**

Miguel Jara's James Beard Award–winning burrito has hardly changed since 1972: grilled meats, slow-cooked beans, flour tortillas, just-made salsa, period. *11am-8:45pm Wed-Sun*

La Corneta Taqueria $

46 P122 **B5**

Roving mariachis serenade Mission families feasting on extra-special burritos with plump prawns, velvety pinto beans and ultrafresh salsas. *10am-9pm*

Pancho Villa $

47 P124 **C3**

Meal-sized 'baby burritos' are not to be confused with the baby-sized regular – choose veg or meat and slather with salsas. *10am-10pm*

Taqueria El Farolito $

48 P122 **B5**

Follow late-night lines into this no-frills, cash-only taqueria for meat-packed, avocado-studded, tinfoil-wrapped, forearm-sized burritos. *10am-1:45am Sun-Thu, to 2:45am Fri & Sat*

Special-Occasion Dining

San Ho Won $$$

49 P122 **C3**

The minimalist dining room showcases sumptuous Korean flavors – *jebi churi* filet packs more flavor than an entire steakhouse, and mouthwatering *banchan* (sides) satisfy soul-deep cravings. *5-9:30pm Thu-Sun, to 10pm Fri & Sat*

Flour + Water $$

50 P122 **C3**

Rustic yet elegant Italian dishes: classic mortadella-stuffed tortellini, creative duck and butternut garganelli, memorable honey-drizzled *matsutake* mushroom pizza. *5-9:30pm*

Farmhouse Kitchen Thai Cuisine $$

51 P122 **C3**

California farm-to-table meets Thai festival fare, with turmeric-laced Sonoma fried chicken and Make a Wish cocktails served in genie's lamps. *11:30am-2pm & 5-8:30pm Sun-Thu, 4:30-9:30pm Fri & Sat*

Donaji $

52 P122 **B5**

Celebrate Oaxacan-Californian style, with deep flavors and organic ingredients – red-mole-braised short ribs, black mole chicken tinga enchiladas, Oaxacan chocolate-churro s'mores. *5-10pm Wed-Thu, to 10:30pm Fri & Sat*

Vegetarian & Vegan

Shizen $$

53 P124 **C2**

No boring cucumber sushi rolls here – discover marinated mushroom 'secret weapon' rolls and the 'prime suspect' (tempura asparagus with egg-free gochujang aioli). *5-9pm Sun-Thu, 4-9:30pm Fri & Sat*

La Palma Mexicatessen $

54 P122 **D5**

The Mission motherlode of handmade tamales, *huaraches* (stuffed masa), and *pupusas* (tortilla pockets) with vegan masa and vegetarian (or meat) fillings. *8am-5pm Wed-Mon*

Udupi Palace $

55 P124 **C6**

Hot dates get hotter over 2ft-long paper *dosa* (lentil-flour pancakes) and satisfying *idli* (fluffy lentil-rice cakes) with spicy sambar and coconut chutney. *noon-8:30pm*

Burma Love $$

56 P124 **B1**

Flavors here hug your tongue, then deliver a swift kick – get fermented tea-leaf salad, caramelized eggplant, coconut sticky rice and top-notch cocktails. *11:30am-3pm & 5-10pm*

Mission Mezze

Komaaj Mazze & Wine Bar $$

57 P122 **A7**

Brilliant flavors rarely found outside northern Iran – pomegranate-glazed smoked trout, Persian cucumbers with *dalar* dressing – with Armenian wines made from Iranian grapes. *5:30-9pm Tue-Thu, noon-3pm & 5:30-10pm Fri-Sun*

Reem's $

58 P122 **B5**

Acclaimed Syrian-Palestinian chef/owner Reem Assil creates sensational, sustainable Palestinian Californian comfort food, including 'Pali-Cali' flatbread with sumac-laced chicken and caramelized onions. *11am-3pm & 5-9pm Tue-Sat*

Freekeh $

59 P124 **B3**

Share classic dips and tangy *musakhan* (sumac chicken or mushrooms rolled into lavash) with Lebanese arak-spiked lemonade. *5:30-9pm Tue-Sun, 10am-2:30pm Sat & Sun*

Old Jerusalem $

60 P122 **B6**

Bond over generous portions of Palestinian and Syrian classics – shawarma, *mansaf* (lamb pilaf), *ful* (fava dip) – plus *kenafeh* (cheese pastry) hot from the family-heirloom griddle. *11am-10pm Wed-Mon*

Baked Goods

Craftsman & Wolves $

61 P124 **C5**

Break breakfast rules with the Rebel Within, a cheesy muffin with a soft-boiled egg baked inside – and/or seasonal mini-cakes, like yuzu coconut or cassis-champagne mousse. *7:30am-3:30pm Mon-Fri, 8am-4pm Sat & Sun*

Tartine $

62 P124 **B4**

Riches beyond your wildest dreams: butter-golden *pain au chocolat*, creamy cappuccinos, gooey ham-and-cheese croque monsieurs with béchamel. *7:30am-6pm*

Stonemill Matcha $

63 P124 **C3**

Teatime here means dreamy baked goods with SF-favorite Asian flavors: black-sesame cream puffs, flaky matcha croissants, chicken *katsu* milk-bread sandwiches. *10am-4pm Mon-Fri, 9am-5pm Sat & Sun*

Black Jet Baking $

64 P122 **C8**

Artisan bakers reinvent nostalgic packaged treats with California-fresh ingredients – get the flaky toaster pastries with housemade jam – and serve seasonal pizza slices. *8am-2pm Tue & Wed, to 4pm Thu-Sun*

Ice Cream

Garden Creamery $

65 P124 C5

Organic cream and hand-picked fruit make luxurious textures and intense flavors, like black sesame and 'strawberry on steroids.' *6-10:30pm Wed-Fri, noon-9:30pm Sat & Sun*

Mitchell's Ice Cream $

66 P122 A7

Since 1953 happy dances erupt on Mission sidewalks for tropical flavors like *macapuno* (young coconut), Kahlua mocha and *ube* (purple yam). *11:30am-11pm*

Humphry Slocombe $

67 P122 E1

Treat your taste buds to original flavors – Vietnamese coffee, bourbon and cornflakes, goat-cheesecake – drizzled with California olive oil and sea salt. *1-10pm*

Bi-Rite Creamery $

68 P124 A4

Even VIPs humbly queue behind velvet ropes for Sonoma honey-lavender or salted-caramel ice cream with housemade hot fudge. *noon-9pm*

Drinking

Iconic Bars

Royal Cuckoo Organ Lounge

69 P122 A7

DJ starts playing the organ, some dude picks up a trumpet, and a *lucha-libre*-masked customer yells, 'Yesss, Chet Baker is my jam!' So begins another epic, Cuckoo night. *6pm-midnight Mon, 4pm-2am Tue-Thu, from 3pm Fri-Sun*

Pop's Bar

70 P122 D5

Approach the 1937 deco bar for cocktails named after lowrider cars – get the classy Cutlass (rye, Avena, Aztec chocolate bitters) – that kick into overdrive when DJs spin. *6am-2am*

Zeitgeist

71 P124 B1

At this biker beer garden, you've got two seconds to choose a craft beer from 64 on tap – tough but fair. *2-11pm Mon-Wed, to midnight Thu & Fri, noon-1am Sat, noon-9:30pm Sun*

Homestead

72 P122 C3

Your friendly Victorian corner dive c 1893, with carved-wood bar, cast-iron fireplace and Mission characters galore – when Iggy Pop hits the jukebox, stand back. *3-11pm Sun-Thu, to 2am Fri & Sat*

Cocktails

Trick Dog

73 P122 C3

Each new menu captures an SF obsession – Whole Earth Catalog, Mission muralists, death-defying circus acts – proof that the bar often called America's best never runs out of tricks. *4pm-midnight Sun-Thu, to 2am Fri & Sat*

Dalva & Hideout

74 P124 B3

Discuss Roxie movies over Altered States (mezcal, vermouth, gentian) or dish Dolores Park gossip in backroom Hideout with a Friend of the Devil (rye, stout, amaro). *5pm-midnight Sun-Tue, to 2am Wed-Sat, Hideout from 7pm*

%ABV

75 P124 B3

Discerning drinkers recognize the name ('percent alcohol by

PAULAAH293/SHUTTERSTOCK

Pop's Bar (p137)

volume') and appreciate the craft – tangerine oil in martinis, hand-cut ice cubes in Japanese malt whiskey. *4pm-2am*

Elixir

76 P124 **B3**

SF's first certified-green bar is an 1858 Wild West saloon with organic whiskey cocktails that inspire air-guitar-rocking to the killer jukebox. *4pm-midnight Sun-Wed, to 2am Thu & Fri, noon-2am Sat*

Coffee

Finjan Qahwa

77 P122 **A7**

Conversation flows easily over shared baklava and mellow, yellow Yemeni coffee, served in brass teapots or in iced lattes. *7am-10pm Sun-Thu, to 11pm Fri & Sat*

Ritual Coffee Roasters

78 P124 **C6**

Devotees queue for house-roasted small-batch coffee with distinctive flavor profiles – descriptions comparing roasts to grapefruit peel or toasted hazelnut aren't exaggerating. *6:30am-7pm*

Four Barrel Coffee

79 P124 **B2**

Surprise: SF's hippest cafe is also the friendliest, with upbeat baristas handling pour-overs, a sunny parklet, gallery-worthy art, and no outlets or wi-fi to hinder conversation. *7am-5pm*

Manny's

80 P124 **C3**

Other cafes serve coffee but Manny's serves community, with laugh-it-off comedy shows and forums on SF hot topics from climate to cannabis – plus tasty *cortados*. *8am-8pm Mon-Fri, from 9am Sat & Sun*

Shopping

Books

Adobe Books & Arts Coop

81 P122 **B5**

Wall-to-wall inspiration – just-released fiction, limited-edition art books, rare cookbooks, well-thumbed poetry – plus zine-launch parties, comedy nights and art openings. *noon-7pm*

Medicine for Nightmares

82 P122 **C5**

Part bilingual bookstore, part community center: new and used bilingual titles in the front, local art shows and events in the back, including free live jazz, multilingual poetry readings and Howard Zinn history talks. *12:30-10pm Tue-Thu, to 11pm Fri & Sat, to 9pm Sun & Mon*

826 Valencia

83 P124 **C5**

When you're running low on pirate supplies and/or freshly published ideas, count on this nonprofit for spyglasses and McSweeney's latest publications – sales support on-site tutoring for youth. *noon-6pm*

Dog Eared Books

84 P124 **C5**

Trust staff picks here, featuring well-curated selections of local authors, graphic novels and zines – sell vacation reads you've finished and score new/used books. *10am-10pm*

Mission Makers

Nooworks

85 P124 **B2**

SF-made all-gender jumpsuits, tops and sundresses are Insta hits with limited-edition, local-artist-designed graphic prints – rainbows and tigers, or mystical Tarot symbols – and back-room sales racks hold scores galore. *11am-7pm*

Open Editions

86 P124 **C5**

Arty sportswear designed by local artists: Stephanie Syjuco's battleship-dazzle-pattern hoodies, Mitsu Okubo's *Sigh*Twomble' caps, bandanas with Bob Aufuldish's 1996 dingbat typeface. *11am-7pm*

Gravel & Gold

87 P124 **C6**

Get back in touch with nature and California's hippie roots with relaxed, sustainable Cali clothing – breezy smock-dresses, hand-printed cotton tops, raffia bucket hats, train-conductor-striped chore jackets. *noon-7pm*

Ian James

88 P124 **B2**

Most days Ian's making stylish leather satchels in his storefront studio, with a signature X pattern and subtle contrasting outstitching – plus clever cardholders for Mission nights out. *noon-6pm Thu-Sun*

Heath Ceramics & Newsstand

89 P122 **C2**

The source of handmade stoneware you've spotted at top SF restaurants, featuring ceramist Edith Heath's original midcentury lines and new colors – plus local artisan pop-ups. *10am-6pm*

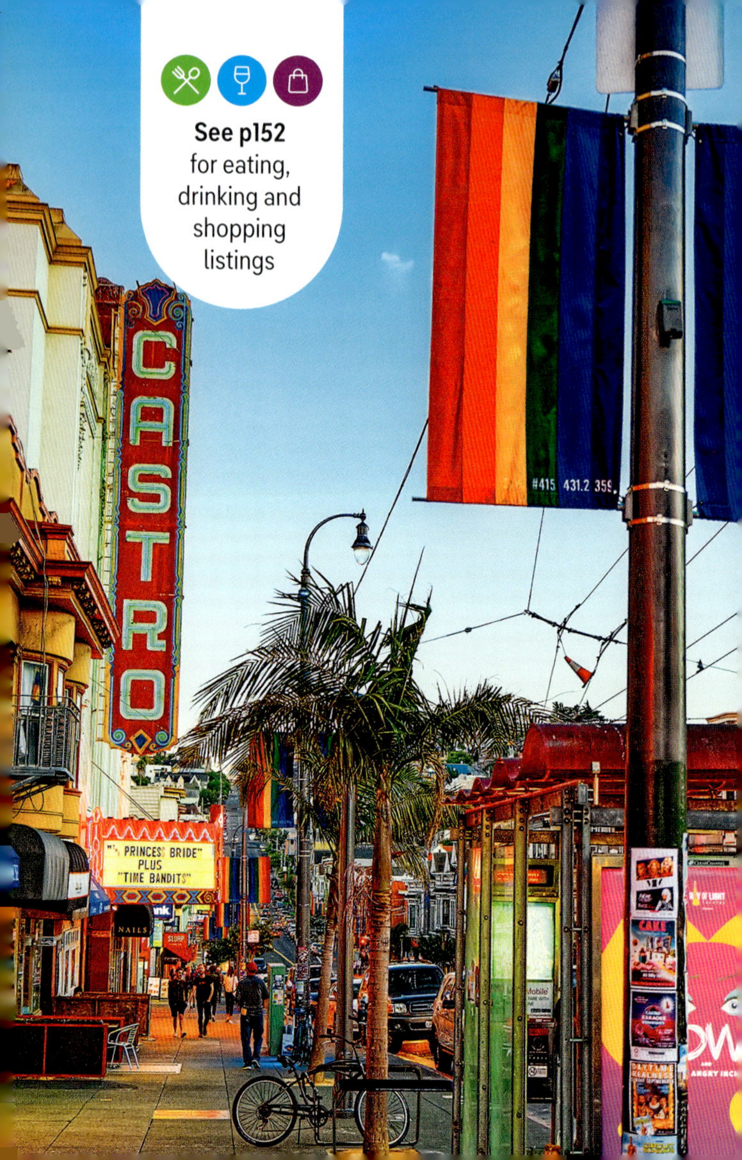

See p152
for eating,
drinking and
shopping
listings

Explore
The Castro

Researched by
Dylan Lalanne-Perkins

Welcome to the gayborhood! Rainbow flags gaily wave hello at the world's premier LGBTQ+ culture destination, spiritual home to club kids, career activists, leather daddies and drag stars alike. Castro nightlife is urban-legendary, but when the sun comes out, the Castro really shines – being out in broad daylight is a freedom this community fought for, and thoroughly enjoys – especially on weekends, when crowds come to people-watch, shop and drink. The little neighborhood under the giant rainbow flag is a global symbol of freedom, and you're about to see exactly why.

Getting Around

Train
Metro K, L and M trains run beneath Market St to Castro Station. J trains travel from down-town along Church to 18th St and beyond.

Streetcar
Vintage streetcars operate on the F-Market line, from Fisherman's Wharf to Castro St.

Bus
The 24 connects the Castro to bustling Divisadero St, and the 33 goes to the Haight and the Mission.

THE BEST

CITY VIEWS Corona Heights Park (p148)

LIVE MUSIC Cafe du Nord (p147)

MUSEUM GLBT Historical Society Museum (p149)

DANCE FLOOR QBar (p154)

CALIFORNIA CUISINE Frances (p153)

Castro St (p144)
V_E/SHUTTERSTOCK

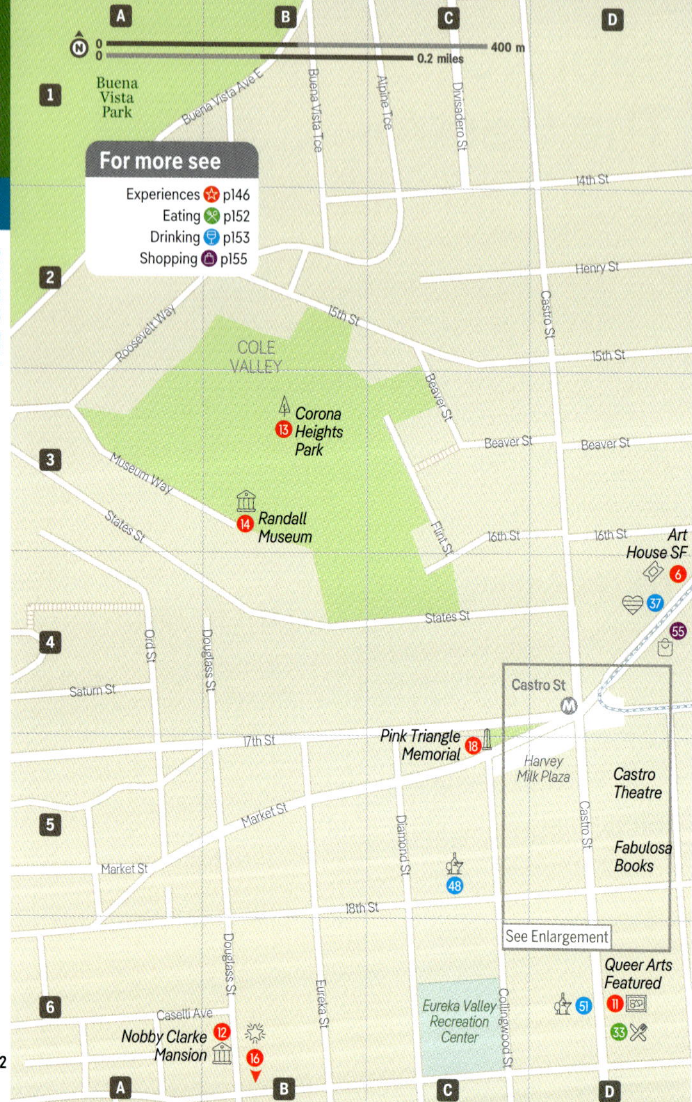
A
B
C
D
1
2
3
4
5
6
0 400 m
0 0.2 miles
Buena Vista Park
Buena Vista Ave E
Buena Vista Tce
Alpine Tce
Divisadero St
14th St
Henry St
Castro St
15th St
Roosevelt Way
COLE VALLEY
Corona Heights Park
13
Beaver St
Museum Way
Randall Museum
14
States St
Flint St
16th St
Art House SF
6
37
55
Ord St
Douglass St
Saturn St
Castro St
Pink Triangle Memorial
18
Harvey Milk Plaza
Castro Theatre
17th St
Market St
Diamond St
Fabulosa Books
48
18th St
See Enlargement
Queer Arts Featured
11
51
33
Eureka St
Eureka Valley Recreation Center
Collingwood St
Caselli Ave
Nobby Clarke Mansion
12
16
For more see
Experiences p146
Eating p152
Drinking p153
Shopping p155

E
F
G
H
1
2
3
4
5
6
Walter St
Market St
14th St
Church St
The Academy SF
Swedish American Hall & Cafe du Nord
Henry St
THE CASTRO
Noe St
15th St
Dolores St
Sanchez St
Church St
Flore Dispensary
Market St
16th St
The Hope for the World Cure
Pond St
Prosper St
0
50 m
Castro St
17th St
17th St
Market St
Harvey Milk Plaza
Jane Warner Plaza
Castro Theatre
17th St
Ford St
Castro St
THE CASTRO
Noe St
18th St
MAG Galleries
Gear Up
Strut
Fabulosa Books
18th St
Hancock St
Rainbow Honor Walk
GLBT Historical Society Museum
19th St

WALKING TOUR

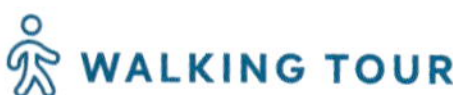

Walk the Castro

Mornings are quiet, but the Castro kicks into gear in the afternoons and evenings, especially on weekends, when crowds come to people-watch, shop and pass the time at gay bars. At night, semi-clad partiers and buttoned-up moviegoers mingle on the Castro's wide sidewalks.

START	END	LENGTH
Twin Peaks Tavern	Barbie Doll Window	0.3 miles; 10 mins

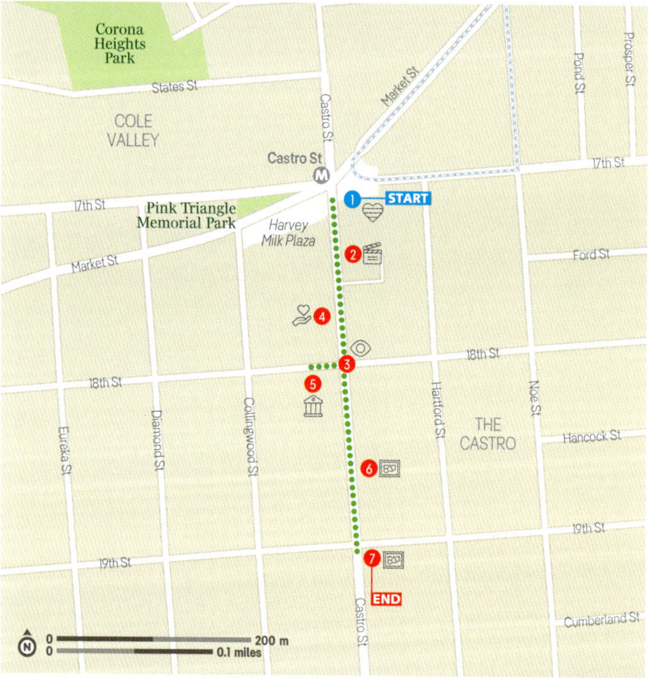

1 Twin Peaks Tavern

As soon as you arrive in the Castro, vintage rainbow neon arrows point the way to a local landmark: opened in 1935, **Twin Peaks Tavern** (p154) became the world's first gay bar with windows open to the street in 1971. Toast Pride at the carved-wood bar, or nab a window seat for the Castro's best people-watching.

2 Castro Theatre

Look up: the **Castro Theatre** (p146) marquee is winking its neon welcome. Architect Timothy Pflueger's 1922 deco designs were being restored at the time of research, though plans to remove the original velvet cinema seats have sparked debate. Lines wrap around the block for movie premieres, drag legends and A-list LGBTQ+ comedians.

3 Rainbow Honor Walk

Watch your step on Castro St – you might step on Virginia Woolf or James Baldwin. They're among the 68 trailblazing LGBTQ+ icons featured in bronze sidewalk plaques along the **Rainbow Honor Walk** (p146).

4 Strut

On crowded Castro St today, you'd never guess how hauntingly empty it was during the AIDS epidemic. In 1982 the nonprofit San Francisco AIDS Foundation was formed to take preventive action, and set global standards for humane care. Today, it provides the now-thriving community with free and low-cost health services at **Strut** (p150). If it's not a busy weekend, you might pop in to thank a front-desk volunteer for their work.

5 GLBT Historical Society Museum

Detour off the main stretch to **America's first gay museum** (p149), capturing proud moments and historic challenges through stories and artifacts – including Harvey Milk's worn-out shoes from civil-rights marches, Gilbert Baker's handsewn 1978 rainbow flag and disco-diva Sylvester's glamorous stage wear.

6 Harvey Milk's Castro Camera

Strut over the rainbow-pinstriped crosswalks to **Queer Arts Featured** (p148). This storefront may look familiar: this was once Harvey Milk's camera shop, as featured in the Academy Award–winning biopic *Milk*. Here, the Mayor of Castro St continues to watch over his neighborhood from the window mural.

7 Barbie-Doll Window

No loop through the Castro would be complete without a peek at the **Barbie-Doll Window**, featuring trans Barbies and Billy Dolls, a gay alternative to Ken who's more than just a little anatomically correct. Dolls are dressed – well, some of them – in outrageous costumes and arranged in protest lines, complete with signs. One says it best: 'It's Castro, Bitch.'

EXPERIENCES

Enjoy a Show at the Deco-Fabulous Castro Theatre

ENTERTAINMENT

MAP: 1 P142 **G5**

Follow the yellow-brick road to the **Castro Theatre** (*castrotheatre.com*), with its towering marquee welcoming folks to SF's legendary gay neighborhood. The baroque facade hints at the ornate interior – architect Timothy Pflueger's Spanish-Moorish-Asian decor allegedly inspired the *Wizard of Oz* set.

For over a hundred years, this has been the place for all-star drag revues, A-list queer comedy and film-festival premieres – including the world's biggest LGBTQ+ film fest, Frameline. Showtime starts at the Castro when the mighty organ rises – and no, that's not a euphemism – playing show tunes and leading crowd sing-alongs to Judy Garland's anthem 'San Francisco.' At audience-participation events, everyone is given kits containing glow sticks, bubbles and noisemakers to punctuate the movie's most dramatic moments.

At the time of research, the Castro Theatre was under construction with a hopeful reopening set for late 2025. The renovation and historic restoration, not without neighborhood controversy, plans to allow space for an expanded live-music repertoire.

RAINBOW HONOR WALK

Cruising around the Castro, you're always in good company. Along Market and Castro Sts, the gold sidewalk plaques of the **Rainbow Honor Walk** celebrate LGBTQ+ heroes, with a total of 68 trailblazers pointing the way forward. Watch your step, don't tread on literary giant James Baldwin, Nobel Laureate Jane Addams, or local icons like trans activist Lou Sullivan and San Francisco's Absolute Empress José Sarria, founder of the Imperial Court System.

MAP: 2 P142 **G6**

People-Watch at the Plaza

OUTDOORS

Follow the yellow-brick road to **Jane Warner Plaza** (MAP: 3 P142 **H4**), named for the pioneering lesbian officer who patrolled the Castro. Historic streetcars that look like colorful toy trains make their last stop here, do a perfect pivot turn, and head back to Fisherman's Wharf. Rainbow-themed seating and bizarre public art make for prime people-watching – including glimpses of Castro nudists on sunny days, legally obliged to cover up with strategically placed socks. Somewhere over the rainbow (across the street) is **Harvey Milk Plaza** (MAP: 4 P142 **G4**), where a huge rainbow flag flaps – currently under construction with fundraising still underway to transform the space into an additional public gathering space for the neighborhood.

Read the Rainbow at Fabulosa Books

BOOKSTORE

MAP: 5 P142 **G5**

True to its name – 'Fabulosa' means 'fabulous' in Polari, 19th-century gay theater slang – beloved neighborhood bookstore **Fabulosa Books** (*fabulosabooks.com*) carries a selection as colorful as the Castro's rainbow crosswalks. With an eclectic mix of genres, ranging from Lesbians!! to Gender-Funky Sci-Fi, Fabulosa Books embraces a spirit of inclusivity, carrying literature that represents all identities (including straight people). Whether you're digging through bins of vintage ephemera for a punk zine or retro skin mag, or browsing a display of forgotten literary masterpieces, you'll find something you never knew you'd love. Author readings here are magnets for local characters, and Books Not Bans, a nonprofit effort sending LGBTQ+ books to communities across the country where access is restricted, operates out of the (literal) closet in the back.

Gallery-Hop During the Castro Art Walk

EVENT

See what the Castro's creative community has been dreaming up lately at the monthly **Castro Art Walk** (*castroartwalk.com; free*), held the first Friday of each month from 5pm to 8pm. Bounce from **Art House SF** (MAP: 6 P142 **D4**; *arthousesf.com*) to **MAG Galleries** (MAP: 7 P142 **F5**; *mag-galleries.com*) to the collection of neighborhood businesses that have transformed into art exhibitions showcasing local talent. Members-only LGBTQ+ social club **The Academy SF** (MAP: 8 P142 **F2**; *academy-sf.com*) opens its doors to the art-loving public and **Flore Dispensary** (MAP: 9 P142 **E3**; *floredispensary.com*) displays work in the window under the 'queer weed' sign. For the complete list of participating local businesses and artists each month, check the art-walk website.

Listen to Indie Music at Underground Cafe du Nord

LIVE MUSIC

MAP: 10 P142 **F2**

The Castro was once known as Little Scandinavia after the sailors who docked here – and the secret to their community spirit was the speakeasy running in the basement of their local meeting hall since 1907. Today the updated **Cafe du Nord** (*cafedunord.com;*

NOBBY CLARKE'S FOLLY
The strange **Nobby Clarke Mansion**, notable for its several turrets, gables and unique shingle pattern on the roof, was built in 1892 by Alfred E Clarke, an attorney who amassed a fortune by dubious means. Looking for sunnier weather than swanky Nob Hill afforded, he spent millions in today's money – the typical cost of housing in modern SF but an unheard of expenditure for the time – building this baroque Queen Anne, only for it to go uninhabited after construction when his wife refused to move in. Snob Hill socialites dubbed the house 'Nobby Clarke's Folly.'
MAP: 12 P142 **B6**

tickets $18-35) speakeasy is an atmospheric singer-songwriter hotspot, hosting prolific artists like Cat Power, Bon Iver and St Vincent, while the upstairs **Swedish American Hall** *(swedishamericanhall.com)* hosts folkYEAH! indie-breakthrough showcases. A few nights a month, laughter reverberates below street level as comedians take over the intimate stage for an evening of stand-up, with some all-ages shows; most are 21-plus.

View LGBTQ+ Art at Queer Arts Featured

GALLERY

MAP: 11 P142 **D6**

It's no secret that the Castro is queer – after all, this neighborhood is home to the artist-led gallery and retail space **Queer Arts Featured** *(queerartsfeatured.com)*. Located in the historic storefront that once housed Harvey Milk's Castro Camera, and was more recently the center for the Human Rights Campaign, Queer Arts Featured upholds this legacy by celebrating and promoting local artists across the LGBTQ+ spectrum. Shop for tarot decks featuring queer icons throughout history – Oscar Wilde lounging on a marble throne is Justice, while ACT UP protesters are the transformative Death card – or feed your imagination with an evening of Queer Bedtime Stories where anyone is welcome to bring a reading to share or simply listen along.

Summit Corona Heights

PARK

MAP: 13 P142 **B3**

If there's one thing San Francisco has in ample supply, it's jaw-dropping views – a reward for the uphill battle you must embark on to reach them. For romantic sunsets with panoramic views from the Castro to the bay, scramble up the red rocks of the 520ft-high peak at **Corona Heights Park**. Face southeast as the sun sets, and watch rainbow lights twinkle welcomes across the Castro. Be sure to bring a jacket with you once afternoon fog blows in – you'll be glad to have it.

Discover Scientific Wonders

MUSEUM

MAP: 14 P142 **B3**

While adults are asleep downhill, eight-year-olds are making scientific discoveries at the **Randall Museum** *(randallmuseum.org; free)* atop Corona Heights Park. After Josephine Randall became a pioneering Stanford zoologist in 1910, she turned a jail into a kids' science and arts center as San Francisco's first Rec & Parks Superintendent. Highlights include state-of-the-art science and tech labs, woodworking and ceramics studios, a habitat for 100 stray and wounded animals, plus Lionel trains chugging along the expansive Golden Gate Model Railroad. Check the website for wonder-inspiring hands-on workshops, often available on a walk-in basis.

Time-Travel Through Queer Public History

MUSEUM

MAP: 15 P142 **G6**

America's first queer-history museum, the **GLBT Historical Society Museum** *(glbthistory.org; admission $10)* showcases a century of San Francisco LGBTQ+ ephemera – including Harvey Milk's campaign literature and Keith Haring's posters urging SF to 'Act Up Fight AIDS' – alongside exhibits highlighting queer culture and movements throughout history. Since 1985 the GLBT Historical Society, which sponsors the museum, has

FIND OUT WHAT'S GOING DOWN IN THE CASTRO

Bay Area Reporter

If you don't spot a free copy of this LGBTQ+ community newspaper with stellar event listings in Castro cafes or bookstores, find the latest issues and records since 1971 at *ebar.com*.

Noticeboard

Check out the outdoor bulletin board at 18th and Castro St to see what's happening in the Castro now: circuit parties, drag political fundraisers, bands seeking guitarists and – the perennial favorite – missed connections, documenting brief, anonymous encounters of any and all kinds.

Flyers

Wrapped around every post along the main drag are colorful posters for myriad events, like a trans-temporal evening for the gender playful, a cowboy vs aliens dance party or a David Lynch tribute show (Mulholland Drag).

worked to collect and preserve community history. Visits here are bonding experiences for LGBTQ+ community and civil-rights allies alike, with moving multimedia stories sharing deep struggles and sheer queer joy. The shop features books researched at the museum, historic event posters – yes, SF's 1970 Gay-In was an actual event – and fridge magnets echoing Harvey Milk's words: 'You gotta give 'em hope.' Indeed.

Race Down Concrete Slides at Seward Mini Park

PARK

MAP: 16 P142 **B6**

Climb steep hills to **Seward Mini Park** – and ride back down on one of the city's hidden concrete slides! Designed by a local high-schooler, winner of a competition put on by sculptor Ruth Asawa, the **Seward Street Slides** have been entertaining generations of San Franciscans since 1973. Cardboard is necessary for descents, and there's usually a stack by the slides – BYO waxed paper for faster speeds, and be sure to wear sturdy pants. Bring kids: a park sign reads 'No adults unless accompanied by children.' Neighbors don't love noise, but sometimes it can't be helped… *wheeee!*

Seize the Night

MARKET

Every third Friday of the month from 5pm to 10pm, the neighborhood gets all dolled up for the **Castro Night Market** *(castronightmarket.com)*, a showcase of Castro-based queer-owned businesses, celebrating community and supporting the ultra-local economy. Vendor booths line 18th St between Collingwood and Hartford, selling handmade wares: ceramic vases with an ancient Greco-Roman aesthetic (phalli intact), baskets of crocheted strawberries, tote bags adorned with vintage pulp-novel covers, and small leather goods and accessories, like teddy bears in full bondage gear. Food stands fill the air with the aroma of Latin-inspired gourmet burgers, Peruvian-fusion ceviche bowls and tea-infused ice cream. On stage, DJs spin dance beats while go-go dancers in fairy wings draw a crowd.

Receive Life-Saving Care & Enjoy Life-Affirming Art

HEALTHCARE

MAP: 17 P142 **G5**

In the 1980s and '90s, the AIDS epidemic devastated the Castro – but amid incalculable loss, the community got organized. The Castro's resurgence is a testament to the groundbreaking healthcare pioneered by community organizations including San Francisco AIDS Foundation, the nonprofit behind **Strut** *(sfaf.org)*. This landmark health and wellness center offers free and low-cost services for all, including PrEP prophylaxis, health screenings, walk-in counseling, substance-abuse treatment, and support groups. ID is required, and privacy assured. Book appointments or expect waits for walk-in clinical services.

When cheers and wolf whistles burst out of the center's giant glass doors, you know it must be that time of the month again – every third Tuesday, Strut hosts the city's most unique (and most rambunctious) open-mic night. This health organization has a rotating event calendar that rivals that of any gay bar: Beyond Binary, an afternoon of art and activities for intersex and non-binary community members of any age, every third Monday; art openings in the gallery space; and staged readings of plays.

BEST PUBLIC ART

Pink Triangle Memorial

MAP: 18 P142 **C5**

Triangular granite columns sprout from the grass and a rose-quartz-filled triangle rests in the center, dedicated to the thousands of queer lives lost during the Holocaust.

The Hope for the World Cure

MAP: 19 P142 **E3**

This mural tells a kaleidoscopic story about the chaos of the AIDS epidemic and the solidarity of the global queer community.

Gear Up

MAP: 20 P142 **E5**

Serge Gay Jr's mural symbolizes a person getting their armor ready for a march on the streets – the black leather jacket has pins and patches reflecting the Civil Rights movement, women's rights, LGBTQ+ rights and the Black Lives Matter movement, plus the faces of Marsha P Johnson, James Baldwin and Malcolm X.

LISTINGS

Best Places for...

$ Budget $$ Midrange $$$ Top End

Eating

Coffee & Pastries

Poesia Cafe $

Ultra-local produce and premium Italian imports combine to make buttery *cornetto* pastries and traditional focaccia, plus some truly killer espresso. *8am-6pm Sun, to 5pm Mon, 7:30am-5pm Tue-Thu, 7:30am-6pm Fri & Sat*

Cafe de Casa $

Dark-roast Brazilian coffee and colorful Brazilian fare to match the Castro's rainbow spirit – the *pão de queijo* (cheese-ball bread) sandwich is genius. *8am-6pm Mon-Sat, to 5pm Sun*

Thoroughbread & Pastry $

Enjoy warm chocolate bread, olive *fougasse* and sourdough sandwiches – pastries with pedigree, creations of Michelin-starred Michel Suas, founder of the SF Baking Institute. *8am-4pm Wed-Fri, to 5pm Sat & Sun*

Casual Brunch & Lunch

Kitchen Story $$

24 F3

Korean-inspired scrambles and thick Millionaire's Bacon make this one of SF's best brunch spots – and the most popular, so be sure to go early. *9am-2pm Mon-Fri, to 2:30pm Sat & Sun*

Dinosaurs Sandwiches $

25 E3

Monster banh mi stomp hunger with your choice of beef, lemongrass chicken, portobello, or pork with pâté on crusty French bread with all the fixings – jalapeños, mayo and pickled vegetables, cilantro and Sriracha hot sauce are optional. *10am-7pm*

Gai Chicken Rice $$

Who's got the solution to cold snaps and tentative tummies? This Gai. The tender Hainan-style poached chicken is free-range, accompanied by jasmine or brown rice cooked in chicken broth. Soulful soup gets you back on your feet; sweet Vietnamese coffee gets you Castro-club-hopping. *11am-9pm*

Beit Rima $$$

Palestinian lager pairs with Arabic comfort food: Gazan braised lamb shank, shakshuka, and classic meze with just enough lemon hummus to make you pucker up. *11am-9pm Sun & Tue-Thu, to 9:30pm Fri & Sat*

Fisch & Flore $$$

Enjoy fresh seafood and watch the entire gay world go by from the sun-drenched patio on the most happening corner in the neighborhood. *11am-10pm Fri-Sun*

Cozy Dinners & Date-Night Spots

Starbelly $$$

All the sun-drenched flavors and chill vibes you'd expect from California, with ingredients sourced from the farmers market across the street. Starbelly's Point Reyes blue cheeseburger is the Castro's best burger, especially with housemade bacon. *11:30am-9pm Mon-Thu, to 10pm Fri, 10am-10pm Sat, 10am-9pm Sun*

Frances $$$

 **E4**

Seasonal menus show-case rustic flavors and luxurious textures with impeccable technique – handmade pastas, juicy steaks, lumberjack date cake to satisfy your discerning lumberjack date – plus top-notch Italian and cult Californian wine. Tasting menus are excellent value here (from $65). *5:15-9:15pm Tue-Sat*

Poesia $$$

 **H5**

Get cozy at this bay-window *osteria* with feel-good handmade pastas and excellent DOC Italian wines by the glass. Arrive before 6:30pm for half-off happy-hour negronis and Aperol spritz, plus bargain crostini. Fun fact: Oprah ate here when she visited the Castro. *5-9:30pm*

Blind Butcher $$$

 **H5**

Intimate seating and moody lighting make this a popular date-night spot for meat-lovers – best steak in the Castro! – and vegetarians alike. *5-10pm Mon-Fri, 11am-3pm & 5-10pm Sat & Sun*

Anchor Oyster Bar $$$

 **D6**

Since 1977 Anchor remains Castro's port of call for sustainably sourced local oysters, Dungeness crab and San Francisco's famous *cioppino* (seafood stew). No reservations – get on the list, then chill with a glass of wine until called. *2-8pm Thu-Mon*

Late-Night Delights

Orphan Andy's $$

34 **H4**

Bask in flamboyant flair at this local haunt, serving up retro realness alongside an expansive repertoire of classic diner staples. *24hr*

Hot Cookie $

 **G4**

If the smell wafting down Castro St isn't enough to draw you into tiny Hot Cookie, maybe this will: freshly baked phallic-shaped treats of firm macaroon cookie dough dipped in white or dark chocolate, and a wall of hot customers posing in eye-catching branded underwear. *11am-11pm Sun-Thu, to 2am Fri & Sat*

Drinking

Gay Clubs

440 Castro

 **G5**

Two-for-one Woody Wednesdays and Monday's Underwear Party welcome bears (the term was coined in SF) and Peter Pans alike – but if you think 440's Battle of the Bulge contest has something to do with WWII, this is not your bar, honey. *noon-2am*

Beaux

 **D4**

The candy store of Castro clubs, Beaux serves every gay flavor, from Pan Dulce Wednesdays to go-go Manimal Fridays to straight-friendly weekend drag brunches (reserve ahead). *3pm-2am Mon-Fri, from noon Sat & Sun*

The Cafe

 **G4**

With a Harvey Milk mural and rainbow light-up dance floor, this is the obvious place to throw your own coming-out party. Kick-ass sound and trippy light shows pack the dance floor; parties range from Latinx Picante Thursdays to lesbian Sugar Saturdays. *10:30pm-2am Thu, from 8pm Fri, from 9pm Sat*

QBar

 G5

Determined 20-something club kids shimmy and shout over pop remixes on the cramped dance floor, while smokers flirt on the patio. Busy bartenders mix mean dirty martinis and lemon drops, if you ask nicely. *9pm-2am Mon-Wed, to 1am Thu, 5pm-2am Fri-Sun*

Historic Gay Bars

Twin Peaks Tavern

40 G4

The first gay bar in the world to install windows open to the street. Nab an outdoor seat on sunny afternoons for prime people-watching, cozy up to the Victorian carved-wood bar for cocktails, or grab a booth to review Castro shows over wine by the glass. *noon-2am*

Moby Dick

 E5

You can call anyone Ishmael here, as long as you're buying. The fish tank over the bar is mesmerizing – there's something thrusting out of the coral, and it's definitely not fishy. The sign has been a Castro photo-op since 1977. Cash only. *noon-2am*

Midnight Sun

42 H6

'Servicing the Castro for over 50 years' is no small claim to fame – and Midnight Sun lives up to its motto daily with a steady flow of good vibes and strong drinks (two for one until 9pm every day). *2pm-midnight Mon-Wed, to 2am Thu & Fri, 1pm-2am Sat, 12:30pm-midnight Sun*

Neighborhood Hangs

Toad Hall

 G6

It's named after a famous 1970s Castro gay bar, as seen in the movie *Milk* – and the front bar does look like a 1970s suburban den. *4pm-2am Mon-Thu, from 3pm Fri, 2pm-2am Sat, 1pm-2am Sun*

Mix

44 H6

Living up to its name with a full rainbow of colorful neighborhood characters – acclaimed lesbian playwrights, AIDS LifeCycle champs and off-duty drag queens alike. The front bar is snug and sociable, the smokers patio is where the action is. *noon-2am Mon-Sat, from 7am Sun*

Sports Fans & Jock Lovers

Lookout

45 E3

Soon there may be a groove worn across Market St between the Castro's biggest gym and this rooftop bar, where post-workout crowds gather. Grab a drink and listen to stripped-down rugby players deliver truth in advertising at Jock, the Sunday-afternoon fundraising party for LGBTQ+ sports teams. *3:30pm-midnight Tue & Wed, to 2am Thu & Fri, noon-2am Sat, 1pm-midnight Sun*

HiTops

 F3

At Castro's first gay sports bar, you can wear rainbows and team colors. Giant-screen TVs and supersized snacks set the scene for instant bonding – and Thursday Gym Class amps up locker-room antics with go-go boys. *noon-midnight Mon-Thu, to 12:30am Fri & Sat, 11am-midnight Sun*

Classy Cocktails, Microbrews & Wines

Blackbird

 G2

Mysterious tinctures and housemade bitters turn creative cocktails into irresistible potions, luring crowds to this cozy neighborhood den. *5-11pm Mon, to midnight Tue-Thu, 4pm-2am Fri, 2pm-2am Sat, 2-11pm Sun*

Lobby Bar

 C5

The retroglam tavern downstairs at Hotel Castro, serving up signature cocktails for out-of-towners and neighborhood regulars alike. *3-10pm Sun, 5-11pm Wed & Thu, 5pm-midnight Fri, 4pm-midnight Sat*

Copper Bar

 G6

Cozy, copper-covered spot for swanky bar food and unique microbrews – check out tasting flights to sample everything from Copper IPA to Castro Cream. *4-11pm Mon-Wed, from 11am Sun & Thu, 4pm-1am Fri & Sat*

Blush!

 G5

Kick back on red-velvet sofas and pair a happy-hour glass (half-off 'til 6pm Monday to Friday) with tarot readings and live music. *4pm-midnight Mon-Thu, to 1:30am Fri, 3pm-1:30am Sat, to midnight Sun*

Swirl

 D6

Come as you are – pinstripes or leather, gay, straight or whatever – this wine-shop bar has universal appeal and reliably delicious bottles. *11:30am-9pm*

Shopping

Him & Home

Apothecarium

 H1

What's that alluring frosted-glass emporium? It's America's best-designed marijuana dispensary, according to *Architectural Digest*. Consult expert staff about edibles for your desired state – then you can really appreciate the local art on thoughtfully provided designer couches (21-plus only; ID required). *9am-9:30pm*

Cliff's Variety

53 G5

Hardware maestros at this 1936 general store, famous for gasp-worthy window displays, won't raise an eyebrow if you express a dire need for a jar of rubber nuns, silver body paint and towering pink wigs – though they might angle for an invitation. *10am-6:30pm*

Local Take

 H4

Take in the local scenery with a Castro Theatre marquee print, F-line streetcar T-shirt or belt buckle featuring vintage Muni maps, and support SF's creative economy. *11am-7pm*

Stag & Manor

 D4

Dashingly handsome decor from this indie design boutique lets you take the Castro home. Brass-ball lanterns wink welcome at guests and fair-trade throw pillows show dates how thoughtful yet laid-back you are. *noon-6pm Tue & Sat, to 5pm Wed, Fri & Sun, to 6:30pm Thu*

Bookstores

Omnivore Books

56 G6

Salivate over signed cookbooks by chef-legend Alice Waters, satisfy insatiable appetites with specialty titles covering ancient Filipino diets, Lebanese preservation methods and DIY moonshine, and attend events with star chefs and food luminaries like Michael Pollan. *11am-6pm Mon-Sat, noon-5pm Sun*

Fabulosa Books

  G5

For vacation reading that matches the scenery, head to the Castro's indie bookstore for a wide selection of San Francisco literature and LGBTQ+ novels censored elsewhere. The bulletin board at the back will give you the lowdown on literary events and local activism. *10am-9pm Sun-Fri, to 10pm Sat*

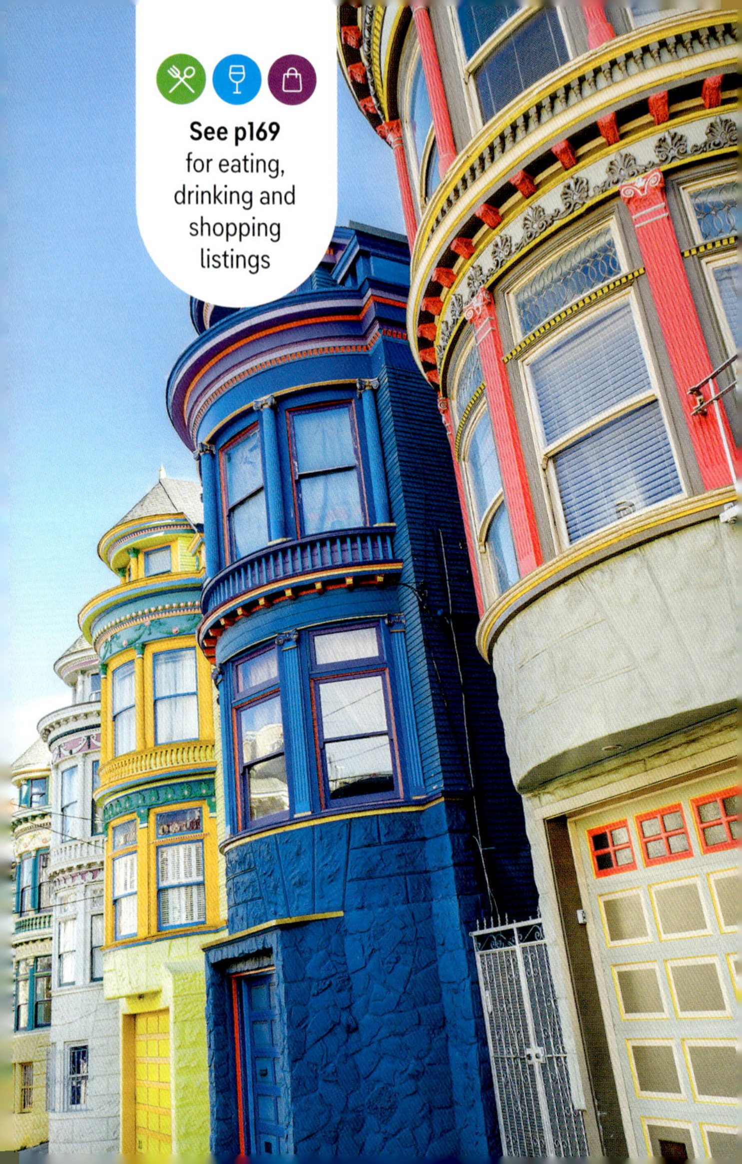
See p169
for eating,
drinking and
shopping
listings

Explore The Haight & Hayes Valley

Researched by Dylan Lalanne-Perkins

In the 1960s thousands of young people from across the country flocked to Haight and Ashbury, drawn in by psychedelic music and tales of free-love communes. Counterculture kids called themselves freaks and flower children; *San Francisco Chronicle* columnist Herb Caen dubbed them 'hippies.' The Upper Haight has hung onto its roots: hippies reminisce about glory days, trailed by teenage relations pretending not to know them, and new-age practitioners load up on chakra-cleansing crystals. Down in the Lower Haight there are mellower vibes – dog walkers mosey like urban cowboys wrangling their herds and cyclists dodge steep hills. Next door in Hayes Valley, Zen monks and jazz legends drift past designer boutiques and some of the city's best restaurants.

Getting Around

Bus

Bus lines 6 and 7 travel along Haight St, connecting downtown to Golden Gate Park. The 22 links the Lower Haight to the Mission and the Marina, while the 43 connects the Upper Haight to the Marina.

Muni

Van Ness station is one block east of Hayes Valley, offering Muni lines across the city. The N line goes through the Lower Haight and onward to Ocean Beach.

BART

Civic Center station is four blocks east of Hayes Valley, with trains to the Mission and the East Bay.

THE BEST

LIVE MUSIC SFJAZZ Center (p167)

ART Haight Street Art Center (p166)

FAMILY-FRIENDLY ACTIVITY Church of 8 Wheels (p166)

ADVENTURE The Wiggle (p165)

COMMUNITY SPACE Patricia's Green & PROXY (p168)

Colorful buildings, Haight & Ashbury (p161)

MICHAEL WARWICK/SHUTTERSTOCK

Haight Street Flashback

Flashbacks are a given in the Haight, where the fog is fragrant downwind of Haight St's legal marijuana dispensaries, and hippie tie-dyes and ideals have never entirely gone out of fashion. In the Upper Haight, watch out for the colorful, historic homes where rock-star residents lived and loved freely.

START	END	LENGTH
Buena Vista Park	Golden Gate Park	1.3 miles; one hour

1 Buena Vista Park

Start in **Buena Vista Park** (p163), with panoramic city views that move San Franciscans to tears. Brave trails weaving uphill, then take Buena Vista Ave West back down to spot Victorian mansions that survived the 1906 earthquake and fire, and the hippie-commune boom during the 1967 Summer of Love.

2 Bound Together Anarchist Book Collective

Heading west up Haight St, you may recognize Emma Goldman in the *Anarchists of the Americas* mural at **Bound Together Anarchist Book Collective** (p165) – if not, staff can recommend biographical comics by way of introduction.

3 Symbionese Liberation Army House

Neighborhood old-timers claim the **Symbionese Liberation Army** used 1235 Masonic Ave as a safe house for kidnapped-heiress-turned-revolutionary-bank-robber Patty Hearst.

4 Grateful Dead House

Like surviving members of the Grateful Dead, the purple Victorian at **710 Ashbury** sports a touch of gray – but during the Summer of Love, this was where the band blew minds, amps and brain cells. After a 1967 drug bust, the Dead held a press conference here arguing for decriminalization, claiming that if everyone who smoked marijuana were arrested, San Francisco would be empty.

5 Janis Joplin's House

And **635 Ashbury St**, the pink building down the block? One of many known SF addresses for Janis Joplin, who had a hard time hanging onto leases in the 1960s – but as she sang, 'Freedom's just another word for nothin' left to lose.'

6 Haight & Ashbury

At the corner of **Haight & Ashbury** (p161), the clock overhead always reads 4:20, better known in 'Hashbury' as International Bong-Hit Time. For trips that became bummers, Haight-Ashbury Free Clinic (p167) offered free recovery treatment to all the neighborhood hippies.

7 Evolutionary Rainbow Mural

Cross Haight and Cole Sts, and across the street from the apartment where Charles Manson once lived, you'll see a Summer of Love relic: Yana Zegri's 1967 **Evolutionary Rainbow** mural. Once a shop owner painted it over – and faced community boycotts until it was restored.

8 Hippie Hill

Follow your bliss to the drum circle at **Hippie Hill** in Golden Gate Park, where free spirits have gathered since the '60s to flail to the beat.

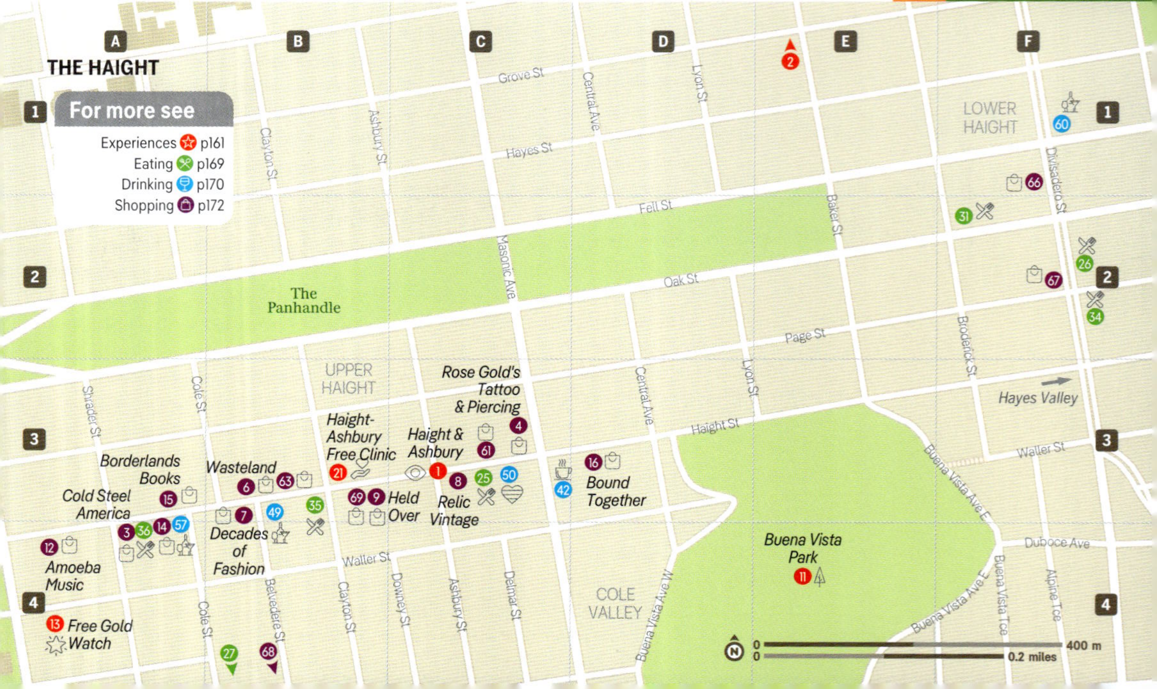
THE HAIGHT
For more see
Experiences p161
Eating p169
Drinking p170
Shopping p172
A
B
C
D
E
F
1
2
3
4
LOWER HAIGHT
UPPER HAIGHT
COLE VALLEY
Hayes Valley
The Panhandle
Buena Vista Park
Grove St
Hayes St
Fell St
Oak St
Page St
Haight St
Waller St
Duboce Ave
Clayton St
Ashbury St
Central Ave
Lyon St
Baker St
Broderick St
Divisadero St
Masonic Ave
Shrader St
Cole St
Belvedere St
Downey St
Delmar St
Buena Vista Ave W
Buena Vista Ave E
Buena Vista Tce
Alpine Tce
Rose Gold's Tattoo & Piercing
Haight-Ashbury Free Clinic
Haight & Ashbury
Borderlands Books
Wasteland
Cold Steel America
Decades of Fashion
Held Over
Relic Vintage
Bound Together
Amoeba Music
Free Gold Watch
0
400 m
0.2 miles

EXPERIENCES

Drop Out at Haight & Ashbury

CROSSROADS

MAP: 1 P160 C3

Was it the fall of 1966 or the winter of '67? As the Haight saying goes, if you can remember the Summer of Love, you probably weren't here. The fog was laced with pot, sandalwood incense and burning military draft cards, and at the corner of **Haight & Ashbury Sts** a cultural revolution began. Decades later, 'Hashbury' remains a counterculture magnet. On average Saturdays here, you can sign Green Party petitions, commission a poem, and hear Hare Krishna on keyboards and Bob Dylan on banjo. The cubic clock on the northeast corner of Haight and Ashbury is frozen at 4:20 – a term coined in the Bay Area circa 1971, now recognized globally as International Bong Hit Time. Though local clockmakers through the years have taken it upon themselves to get the vintage clock running again, stoned pranksters always reset it.

Handmake in the Haight

ART CENTER

MAP: 2 P160 E1

Macramé, stoneware pottery, tie-dyes, tapestries, block prints, stained-glass suncatchers – the Haight's classic hippie handicrafts are undergoing a major revival with hands-on courses at **WorkshopSF** *(workshopsf.org; lessons $50-120)*. Every day of the week, enthusiastic local artists offer adults-only classes

BEST PIERCING & TATTOO STUDIOS

When visiting the Haight, there's always a chance you'll walk away with a more permanent souvenir – get expert service and artistry at these neighborhood institutions:

Cold Steel America

MAP: 3 P160 A4

The city's most acclaimed piercing shop with an expansive inventory of rare antique earrings and a wide array of body jewelry in metal alternatives: glass, silicone, amber, stone, wood and horn.

Rose Gold's Tattoo & Piercing

MAP: 4 P160 C3

Piercers give ear-styling consultations, their expert advice as solid as the 14 karat and 18 karat gold body jewelry on offer, while tattoo artists craft intricate fine-line work.

Idle Hand

MAP: 5 P162 A2

Browse over 500 flash sheets of pre-drawn designs spanning a century of tattoo history, or make an appointment with artists constructing individualized adaptations of classic trad tats. Cash only.

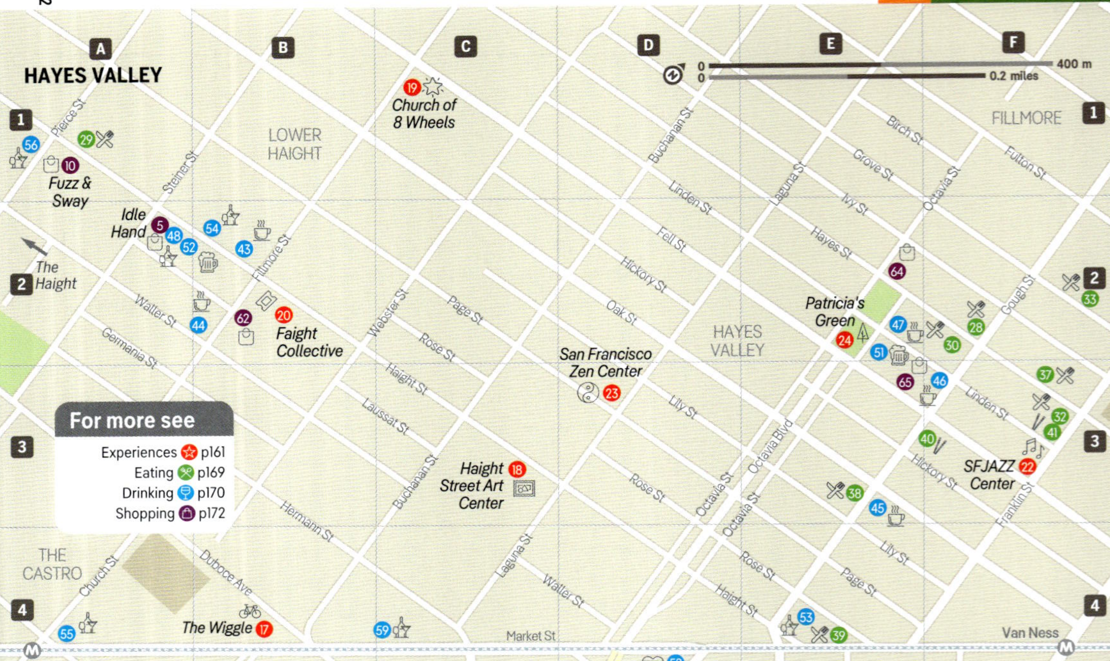
HAYES VALLEY
A
B
C
D
E
F
1
2
3
4
0
400 m
0
0.2 miles
19 Church of 8 Wheels
LOWER HAIGHT
FILLMORE
HAYES VALLEY
THE CASTRO
10 Fuzz & Sway
5 Idle Hand
The Haight
20 Faight Collective
23 San Francisco Zen Center
18 Haight Street Art Center
24 Patricia's Green
22 SFJAZZ Center
17 The Wiggle
Pierce St
Steiner St
Fillmore St
Webster St
Buchanan St
Laguna St
Octavia St
Octavia Blvd
Gough St
Franklin St
Birch St
Grove St
Fulton St
Linden St
Ivy St
Hayes St
Fell St
Hickory St
Oak St
Page St
Rose St
Haight St
Lily St
Waller St
Germania St
Laussat St
Hermann St
Duboce Ave
Church St
Market St
Van Ness
For more see
Experiences p161
Eating p169
Drinking p170
Shopping p172

at this sunny DIY school. Keep your favorite jeans in rotation by mastering the art of Sashiko visible mending or take it easy at a Chill Sketching evening session. Most lessons cost less than $75 – and that homebrew workshop costs less than a round at the bar.

Flashback to the Summer of Love FESTIVAL

Every year since 1977, when Harvey Milk helped organize the first **Haight Street Fair**, the Summer of Love stages a comeback: free music on two stages – funk groups groove in their tie-dye jumpsuits and middle-school rockers headbang – plus vendors selling rainbow macramé and trippy tarot decks, skateboarders performing tricks for the crowd, and pot smoke wafting overhead thick enough to rival the fog.

Wander Through Wardrobes of the Past SHOPPING

The Upper Haight is the place to rock a new old style with vintage concert tees, jumpsuits ready for the disco dance floor, and a steady supply of go-go boots – at reasonable (not bargain) prices, anyone can afford a few fashion risks. Head to **Wasteland** (MAP: 6 P160 **B3**; *shopwasteland.com)*, a converted-cinema vintage superstore, to peruse the wall of prized vintage rock tees and the racks of high-end leather jackets plucked straight off the runway. **Decades of Fashion** (MAP: 7 P160 **B3**; *decadesoffashionsf.com)* is a wearable museum featuring everything from frilly Gilded Age opera gloves to *Dynasty*-era shoulder pads. Travel to the early 20th century at **Relic Vintage** (MAP: 8 P160 **C3**; *relicvintagesf.com)*, an elegant haberdashery of pinstriped suits and poodle skirts. **Held Over** (MAP: 9 P160 **B3**) is the spot for 1970s Western wear and flared denim for days, the perfect pregame for an evening of line dancing (yeehaw!). If you tumble downhill to the Lower Haight, the vintage party keeps grooving at **Fuzz & Sway** (MAP: 10 P162 **A1**), a carefully curated spot for funky maxi skirts and mod dresses.

Walk in Buena Vista Park PARK

MAP: 11 P160 **E4**

True to its name, the hilltop Buena Vista Park offers splendid vistas over the city. Choose any of the secluded trails that weave up the park to enjoy spectacular views on the upper slopes, where the Golden Gate Bridge can be seen peeking through the fog.

Founded in 1867, this is one of San Francisco's oldest parks, populated by stately, century-old coast live oak trees where a world of woodland creatures thrives. Keep an eye out for the dramatic scarlet plumage of a red-breasted sapsucker drilling for sap, and tubby gophers emerging from their burrows to nosh on roots and seedlings. As you wander, peek under your feet for fragments of a forgotten last name – the engraved marble chunks bordering the park's paths are remnants of San Francisco's earliest tombstones. If you go on any nighttime excursions in the park, you are likely to catch a good view of something else: Buena Vista has a longstanding reputation as a gay cruising hotspot.

Shop Bops at Amoeba SHOPPING

MAP: 12 P160 **A4**

Enticements are hardly necessary to lure fans to the West Coast's most eclectic collection of new and used music and video, but **Amoeba Music** *(amoeba.com)* offers listening stations, free zines with uncannily accurate staff reviews, and upwards of 100,000 vinyl records, CDs and cassettes for everything from mainstream hip-hop to obscure jazz, along with DVDs and VHS for anyone looking to ditch streaming once and for all. This cavernous former bowling alley regularly transforms itself into a venue for Live at Amoeba, a free concert and album-signing series. Oh, and when Amoeba's not feeding your record collection, they're running a foundation that's saved one-million acres of rainforest.

Play Retro Pinball at Free Gold Watch ARCADE

MAP: 13 P160 **A4**

The name sounds too good to be true, but you've hit the jackpot: step inside **Free Gold Watch** *(freegoldwatch.com)* to discover a working screen-printing shop absolutely crammed with 50-plus vintage pinball games. Most cost a buck or less to play, including Elvis, Godzilla and SF-favorite Dirty Harry–themed games. Regulars proceed directly to the next level of gamer heaven: the Secret Juju Gallery of rare 1970s games. At the time of research, Free Gold Watch just won big, securing a food and beverage license to be able to serve up arcade staples – pizza, hot dogs and nachos – and craft beers and cocktails. Righteous.

Browse Book Nooks BOOKSTORE

Throw a stone in SF and you'll probably hit a writer (ouch) or reader (ouch again) headed to/from **Booksmith** (MAP: 14 P160 **A4**; *booksmith.com*). Literary figures organize Booksmith book signings, raucous poetry readings and politician-postcard-writing marathons. This is no library, as you'll discover at keg parties where boozy book browsing is encouraged – when you wake up tomorrow amid piles of signed San Francisco novels, you'll know exactly what happened last night.

DEATH OF HIPPIE

On October 6, 1967, the Summer of Love was laid to rest. A mock funeral procession kicked off at Buena Vista Park (p163) with the San Francisco Diggers – a legendary community action and street-theater group famous for giving out free food every day in the Panhandle – carrying a coffin bearing the inscription 'Hippie, Son of Media.' Their message: stop flocking to SF, drawn in by the media's depiction of hippies – instead, 'bring the revolution to where you live.' But Hippie's untimely demise was not enough to snuff out the '60s idealism, still alive in the Haight today.

Explore the outer realms of literature at **Borderlands Books** (MAP: 15 P160 **A3**; *borderlands-books.com)*, a store dedicated to science fiction, fantasy, mystery and horror. Once voted the 'Best Place to Meet a Kinky Space Cadet' by the *SF Bay Guardian*, this shop is a gathering place for the city's more far-out readers.

Since 1976, **Bound Together** (MAP: 16 P160 **D3**; *boundtogether.org)*, a volunteer-run, nonprofit anarchist bookstore, has kept free thinkers supplied with organic-permaculture manuals, social history and radical comics, all while coordinating the annual Anarchist Book Fair, running the Prisoners' Literature Project and retouching the *Anarchists of the Americas* mural – makes us tools of the state look like slackers.

Ride the Wiggle

BIKING

MAP: 17 P162 **B4**

While much of San Francisco is famous for its calf-burning climbs, thousands of cyclists coast through the Lower Haight along **the Wiggle**, a zigzagging path that dodges inclines on the way to Golden Gate Park. The 400ft Duboce Bikeway Mural, *Gateway to the Wiggle*, welcomes riders to this bike highway, celebrating all of San Francisco's forms of carless transportation. Wind through the neighborhood's well-worn grooves, following green signs that guide your way to the park – from there, you can ride through the trees all the way to Ocean Beach. Rent from Bay Wheels, San Francisco's official bike-share program with docking stations all over the city. A single ride gets you 30 minutes for $3.99, then 30¢ for every minute after; day passes are $15.

Psychedelic Poster Prints

ART CENTER

MAP: 18 P162 **C3**

Look for Jeremy Fish's bronze bunny-skull sculpture and enter a wonderland of psychedelia.

The **Haight Street Art Center** *(haightstreetart.org; free)*, open noon to 6pm Thursday through Sunday, is a nonprofit organization dedicated to silk-screened posters – San Francisco's signature art form. Visitors can glimpse posters in progress at the on-site screen-printing studio, plus jaw-dropping gallery shows: rooms plastered floor-to-ceiling in original retro-futurist glam-rock poster prints – think Bowie in metallic platforms, strutting straight out of a moonage daydream. Gracing the stairwell is a hidden SF treasure: Ruben Kaddish's 1937 WPA fresco *Dissertation on Alchemy*, surely the trippiest mural ever commissioned by the US government.

Skate at the Church of 8 Wheels

ROLLERSKATING RINK

MAP: 19 P162 **C1**

At the **Church of 8 Wheels** *(churchof8wheels.com; admission $18)*, worship begins with '80s music blaring from the pulpit and congregants skating backwards under a disco ball, its lights dancing across stained-glass windows. This church-turned-roller-rink is a hit for all ages, with family-friendly skate sessions from 5pm to 6:30pm on Fridays, 2:30pm to 6:30pm on Saturdays, and 6pm to 7:30pm on Sundays and Tuesdays. After that, the floor is for anyone 18 and up looking to get their skate groove on – at goth nights, silent discos and Soul Roll Sundays. Check the calendar for theme nights and rent a pair of skates for just $5.

See What Faight Has in Store for You

ART COLLECTIVE

MAP: 20 P162 **B2**

Looking for an affordable yoga studio? A radically free craft workshop? Comedy show? Place to get a DIY thigh tat? At the crossroads of Fillmore and Haight, the aptly named **Faight Collective** *(thefaight.com)* is the ultimate third place. The street-level Upper Faight serves as a retail space, featuring work from local makers.

UNHOUSED IN THE HAIGHT

From buskers to teens scrounging for bus fare, panhandling – no judgment, no obligation – has been part of the Upper Haight since the '60s, when America's youth first fled here as a place to fit in. But in 2010 San Francisco's controversial Sit/Lie Ordinance targeted the Haight, making 7am to 11pm sidewalk 'loitering' punishable by up to $100 fines – but with limited shelter beds to accommodate unhoused people citywide, many street kids have no place else to go. While you're in town, volunteering or donations to homeless service nonprofits, like Haight Ashbury Food Program, are thoughtful gestures to repay San Francisco hospitality, and ensure everyone has a chance to feel at home here.

Take home the scents of the city with hand-poured zip-code candles, or don a stenciled jean jacket that dares you to 'break fake rules.' Downstairs, Lower Faight is an events space with an unpredictable lineup. Morning Vinyasa yoga flows into afternoon 'Bad Art Club' workshops. By evening, the space transforms into a carnival of open mics, live-music sets, and something called 'collective envisioning.'

Toast Jazz Giants at SFJAZZ

LIVE MUSIC

MAP: 22 P162 **F3**

Jazz legends and singular talents from Argentina to Yemen are showcased at **SFJAZZ Center** *(sfjazz.org; tickets $35-105)*, America's largest jazz center. Enjoy brilliant sound in Miner Auditorium, where the stage is regularly stormed by soul icon Mavis Staples, punk poet Laurie Anderson and Tony-winning dancer Savion Glover. Jazz-themed cocktails are served on the balcony, and you can take them with you to your seat – even upper-tier bargain seats have drink holders (and clear stage views). Hear fresh takes on classic jazz albums and poets riffing with combos in the downstairs Joe Henderson Lab. Test your knowledge of jazz history against stunning tiled murals composed of influential jazz venues across the country.

HAIGHT ST FREE CLINIC

The **Haight-Ashbury Free Clinic**'s original hand-carved 1967 sign still hangs at the eastern corner of Haight and Cole Sts, along with a mural of its motto: 'Healthcare is a right, not a privilege – love needs care.' After a little drug experimentation of his own, a local doctor opened San Francisco's legendary 'hippie clinic' providing judgment-free treatment to the neighborhood's influx of hippies. Support flooded in from SF big-shots, most notably concert producer Bill Graham, and for over 50 years, this clinic was a safe haven running life-saving, substance-abuse treatment, health screenings, and mental-health and women's-health services, all free or low-cost.

MAP: 21 P160 **B3**

Meditate at the SF Zen Center

WELLNESS

MAP: 23 P162 **D3**

This Italianate brick landmark that rises from a sea of Victorian flats in Hayes Valley has sheltered people of all faiths. In 1922 Julia Morgan, the first woman to be licensed as an architect in California and designer of famed Hearst Castle, designed this to be the Emanu-El Sisterhood, a residence for low-income Jewish women – note the ironwork stars of David on the 1st-floor loggia. Today, it's the **San Francisco Zen Center** *(sfzc.org; free)*, home to the largest Buddhist community outside of Asia since 1969.

Watch the sunlight fill the Zendo during free morning zazen, every day at 5:25am. Other programs are available on a semi-regular basis – check the calendar for half-day meditations in the lush garden courtyard and fun evening workshops blending the art of breathwork and beatboxing. Every other Thursday at 7pm is Trans Sangha, a meditation group by and for the trans community; beginners and newcomers are always welcome.

Bask at Patricia's Green & PROXY

PARK

MAP: 24 P162 E2

After the 1989 earthquake damaged freeway ramps, San Francisco voters nixed the cement skies of a freeway overpass in favor of a walkable community hub. At **Patricia's Green**, a hip pocket-park featuring Burning Man–inspired sculpture installations, kids scramble up the dome-shaped playground, and in the evenings after a few rounds, adventurous adults take a turn too – especially when neighbors envelop the play structure in a glowing 'sensory tent' filled with dry ice and light shows. Fridays and Saturdays until 10pm, Hayes St is a pedestrianized extension of the park – grab a partner to do-si-do at free line-dancing lessons, available some evenings.

At the eastern end is **PROXY** *(proxysf.net)*, a hamlet of upcycled shipping containers where you can graze your way across gourmet attractions. Spring through fall, free Friday-night 'bike-in' movies are shown on the outdoor projector, screening recent award-winning animations and indie foreign flicks – layer up to stay warm and snag a roll of green turf to lounge on.

Best Places for...

$ Budget $$ Midrange $$$ Top End

Eating

Breakfast & Brunch

Pork Store $$
25 P160 **C3**
A cozy pink diner that's been servin' up pork chops and 'scralifornia' (avocado and fresh *salsa ranchero* scramble) since 1979. *8am-2pm Mon-Fri, to 3pm Sat & Sun*

That's My Jam $$
26 P160 **F2**
It's breakfast time all weekend at this boutique bistro, with photo-worthy Painted Lady Lattes in pastel hues of iconic SF homes. *9am-3pm Fri-Sun*

Zazie $$
27 P160 **B4**
Hearty and wholesome – the line out the door lets you know just how good the homestyle potatoes and bowls of chai tea are. Tip-free. *8am-2pm Mon-Fri, 9am-3pm Sat & Sun*

Chez Maman West $$$
28 P162 **F2**
The restorative brunch everyone needs: buckwheat crepes plumped with prosciutto béchamel, cinnamon-laced berry *pain perdu* and bubbly by the glass. *11:30am-10pm Mon-Fri, from 10:30am Sat & Sun*

Sit-Down Mexican Food

Otra $$
29 P162 **A1**
Start off strong with spicy *salsa macha* on black beans, followed by sweet-potato tacos or cauliflower asparagus enchiladas from this vegetarian-friendly menu. *5-10pm*

Papito Hayes $$
30 P162 **F2**
Cozy and casual spot for well-seasoned enchiladas, tortas and fajitas, and heavy pours of spicy hibiscus margaritas. *11am-9pm Sun-Wed, to 10pm Thu-Sat*

Nopalito $$$
31 P160 **F2**
A beloved San Francisco favorite. Stop in for fresh, organic ingredients in colorful meals that can pierce through even the foggiest of days. *11:30am-9pm Sun-Tue & Thu, to 9:30pm Fri & Sat, 4:30-9pm Wed*

Vegan

Rad Radish $$
32 P162 **F3**
Totally radical, plant-based menu that satisfies all munchies: Pineapple Express Impossible burgers, 'chicken' caesar wraps and sides of chili-crisp cauliflower. *9am-9pm Mon-Fri, from 10am Sat & Sun*

Om Sabor $$
33 P162 **F2**
Creative, eco-friendly spins on nostalgic faves for the all-vegetarians occasionally, secretly missing their meat-eating days. Located inside cocktail audiophile lounge Phonobar. *5-10pm Wed-Sat, to 9pm Tue*

Quick & Casual

Little Chihuahua $

34 P160 **F2**

Who says sustainable, organic food has to be expensive? Grass-fed meats and organic veggies and beans are packed into giant burritos (the two-meal kinda deal), all washed down with craft beer or wine in a can. *11am-10pm Mon-Fri, from 10am Sat & Sun*

Street Taco $

35 P160 **B3**

Haight skateboarders swerve here for legit Mexico City fare on hand-made organic tortillas. Flavors come on strong with fresh housemade salsa and that mouthwatering aroma is *al pastor* (grilled pork) hot off the rotisserie – expect a wait. *11am-10pm*

Escape from New York Pizza $

36 P160 **A4**

The Haight's obligatory mid-bender stop for a hot slice. Pesto with roasted garlic and potato will send you blissfully off to carb-loaded sleep, but the sun-dried tomato with goat's cheese, artichoke hearts and spinach will recharge you to go another round. *10am-10pm Sun-Wed, to 11pm Thu, to 2am Fri & Sat*

Hayz Dog $

37 P162 **F3**

The best hot dogs in San Francisco: signature Hayz has got kimchi relish, scallions and kewpie, or get the vegetarian ode to elote with smoked paprika aioli and cotija. Grab it to-go and take your dog for a walk in the park. *11am-9pm Sun-Wed, to 11:30pm Thu-Sat*

Upscale Meals

Rich Table $$$

38 P162 **E3**

Impossible cravings begin with mind-bending dishes: porcini doughnuts, Dungeness crab latkes and only-in-SF pasta inventions like sea-urchin *cacio e pepe*. Book two to four weeks ahead – otherwise you'll need to bide your time at the bar, and hope for an opening before the California wine runs dry. *5-10:30pm Tue-Sat*

Zuni Cafe $$$

39 P162 **E4**

Turning basic menu staples into gourmet go-tos since 1979 – caesar salad with house-cured anchovies, brick-oven-roasted free-range chicken with Tuscan-bread salad and mesquite-grilled, grass-fed burgers on focaccia. *11am-3pm Fri-Sun, 5-9:30pm Tue-Sun*

Dumpling Home $$$

40 P162 **F3**

Fancy dining without the price tag at this casual, Michelin-approved spot that excels in soup dumplings – supple and full of a variety of meats. *11:30am-2:15pm & 5-8:15pm Sun-Thu, to 8:45pm Fri & Sat*

Nojo Ramen Tavern $$$

41 P162 **F3**

Find moments of clarity on foggy Hayes Valley nights with eye-opening bowls of proper ramen. Housemade broth brings bottomless flavor to modest bowls of noodles, topped by house-specialty chicken. Get the optional 'spice bomb.' *5-9pm Mon-Thu, 11:30am-2:30pm & 5-9:30pm Fri-Sun*

Drinking

Coffee Shops

Coffee to the People

42 P160 **C3**

The people united will never be decaffeinated at this radical coffeehouse. Choose a bumper-sticker-covered table, admire the macramé and browse consciousness-raising books. Hemp-milk cappuccinos are an acquired taste and beware the fair-trade quadruple-shot Freak Out. *7am-5pm Sun-Fri, to 6pm Sat*

Cafe International

 P162 **B2**

Fuel up with a Turkish coffee and an avocado bagel at a splatter-painted table on the back patio while a jazz band – likely a group of pensioners and their 11-year-old drummer – plays in the corner. *7am-4:30pm*

Le Cafe du Soleil

44 P162 **B2**

Bright outdoor seating invites you to linger over a fresh brew, paired with a croque monsieur or croque madame, the power couple of Saturday mornings. *7am-5pm*

LOQUAT

45 P162 **E3**

Featuring foods of the Jewish diaspora – don't skip out on cinnamon date babkas or seasonal veggie bourekas – and coffee from local roaster Four Barrel Coffee. *8am-5pm Wed-Mon*

Blue Bottle Coffee Kiosk

46 P162 **F3**

Don't mock SF's coffee geekery until you've tried the elixir emerging from this back-alley garage-door kiosk that built its reputation with micro-roasted organic coffee. Expect a (short) wait and sit outside on creatively repurposed traffic curbs. *6:30am-6pm Mon-Thu, to 7pm Fri-Sun*

Ritual Coffee

 P162 **E2**

The Hayes Valley shipping-container outpost of the Mission roastery offers creamy single-origin espresso and powerful pour-overs to rival those at Blue Bottle around the corner – but beware, those are fighting words among SF's hardcore coffee loyalists. *6:30am-7pm Mon-Fri, to 8pm Sat & Sun*

Neighborhood Dives

Noc Noc

48 P162 **A2**

Who's there? Trance DJs, anarchist hackers, Burning Man founders, that's who. At the Haight's original '90s post-apocalyptic cave rave, happy hour lasts until 7pm daily with $5 local drafts (no PBR here). *5pm-1am Sun-Thu, to 2am Fri & Sat*

Aub Zam Zam

 P160 **B3**

Persian arches, *One Thousand and One Nights* murals, 1930s jazz on the jukebox and top-shelf cocktails at low-shelf prices have brought bohemian bliss to Haight St since 1941. Phones down; cash only. *3pm-2am Mon-Fri, from 1pm Sat & Sun*

Mary's

 P160 **C3**

This queer dive has been pouring barrel-aged cocktails since the '70s, making it the longest-running and last-remaining relic of the Haight's past as a pre-Castro LGBTQ+ enclave. *3pm-2am Mon-Fri, from noon Sat & Sun*

Beer-Lovers

Biergarten

51 P162 **E2**

The faintest ray of sunshine brings lines for beer and bratwurst – wear sunblock, order two rounds of seasonal Fort Point brews at once, and get the pickled deviled eggs and pretzels to share at communal picnic tables. *4-8pm Wed & Thu, 2-9pm Fri, 1-8pm Sat, 1-7pm Sun*

Toronado

52 P162 **A2**

Glory hallelujah, beer-lovers: your prayers

are answered. Genuflect before the chalkboard altar that lists 40-plus beers on tap and hundreds more bottled, including sensational seasonal microbrews. *11:30am-2am*

Wine Bars

Hôtel Biron

53 P162 **E4**

Duck into the alley to find this walk-in wine closet, with standout small-production Californian, French and Italian vintages, and just a few tables for two. *5-11pm Mon & Tue, to midnight Wed-Sat, to 10pm Sun*

Uva Enoteca

54 P162 **B2**

Servers dole out sass, sound advice, and top-notch Soave and Montepulciano by the taste or carafe with pairings of local veggie charcuterie boards. *5:30-9pm Mon-Thu, to 9:30pm Fri & Sat, to 8:30pm Sun*

Millay

55 P162 **A4**

A vibey fuchsia date-night spot with the city's most expansive selection of sake, plus organic wines, and Japanese fusion snacks and tinned fish. *5-10pm Mon, Wed & Thu, 5pm-midnight Fri, 3pm-midnight Sat , 3-8pm Sun*

Classy Cocktails

Stoa

56 P162 **A1**

Find unexpected bar bites at this classy, creative cocktail lounge – everything on the menu is gluten- and dairy-free, from savory grilled mochi to strawberry empanadas. *4-10pm Mon-Thu, to midnight Fri & Sat*

Alembic

57 P160 **A4**

The Victorian tin ceilings are hammered, and you could be too unless you order tasty bar bites with these dangerously dainty cocktails – all expertly crafted from 250 specialty spirits. *4pm-midnight Wed-Sat, 2-10pm Sun*

Bars with Live Music

Martuni's

58 P162 **D4**

The city's top piano bar, where the rainbow spectrum of regulars have memorized the words to every show tune. Sing-alongs are a given – especially after a couple of world-famous lemon drops or top-notch martinis. *4pm-2am*

Mint

59 P162 **C4**

Big voices at this karaoke bar could rattle pennies in the US mint uphill. If you can't decide what to sing from the 30,000-plus playlist, know this: the two-drink minimum practically guarantees applause. *5pm-2am Mon & Wed-Fri, from 4pm Sat & Sun*

Madrone Art Bar

60 P160 **F1**

SF artist Tom Marioni famously said 'drinking beer with friends is the highest form of art' – but at this Victorian parlor-art bar, make it a Madroni. Join crowds grooving and bumping into rotating art installations on Motown Mondays or global disco parties. *4pm-2am Mon-Sat, 3pm-1:30am Sun*

Shopping

Local Brands

Piedmont Boutique

61 P160 **C3**

'No playing in the boas,' says the sign inside the door – a rule gleefully ignored by drag stars, Burning Man costumers and people who take Halloween dead seriously (read: all SF). Since 1972 Piedmont's signature costume getups have been designed and sewn in the city. *11am-7pm*

Upper Playground

62 P162 **B2**

Blend into SF scenery with a locally designed 'Golden State of Mind' hoodie, tectonic-plate map tee, and snap-back cap featuring the elusive Golden Gate Park coyote by SF's own Jeremy Fish. *noon-7pm*

FTC Skateboarding

63 P160 **B3**

Big air and big style at this SF skateboard outfitter – rock the SF look with 'For the City' chore jackets and caps, and show insider flair as you grab air with decks designed by local guest artists. *11am-6pm*

Marine Layer

64 P162 **E2**

Get California cool without getting shivers in 'absurdly soft' tees, which this clever SF company makes by blending cotton and recycled beechwood yarn. Add a 'shacket' (heavyweight flannel overshirt) or canvas chore coat for chilly Ocean Beach bonfires. *11am-7pm Mon-Sat, to 6pm Sun*

Geek Culture

Isotope

65 P162 **E3**

At this comic-book lounge, flip through superhero serials, eye the toilet seats signed by famous illustrators, then head upstairs to relax on comfy leather sofas with local graphic novelists, some of whom lead workshops here. Don't miss signings and free comic-book days. *11am-6pm Mon-Sat, to 5pm Sun*

Gamescape

66 P160 **F1**

Since 1985, this has been the city's tabletop gaming headquarters. Find award-winning Euro-games, local-designed cooperatives and hobby gaming supplies – and hang around the back tables for indie board-games nights and card tournaments. *11am-7pm Mon-Sat, to 6pm Sun*

Comix Experience

67 P160 **F2**

Comic-book deep cuts, signed first editions and kid-friendly graphic novels all find their home in this tiny neighborhood shop. Join the club to get the best graphic novel of the month at your doorstep, wherever that may be. *11am-6pm*

New-Age Wonders

Sword and Rose

68 P160 **B4**

Candlelight glows onto tarot decks and glass jars shimmer with ritually prepared, consecrated powder incense. Behind velvet curtains, practitioners offer tarot, palmistry and astrology readings to help illuminate the path. Appointments are best, but wanderers might snag a walk-in spot if the timing is right. *noon-6pm*

The Love of Ganesha

69 P160 **B3**

The prize jewel of crystal shops, carrying everything from amethyst to zircon. If you're lucky, the back meditation room will be open – recharge before hitting more Haight St shops. *11am-5:30pm*

See p186
for eating, drinking and shopping listings

Researched by Alison Bing

Explore Golden Gate Park & the Avenues

Bison roam, penguins waddle, hippies drum and surfers rip along San Francisco's most outlandish stretch of scenery: 50-block-long Golden Gate Park. Along the residential avenues flanking the park, you'll find Korean BBQ, Gaelic jam sessions, French pastries and Hong Kong movie matinees. This is one chill global village, where hard-core surfers and gourmet adventurers hang out and chow down. South of Golden Gate Park are candy-colored Sunset District homes, mom-and-pop restaurants on Irving St, and surf hangouts around Judah and 45th. North of the park are the Richmond's indie boutiques and cinemas, plus some of SF's best bakeries, bars and affordable dining.

Getting Around

Walk

Paved paths and trails criss-cross Golden Gate Park.

Bicycle

Pick up rentals inside the park at Parkwide Bike and Surrey.

Streetcar

The N line runs from downtown through the Sunset to Ocean Beach.

Bus

Buses 1, 2, 5, 21, 31 and 38 run from downtown through the Richmond; 7 and 6 head from downtown through the Haight to the Sunset; 33 connects the Richmond, Haight, Castro and Mission. North–south buses 28, 29 and 44 cut across the park.

Ocean Beach (p181)

AHMAD T NAJEEB/SHUTTERSTOCK

THE BEST

URBAN WILDERNESS Golden Gate Park (p178)

GLOBAL ART de Young Museum (p179)

WILDLIFE ENCOUNTERS California Academy of Sciences (p178)

END-OF-THE-WORLD VIEWS Lands End (p183)

BEACH WALKS Ocean Beach & Sunset Dunes (p181)

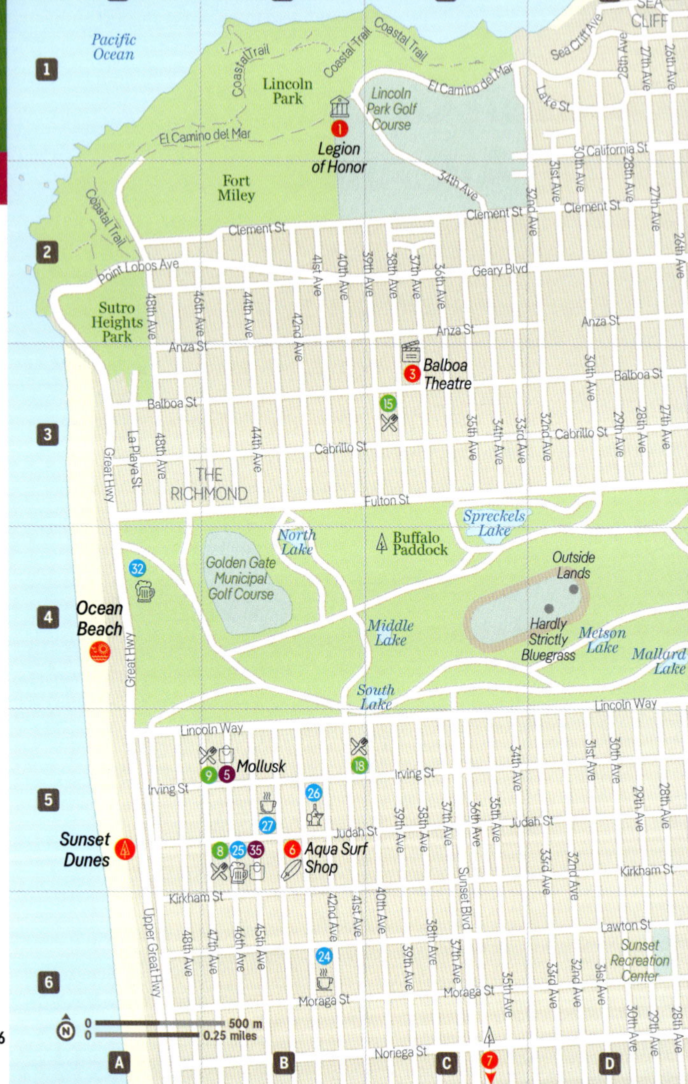
Pacific Ocean
Lincoln Park
Coastal Trail
El Camino del Mar
Lincoln Park Golf Course
Legion of Honor
Fort Miley
34th Ave
SEA CLIFF
Sea Cliff Ave
Lake St
California St
Clement St
Point Lobos Ave
Geary Blvd
Sutro Heights Park
Anza St
Balboa Theatre
Balboa St
Cabrillo St
THE RICHMOND
Fulton St
Great Hwy
La Playa St
North Lake
Buffalo Paddock
Spreckels Lake
Outside Lands
Golden Gate Municipal Golf Course
Ocean Beach
Middle Lake
Hardly Strictly Bluegrass
Metson Lake
Mallard Lake
South Lake
Lincoln Way
Mollusk
Irving St
Judah St
Sunset Dunes
Aqua Surf Shop
Kirkham St
Upper Great Hwy
Sunset Blvd
Lawton St
Sunset Recreation Center
Moraga St
Noriega St
500 m
0.25 miles

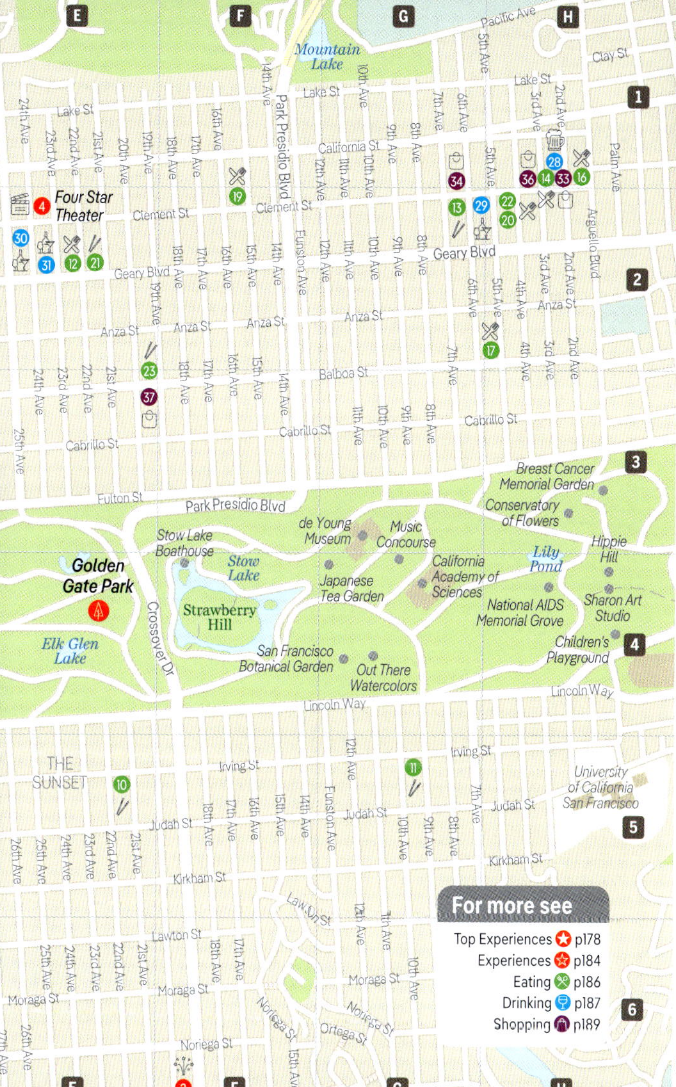
Mountain Lake
Pacific Ave
Clay St
Lake St
California St
Clement St
Geary Blvd
Anza St
Balboa St
Cabrillo St
Fulton St
Park Presidio Blvd
Arguello Blvd
Palm Ave
Funston Ave
Four Star Theater
Golden Gate Park
Elk Glen Lake
Crossover Dr
Stow Lake Boathouse
Stow Lake
Strawberry Hill
de Young Museum
Music Concourse
Japanese Tea Garden
California Academy of Sciences
Lily Pond
National AIDS Memorial Grove
San Francisco Botanical Garden
Out There Watercolors
Breast Cancer Memorial Garden
Conservatory of Flowers
Hippie Hill
Sharon Art Studio
Children's Playground
Lincoln Way
Irving St
Judah St
Kirkham St
Lawton St
Moraga St
Noriega St
Ortega St
THE SUNSET
University of California San Francisco
For more see
Top Experiences p178
Experiences p184
Eating p186
Drinking p187
Shopping p189

★ TOP EXPERIENCE

Golden Gate Park

Everything San Francisco holds dear can be found in Golden Gate Park: free spirits and free music, bountiful butterflies and underground art, loud dahlias and hushed redwood groves, tiny bonsai and massive bison. Landmarks celebrating nature, music, art and science are dotted across the park's 1017 acres.

MAP P176 **E4**

PLANNING TIP
John F Kennedy Dr is pedestrian-only starting at 9th Ave, but you can also bicycle around the park. Pick up bike rentals near the Japanese Tea Garden at **Parkwide Bike and Surrey** *(parkwide.com)*.

Scan this QR code for park events and information.

Natural Wonders

SF's mile-wide and 3-mile-long wild streak starts with the **Conservatory of Flowers** (pictured; *gggp.org; adult/youth & senior/child $17/7/3)*, an 1878 greenhouse lined with rare orchids, lilies and carnivorous plants – check online for holiday light shows and art events. **Combined tickets** *(adult/youth & senior/child $33/21/9)* offer same-day admission to the Japanese Tea Garden (p180) and 55-acre **San Francisco Botanical Garden**, which covers a world of flora from South African savanna to New Zealand cloud forest. Plants here are serenaded by professional musicians at **Flower Piano** *(gggp.org/flowerpiano)*.

Wildlife Encounters

At the park's wild western edge, bison have roamed the **Buffalo Paddock** since 1889. Blue butterflies alight on your shoulders in the **Osher Rainforest Dome**, starfish wave hello in **Steinhart Aquarium** and penguins waddle the African Hall at **California Academy of Sciences** *(calacademy.org; adult/child from $49/45)*, championing weird, wild science since 1853. Night owls party at **NightLife** *($25; 6-10pm Thu; 21-plus)* events, featuring themed cocktails and **Planetarium** shows. Kids may not technically sleep during **Academy Sleepovers**, but they might jump-start science careers.

BENJAMIN HEATH FOR LONELY PLANET

Art in the Park

The park's star art attraction is the **de Young Museum** *(famsf.org; adult/youth $20/free)*. Main-floor exhibits range from Inuit carvings to California prison photography; upstairs features Oceanic carvings and vast textile collections; basement retrospectives range from surrealist Frida Kahlo to photographer Ansel Adams. For park panoramas, take the elevator up the 144ft observation tower – or cloud-watch in James Turrell's **SkySpace** installation, hidden under **Osher Sculpture Garden**. Access is free to the tower, cafe and store; ticket includes free same-day entry to the Legion of Honor (p184). City-supported nonprofit **Sharon Art Studio** offers workshops to create your own masterpieces *(ages 18-plus; one- to three-day workshops $150-350)*, and **Out There Watercolors** *(outtherewatercolors.com; $120 per hour for up to four people)* runs outdoor-painting expeditions to capture park scenery for ages 12-plus.

QUICK BREAK
Inside the park, dining options are limited – best choices are the **de Young Museum cafe** (admission not required) or the **food trucks** that congregate across from the Japanese Tea Garden.

WHERE KIDS GO WILD

Kids flock to the park's historic **children's playground** to ride the vintage 1912 **carousel** *(adult/child $2.50/1)*, scoot down 1970s concrete slides and scale the climbing wall.

FLOAT YOUR BOAT

When the weather's behaving, pedal boats and rowboats are available daily at the restored 1946 **Stow Lake Boathouse** *(row/pedal boats $26/32.50)*.

Park Festivals & Concerts

Golden Gate Park has hosted epic festivals ever since the 1967 Human Be-In urged free spirits to 'tune in, turn on, drop out' – including the free annual **420 Festival** *(420hippiehill.com)*, named after International Bong Hit Time (4:20pm). Free outdoor concerts are held from March through November at Golden Gate Park's **Music Concourse Bandshell** *(sfrecpark.org/1570/Golden-Gate-Bandshell-Concerts)*, including Friday musical happy hours, Sunday reggae and Wednesday singer/songwriters.

Mega music festivals are held around the Polo Fields – notably free **Hardly Strictly Bluegrass** *(hardlystrictlybluegrass.com)*, the first weekend in October, and alt-Coachella fest **Outside Lands** *(sfoutsidelands.com)*, the first weekend in August. Hardly Strictly Bluegrass stages 75-plus acts across six stages, including bluegrass legends (Emmylou Harris, Gillian Welch), singer/songwriters (Elvis Costello, Rickie Lee Jones) and musical rebels (Gogol Bordello, Patti Smith). Score Outside Lands tickets mid-May to attend the August music festival *Billboard* calls America's best, featuring marquee pop (Doja Cat, Tyler the Creator), artsy alt-rockers (Lorde, Beck) and icons (Tribe Called Quest, Big Freedia).

Meditative Moments

Since 1894, the 5-acre **Japanese Tea Garden** *(gggp.org; adult/youth & senior/child $15/7/3; first hour free)* has blushed pink with cherry blossoms in spring and turned flaming red with maple leaves in fall. Don't miss the meditative **Zen Garden** and **Tea House** fortune cookies (introduced right here). For peaceful reflection ringed by redwoods and paving-stone tributes, step into the **National AIDS Memorial Grove** – founded in 1991 to commemorate millions of lives lost to the AIDS epidemic. At **Breast Cancer Memorial Garden** off Conservatory Dr, the secluded hilltop is ringed with benches and flowers.

★ TOP EXPERIENCE

Ocean Beach & Sunset Dunes

At atmospheric Ocean Beach, the sun sets over the Pacific – though fog banks may swallow it first. Standing on golden sand with your back to the city, you can watch the Pacific ebb and flow, with only a few brave surfers to remind you what century you're in.

MAP P176 **A4** & **A5**

Ocean Beach

San Francisco's 3.5-mile city beach is not like most California scenes in Hollywood movies – this moody, misty setting is better suited to meditative solo walks or bonding with friends. This was the original site of Burning Man; bonfires are allowed in artist-designed fire pits from March to October until 9:30pm. Swimmers, beware riptides; beach-combers, mind sneaker waves. Face the Pacific and spot surfers, passing ships and sea lions bobbing in the waves.

Sunset Dunes

At the southern end of Ocean Beach is a 50-acre waterfront park called Sunset Dunes. By popular vote in 2024, San Francisco converted a section of highway to park trails for joggers, cyclists, skaters and walkers to enjoy. Stick to paths in areas undergoing habitat restoration and keep dogs on a leash to protect wildlife. The dunes offer shelter for birdwatching – including skittish snowy plover shorebirds in winter – plus picnics and outdoor painting expeditions with Out There Watercolors (p179). To paint the sunset, pick up art supplies at nearby Case for Making (p189), where artisans make pigments specifically to capture subtle Pacific hues.

PLANNING TIP
Take a mid-beach break for food, drink, bathrooms and inspiration at the **Beach Chalet** (p189), with splendid 1930s frescoes that celebrate the building of Golden Gate Park.

Scan this QR code for events and information.

Lands End Hike

Enter another world as you walk along the edge of the continent, through a rugged landscape that rewards you with unexpected beauty: Victorian ruins, hidden sea caves, art treasures, mosaic byways and your new favorite movie.

START	END	LENGTH
Lands End Lookout	Four Star Theater	2.8 miles; three hours

1 Lands End Lookout

Across from restored 1885 Sutro Heights Park, **Lands End Lookout Visitor Center** *(nps.gov/goga)* offers trail maps and Pacific panoramas. Ancient mapmakers had a point: if ever there were a place for mermaids, monsters and magic, this is it.

2 Sutro Baths

Head downhill to **Sutro Baths**, where Victorian dandies and working stiffs once bathed in woolen rental swimsuits. Millionaire Adolph Sutro opened indoor pools here in 1896 to 10,000 bathers – but bouncers denied Black San Franciscan John Harris entry. He sued Sutro and won a landmark case desegregating community facilities. To lure crowds, Sutro added trapezes, ice rinks and wildly popular Egyptian mummies. After two world wars and the Great Depression, Sutro Baths went bust, and developers started razing them for high-rise condos. Public uproar ensued, and the ruins became parkland instead.

3 Clifftop Trails

Hike Sutro Baths Upper Trail northeast to the **Coastal Trail**, winding along Lands End bluffs. Get giddy views framed by wind-sculpted pines – including glimpses of coastal shipwrecks, frolicking sea lions, and the Golden Gate Bridge (p46). After you pass the clifftop overlook for Seal Rocks Beach, swing onto the **Lands End Trail** toward the Legion of Honor.

4 Legion of Honor

Through the grand colonnaded courtyard, past Rodin's sculpture of *The Thinker*, you'll reach the **Legion of Honor** (p184) entrance. To see contemporary art interact with the Legion's priceless treasures, get a ticket – if you arrive at 4:30pm, you've got 45 minutes to visit for free. Or head directly to the museum cafe for cool drinks, warming espresso and tasty pastries.

5 Lincoln Park's Tiled Steps

The Legion crowns 100-acre Lincoln Park, where America's coast-to-coast Lincoln Hwy officially ends. Follow the drive downhill through Lincoln Park, which was San Francisco's cemetery until 1909 – now it's a public golf course. Swing left after the golf clubhouse toward artist Aileen Barr's deco-inspired tiled **Lincoln Park Steps** *(lincolnparksteps.org; free)* – one of SF's best selfie spots – and descend to California St.

6 Four Star Theater

Walk to Clement St and window-shop your way to **Four Star Theater** (p184). Join local crowds at this neighborhood nonprofit cinema for weekend matinees or free family-friendly 10am movies, or get tickets to whatever's showing tonight – you've earned downtime with popcorn.

EXPERIENCES

See Legion of Honor Masterpieces

MUSEUM

MAP: 1 P176 **B1**

A museum as eccentric and illuminating as San Francisco itself, the **Legion of Honor** *(famsf.org; adult/youth $20/free)* is a monumental gift to the city from 'Big Alma' de Bretteville Spreckels. The Legion's eclectic collection ranges from ancient to modern – Monet water lilies and John Cage soundscapes upstairs, ancient cuneiform tablets and Enrique Chagoya's border-crossing Mayan codex downstairs. The Legion invites contemporary artists to engage with the collection, to provocative effect – Wangechi Mutu positioned her bronze *Shavasana* sculpture of two Black women in the long shadow of Rodin's monumental *The Thinker*.

Blockbuster shows range from from Guo Pei's fantasy couture to Picasso's sketchbooks, alongside selections from the **Achenbach Collection**'s 90,000 works on paper. At 4pm on Saturdays, pipe-organ recitals steal the show in the **Rodin Gallery**. Entry to the museum cafe and store is free; museum entry is free after 4:30pm. Tickets cover same-day entry to the de Young Museum (p179).

Catch the Stern Grove Festival

FESTIVAL

MAP: 2 P176 **F6**

America's oldest free music festival has rocked the Sunset's redwood and eucalyptus grove every summer since 1938 – recent headliners include Sleater-Kinney, Diana Ross, Tegan & Sara, Janelle Monáe, X and SF's own Michael Franti. **Stern Grove Festival** *(sterngrove.org)* tickets are available by online lottery: they're released six weeks before shows, and winners have 72 hours to claim them before they're given away to other lucky fans.

Watch Global Films in Community Cinemas

CINEMA

To make the most of foggy weather, nonprofit SF Neighborhood Theater Foundation has refurbished and reinvented two historic Richmond cinemas. Deco 1926 **Balboa Theatre** (MAP: 3 P176 **C3**; *balboamovies.com; tickets $12.50-20)* screens first-run movies, film-fest favorites, silver-screen classics, live comedy and audience-participation cult hits like *Rocky Horror Picture Show*. Before Ang Lee, John Woo and Wong Kar-wai graced global marquees, their films showed at cozy **Four Star Theater** (MAP: 4 P176 **E2**; *4-star-movies.com; tickets $0-20)*. Screening films since 1964, this nonprofit neighborhood cinema features international film-festival contenders, vintage classics,

THANKS, BIG ALMA

Legions of art fans owe thanks to 'Big Alma' de Bretteville Spreckels, the nude sculptor's model who changed the art world. In 1902 she publicly sued the gold miner who deflowered and dumped her for breach of promise – and won. Then Big Alma volunteered to model for Union Sq's *Goddess of Victory* monument, towering triumphantly with a cast-in-bronze wardrobe malfunction. The statue-selection-committee chair was sugar baron Adolph Spreckels, who became Big Alma's 'sugar daddy' and left her his fortune. Big Alma raised funds to rebuild post-earthquake SF, investigated working conditions for women for the US Department of Labor, and donated the Legion and Maritime Museum to her beloved San Francisco.

Japanese anime, movie events with live music, and free family favorites at 10am on weekends.

Explore the Sunset Surf Scene — SURFING

Watching Ocean Beach surfers brave gnarly riptides may leave you with questions, namely: why do they do this, and can I? Dip your toes into SF surf culture at **Mollusk** (MAP: 5 P176 B5; *mollusksurfshop.com*), where legendary shapers (surfboard makers) create limited-edition boards, and surfer-artists show in the back gallery. Surfers browse wetsuits, *Surfer's Journal* back issues and *Surfing Guide to California*, while kooks (newbies) try on Mollusk's 'kelp bed cruiser, wave peruser' T-shirts. Most SF surfers get their start in protected coves, like East Beach at Crissy Field (p48). Check out rental surf gear and surf lessons at **Aqua Surf Shop** (MAP: 6 P176 B5; *aquasurfshop.com; lessons $120-150; rental per day bodyboard/wetsuit $10/15, surfboard $25-35*).

Hike Fort Funston — PARK

MAP: 7 P176 C6

Flower power is taking over **Fort Funston** (*parksconservancy.org; free*), a military installation turned peaceful national park – you'll notice moss on 146-ton WWII guns and wildflowers alongside Nike missile silos, now used as hang-gliding jump sites. For a scenic hike, take the **Sunset Trail** to the beach and back (1.5 miles; one hour). Bring the family – trails are wheelchair and stroller accessible, and dogs are allowed off-leash in many areas. For a longer hike, pick up the Coastal Trail (p183) here and head north toward Sunset Dunes, Ocean Beach and Lands End.

LISTINGS

Best Places for...

$ Budget $$ Midrange $$$ Top End

See p176 for map of locations

Eating

Mega-Flavor Sunset Meals

Thanh Long $$
 8 B5
Classic crab – roasted, tamarind or 'drunken' – with signature garlic noodles and warm An-family welcomes. *4:30-8pm Sun, Wed & Thu, to 9pm Fri & Sat*

Hook Fish Co $
 9 B5
Join surfers at weathered wooden tables for fresh, sustainable Pacific seafood in tacos or burritos, atop salads, or in fish and chips. *11:30am-9pm*

Mini Potstickers $
10 E5
Dumpling experts pack mini-dumplings with Wagyu beef, shrimp and pork, or flavor-bomb veggies. *10:30am-3pm & 5-8:30pm Mon-Fri, 10:30am-8:30pm Sat & Sun*

Manna $
 11 G5
Home-style Korean cooking, including kimchi pancakes, *kalbi* (BBQ short ribs) and *dol-sot* bibimbap (sizzling stone-pot rice); parties of four maximum. *11am-9:30pm Tue-Sun*

Dinner in the Richmond

Aziza $$$
 12 E2
Cal-Moroccan signatures arrive with fragrant fanfare – wild-salmon tagine, braised Sonoma lamb shakshuka, flaky *bastilla* chicken confit – alongside elegant cocktails and mocktails. *5-9:30pm Wed-Sun, brunch 10:30am-2pm Sat & Sun*

Mamahuhu $
 13 G2
California-fresh takes on nostalgic Chinese American diner classics, recreated with sustainable seasonal ingredients – Niman Ranch beef and broccoli, sweet-and-sour cauliflower, organic shiitake-mushroom *mapo* tofu. *11:30am-9pm*

Chapeau $$$
 14 H1
Every diner is treated like a *bon ami* at this family-owned French bistro, where well-priced tasting menus ($50 to $92) feature classics like onion soup, duck cassoulet and coq au vin. *5-9pm Wed-Sun*

The Laundromat $
 15 C3
The only thing you'll clean at this Laundromat is your plate – memorable square pizzas include margherita with vodka sauce and crispy Brussels sprouts with creamy goat's cheese. *8am-2pm & 5-9pm Wed-Sun*

Baked Goodies

Arsicault Bakery $
16 H1
Armando Lacayo left France for Wall St, then ditched NY finance for SF financiers (teacakes) and signature golden, flaky croissants, usually

sold out by lunch. *8am-3pm*

Cinderella Russian Bakery $

 H2

Join generations of SF's Russian Jewish community for just-baked egg-and-green-onion *piroshki*, decadent potato *vareniki* (boiled dumplings) and hearty borscht. *7am-7pm*

Day Moon Bread $

18 B5

Crusty loaves and chewy cookies baked with 100% California-grown wheat are hits at Clement St Farmers Market (9am to 2pm Sun) – score sandwich specials at their storefront. *9am-4pm Thu-Sat*

Breadbelly $

 F2

Between Paris and Singapore on Clement St, Breadbelly bakes black-sesame brambleberry Danish, and spreads coconut-pandan *kaya* on toasted milk-bread – better hurry. *8am-2pm Wed-Mon*

Lunch in the Richmond

Taqueria Los Mayas $

20 H2

Adios, tacos: *Los Mayas panuchos* (bean-filled tortillas) come piled with Yucatecan *cochinita pibil* (tangy barbecued pork) or *poc-chuc* grilled pork, pickled onions, slaw and sensational salsas. *11am-9pm*

Dragon Beaux $$

 E2

Hong Kong meets Vegas at San Francisco's decadent Cantonese restaurant, featuring succulent duck, five-flavor soup dumplings, crab congee and premium teas. *11am-3pm & 5-9pm Mon-Fri, from 10am Sat & Sun*

Bettola $

 H2

Your friendly neighborhood *tavola calda* ('hot table') dishes proper lasagna, prosciutto-loaded white pizza, and brined rotisserie chicken with Italian wine by the glass or carafe. *11am-9pm*

Han Il Kwan $

 E2

Join surfers and grandmas for epic Korean lunch specials: multiple *banchan* (side dishes), sizzling platters of marinated meats, stone bowls brimming with bibimbap. *11am-8pm Sun & Mon, to 9pm Thu-Sat*

Drinking

Sunset Drinks

Andytown Coffee

 B6

Go early for a Snowy Plover – double-shot of espresso (or matcha) with bubbly water, ice and whipped cream – plus Irish soda bread baked on-site. *7am-5pm*

Woods Outbound

 B5

Microbrews with unexpected ingredients – hibiscus, yerba mate, cocoa nibs – and Norcal co-fermented beer/wine, from Albariño blonde to Merlot red ale. *4-10pm Mon-Fri, noon-11pm Sat, 1-8pm Sun*

Palm City Wines

 B5

Sunny corner serving natural wine with hearty hoagies – think skin-contact Ribolla Gialla with shrimp-salad hoagies – plus hot-dish specials on corkage-free Monday/Tuesday. *4-10pm Mon & Tue, noon-9pm Wed-Sun*

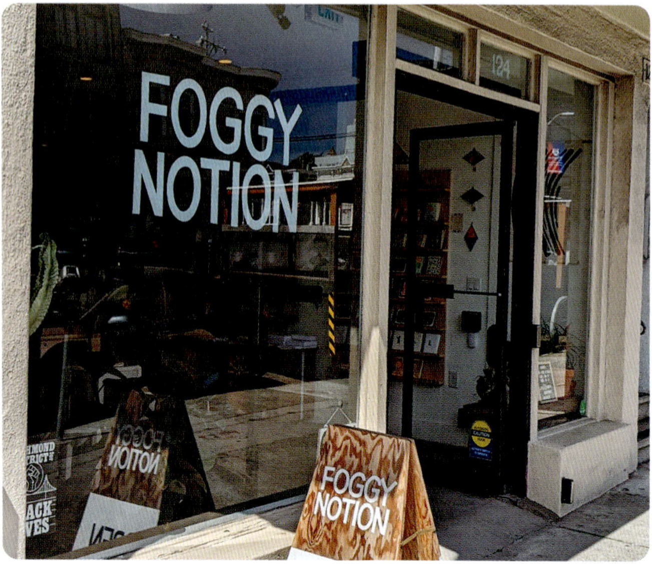

PAULAAH293/SHUTTERSTOCK

Foggy Notion

Judahlicious Vegan Cafe
27 B5
Made-to-order organic smoothies like the N-Line (banana, pineapple mango, coconut) plus organic fair-trade coffee, yerba mate and vegan house chili. *9am-5pm*

Toasts in the Richmond

Plough & Stars
28 H1
Headliners from Ireland to Appalachia play *seisiúns* (jams) here, taking breaks to clink pints of Guinness at union-hall tables. Cover is a bargain ($6 to $20). *3pm-2am Wed-Sun*

High Treason
29 G2
Proof that you can get good vibes and great wines on a beer budget, with cult vintages by the glass, eclectic vinyl, plus winemaker DJs on Mondays. *4-10pm*

Violet's Tavern
30 E2
Toast 5pm to 6pm happy hours with Ultraviolets (pea-flower purple gin cocktails) or alcohol-free Phony Negronis, and stick around for *cioppino Latino*, SF's seafood stew with Peruvian-chili kick. *5-9pm*

Tommy's Mexican Restaurant
31 E2
SF's temple of tequila since 1965 serves pure margarita bliss – enchiladas slow your roll through 400 select blue-agave tequilas. *5-8:30pm Wed-Fri, from 1pm Sat & Sun*

Beach Chalet

 A4

Microbrews with views: watch Pacific sunsets through pints of Riptide Red ale, and admire 1930s frescoes celebrating the building of Golden Gate Park en route to the bathroom. *9am-8pm Mon-Wed, to 9pm Thu & Fri, 10am-8pm Sat & Sun*

Shopping

SF Mementos

Foggy Notion

33 H1

You can't take Golden Gate Park home with you – the city would seem naked without it – but Foggy Notion offers sense memories of SF's urban wilderness: Wild Yonder's 'anti-bad-vibes' bath soak, redwood-printed organic cotton Replant socks, and Clement Street-scented candles. *10am-6pm Mon-Sat, 9am-5pm Sun*

Green Apple Books

34 G1

Stagger out of this literary rabbit hole while you still can, laden with used cookbooks by SF chefs and just-released novels signed by local authors. Check out more books, in-store readings and events at Green Apple Books on the Park (1231 9th Ave). *10am-9pm*

Case for Making

35 B5

Capture SF scenery with sketching notebooks, brushes, palettes and and handmade paints that capture subtle fog and ocean hues. *11am-6pm*

One-of-a-Kind Finds

Park Life

36 H1

Like a multitool of cool, this is a design store, indie publisher, art gallery and HQ for SF Art Book Fair, all folded into one – score finds like Barry McGee's Scooters for Peace tees, book-fair-scented candles, and SF artist Bridget Watson Payne's hand-painted paperbacks. *10am-6pm Mon-Sat, to 5pm Sun*

Love Street Vintage

37 E3

Pull together park festival looks that say 'I'm with the band' with rare vintage at fantastic prices, from psychedelic '60s aloha shirts to embroidered maxi dresses and silver bracelets handmade by hippies. *11am-6pm Thu-Mon*

Tunnel Records

see 4 E2

Duck into Four Star Theater's lobby to find vintage vinyl, mint-condition movie posters and original handbills for legendary SF shows – including a Dead Kennedys' benefit for Jello Biafra's 1979 mayoral run. *noon-6pm Mon-Fri, from 11am Sat & Sun*

POWELL AND MARKET
HYDE AND BEACH
FISHERMANS WHARF
11

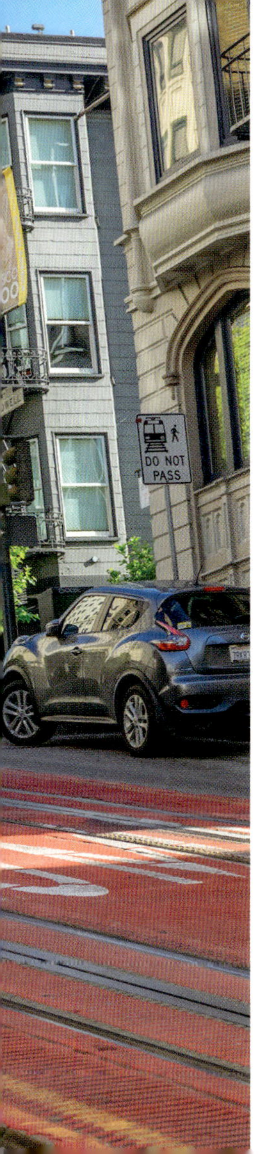

San Francisco Toolkit

Powell-Hyde cable car line
BEN BRYANT/SHUTTERSTOCK

Family Travel

San Francisco sparks imaginations at any age. Even though SF has the fewest kids per capita of any US city, it offers intergenerational bonding experiences galore – especially for outdoorsy, arty, sporty and scientifically curious types.

Pier 39's Bargain Attractions

Pier 39 (p54) offers amusement-park atmosphere without the entry fees. Visit **sea lions** *(free)*, snap family photos at **San Francisco Carousel** *($6 per ride)*, and climb piano-key **Musical Stairs** *(free)* to score discounted **Aquarium of the Bay** tickets at the 2nd-floor **California Welcome Center**.

Playgrounds & Skateparks

The city's busiest, best-equipped playgrounds are at Golden Gate Park, Tunnel Tops, Portsmouth Sq and Dolores Park. Everyone enjoys the intergenerational skate scene at **Potrero del Sol/La Raza Skatepark** (p130), where legendary street skaters graciously give right of way to the littlies in the lower skate bowl. To join in, pick up boards at nearby Mission Skateboards.

GOLDEN GATE PARK ADVENTURES

Park days are action-packed – paddle Stow Lake, skate JFK drive, and meet penguins at California Academy of Sciences.

Scan this QR code to explore park activities:

Rental Gear

Cloud of Goods *(cloudofgoods.com)* rents strollers, wheelchairs and mobility scooters, and **Baby's Away** *(babysaway.com)* rents strollers, car seats and cribs.

Beach Days

Head to Crissy Field's East Beach for sandcastles and picnics with Golden Gate Bridge views.

Kids' Menus

SF is a city of adventurous eaters – small plates and bite-sized portions (like dim sum) make it easy for kids to try food without committing to adult-sized mains. You'll find kids' menus at Wharf and downtown fast-casual joints.

FOTOSLAZ/SHUTTERSTOCK

Accommodations

San Francisco's hotels are clustered downtown and along the waterfront, near major attractions and entertainment venues – hop transit or rideshare to happening neighborhoods.

Where to Stay if You Love...

Nature in the City

The Presidio, Marina & Fisherman's Wharf (p43) Get in touch with nature at Presidio park lodges, Marina motels near Crissy Field, or within earshot of Fisherman's Wharf's barking sea lions.

OUR PICK

We Love to Stay in...

Japantown, Fillmore & Pacific Heights (p105) Live the period-drama fantasy in a grand Victorian parlor, taking tea with visiting dignitaries in a historic Painted Lady B&B – then rock out at legendary Fillmore music venues. Tomorrow you can recover in Japantown spas, picnic at Alamo Sq, browse Divisadero boutiques and slurp noodles in Japan Center. Bliss.

Arts & Nightlife

Downtown, Civic Center & SoMa (p63) Union Sq's historic hotels are near theaters, museums, concert halls and SoMa hotspots, including clubs, bars and legendary LGBTQ+ venues, from leather bars to drag cabarets.

Gourmet Stays

Chinatown & North Beach (p87) Wake up to delectable aromas in this global food and drink destination featuring dim sum, pizza, acclaimed restaurants, wine bars and saloons.

LGBTQ+ Life

The Castro (p141) The historic gayborhood at the heart of SF, with rainbow-flag-flying hang-outs, cafes, bars and club scenes that are gay all day and out every night.

Peace, Love & Vibes

The Haight & Hayes Valley (p157) Begin a new day amid psyche-delic murals, jazz musi-cians and Zen monks in SF's iconic central neighborhoods.

HOW MUCH FOR A NIGHT IN

Landmark hotel
from $220

Historic inn or B&B
$150–270

Hostel
$30–75

Food, Drink & Nightlife

Allergies & Intolerances

Mention any dietary limitations when reserving, and you should be cheerfully accommodated. If you have a food allergy or intolerance, mention it before you order, so your server can double check with the kitchen to ensure your dishes are prepared without that ingredient. Travelers with food allergies should follow doctors' advice, which may include carrying antihistamines or epinephrine in case.

FOOD TRUCKS

Supporting small businesses is delicious: top mobile food vendors flank **Ferry Building farmers market** (p66), **Fort Mason outdoor markets** (p56) and **Presidio Pop Up** (p49).

VEGETARIAN & VEGAN

SF welcomes vegetarians and vegans with options galore, from vegan sushi to acclaimed vegetarian fine dining. Vegetable-forward hotspots are in the Mission and Haight – but restaurants citywide feature vegetarian and vegan dishes. Look for the 'V' symbol highlighting vegetarian signatures on menus, and ask servers about dishes marked as 'vegetarian/vegan optional.'

Sourdough

San Francisco is the home of sourdough bread, with a distinctive tang from local *lactobacillus sanfranciscensis*. You'll recognize SF's signature flavor in sourdough pizza, pancakes, burger buns and baked goods – it can be an acquired taste. If you're not a fan, ask when ordering what menu items are made without sourdough culture.

HOW TO... Pay the Bill

Surcharges Tax (8.625%) and tip (obligatory) add about 25% to 30% to SF restaurant bills. Many restaurants also add a 'Healthy SF fee' of 4% to 7% to defray their costs for workers' healthcare. Some high-end restaurants automatically include a 20% service fee in lieu of a tip – check your bill before you calculate the tip.

Splitting the bill SF restaurants will split the bill two or three ways – ask when your bill is presented. If you're with a group, it's assumed that one or two of you will pay, then settle up with your group the SF way: via a money-sharing app, like PayPal/Venmo.

PRICE RANGES

The following price ranges refer to the average price of a main course.

$ less than $20

$$ $20–30

$$$ more than $30

OPENING HOURS

Lunch Typically 11:30am to 2pm, though not all restaurants open for lunch.

Dinner Around 5:30pm to 9pm; last order may be 8:30pm.

Brunch Served weekends 11am to 3pm.

HOW MUCH FOR A

Burrito
$9–14

Order of three dumplings
$4–12

Slice of pizza
$5–8

Cocktail
$8–16

Espresso
$4–6

Craft beer
$7–9

Glass of NorCal wine
$9–18

FROM LEFT: ANGGALIH PRASETYA/SHUTTERSTOCK, 1000PHOTOGRAPHY/SHUTTERSTOCK

Going Out

At the door Many clubs charge $10 to $30 (often cash) at the door, unless you show up before 10pm or join the club's online guest list. You'll usually only wait 15 minutes to get in anywhere – SF's club scene is inclusive, not VIP-centered.

LGBTQ+ hotspots Find your gay groove in Castro clubs (p153), toast herstory at Mission landmark lesbian bars (p129), and hit drag shows and kink fests in SoMa's Leather & LGBTQ Cultural District (p74).

Straight-friendly venues DJs set the tone at clubs in SF, where the right groove gets everyone on the dance floor – blending gay and straight in a giddy motion blur. Many queer venues welcome straight allies – especially those who tip well – but not all do.

Closing time Last call at many clubs is around 10:30pm weeknights and 1:30am weekends, many close around 2am, though some after-hours SoMa clubs rage until dawn on weekends.

LGBTQ+ Travelers

Doesn't matter where you're from or who's your daddy: if you're here and queer, welcome home.

SF's Queer-Culture Hubs

Other cities have gay neighborhoods, but queer people live, work and play throughout SF. Gay pride literally stops traffic in the **Castro**, where crosswalks are rainbow-striped (pictured) and sidewalk plaques honor LGBTQ+ luminaries whose footsteps you're walking in – including SF supervisor Harvey Milk, who wore holes in his shoes campaigning for civil rights, as seen at the GLBT Historical Society Museum (p149).

The world's first official Trans District (p75) is in the **Tenderloin**, where trans women fought back against police harassment in 1966. SF's official Leather & LGBTQ Cultural District (p74) is in **SoMa**, the heart of SF's club and leather bar scenes.

Polk St served gay sailors since WWII, and North Beach's **Broadway St** was home to America's first lesbian and drag bars in the 1930s – today the lesbian hub is the **Mission** (p129).

HOMOBILES

Get home safely with secure, reliable, donation-based transportation by and for the LGBTQ +community from volunteer-run **Homobiles**. Drivers provide rides 24/7 – for fastest service, text 415-574-5023.

OUR PICKS

YEAR-ROUND PRIDE

June celebrates SF Pride month (p32) and is glorious – but it's not SF's only LGBTQ+ calendar highlight.

April brings Hunky Jesus Contest (p128) and Lesbian Visibility Week.

August is Trans History Month.

September gets kinky at Folsom Street Fair (p75).

October brings Castro Street Fair and National Coming Out Day.

December celebrates Gay Men's Chorus (p128).

EVA CARRE/SHUTTERSTOCK

LGBTQ+ LANDMARK SELFIES

Pose with iconic marquees at Castro Theatre and Brava Theater. Scan this QR code to see what's next at **Brava Theater**.

Resources

SF has two dedicated LGBTQ+ community newspapers. • **Bay Area Reporter** *(ebar.com)* has covered community news and events since 1971. • **San Francisco Bay Times** *(sfbaytimes.com)* offers LGBTQ+ news and calendar listings.

Health & Safe Travel

San Francisco wishes you well, and provides support services so you can enjoy SF life to the fullest.

SAFETY TIPS

Among US cities, SF has comparatively low violent-crime rates. Key concerns are smash-and-grab car break-ins, which you can avoid by taking public transit and rideshares instead of driving. At night in low-lit areas, stash valuables and remove earbuds. Anytime you feel unsafe walking or waiting for transit, hop rideshares.

Free & Low-Cost Health Services

SF is committed to affordable care for all, regardless of insurance or immigration status – see nonprofit **SF Service Guide** *(sfserviceguide.org)* for options. **Lyon-Martin Community Health Services** offers sliding-scale services for women, nonbinary and trans folks. **Strut** (p151) offers sliding-scale counseling, PEP and PrEP HIV prevention, MPOX and Hep C vaccines. **SF City Clinic** provides PrEP, PEP, COVID-19 vaccinations, contraception, STI testing and treatment. City-run **AITC Immunization & Travel Clinic** offers low-cost/free testing and immunizations.

Insurance

Check if your health-insurance policy covers travel to California. If it doesn't, consider travel insurance.

Emergency Care

SF has excellent medical facilities and urgent-care centers in every neighborhood. Major hospitals with ERs include **University of California San Francisco Medical Center** and **San Francisco General Hospital**.

CRISIS SUPPORT

Drug & Alcohol Emergency Info Line helps prevent suicide and overdoses. **Trauma Recovery & Rape Treatment Center** provides support services.

QUICK INFO

Security

Don't leave laptops unattended in cafes.

Privacy

In California, you can't be recorded without your consent.

Marijuana

Weed is legal for adults aged 21-plus with ID in California; driving under the influence isn't.

Responsible Travel

Follow these tips to leave a lighter footprint, support local and have a positive impact on communities.

Help Keep SF Green

Every San Franciscan lives within a 10-minute walk of open park space – the first city worldwide to achieve this green goal. Cheerful sidewalk planters and converted-driveway gardens around SF help support rare species like the Franciscan manzanita and blue Mission butterfly, making SF the world leader in urban biodiversity. Show your support for SF and its butterflies by using zero-emissions transportation and supporting green initiatives, like citywide composting.

Hop a Cable Car

SF cable cars are more than 150 years old, but they're forward-thinking – they're propelled along tracks uphill by renewable hydroelectricity, with some help from gravity on downhill slides.

OUR PICK

Peace, Love & Lunch

In the '60s, Haight hippies and Black Panthers distributed free food around the Bay Area – now you can catch those neighborly vibes by volunteering at historic **Haight Ashbury Food Program** *(thefoodprogram.org)*.

Get Thrifty

When you score SF vintage bargains, everyone wins – you save money and score one-of-a-kind souvenirs, the environment breathes a sigh of relief, and San Franciscan fabulousness stays in circulation. SF's vintage hotspots include the Haight (p163), Mission and North Beach.

FROM LEFT: JACK-SOOKSAN/SHUTTERSTOCK, MAREKULIASZ/SHUTTERSTOCK, ERMAK OKSANA/SHUTTERSTOCK

Resources

- **San Francisco Environment Department** *(sfenvironment.org/events)* – join SF environmentalists in action.
- **San Francisco Bicycle Coalition** provides SF street cycling maps to promote fun, emissions-free transit.

BRING A BAG

San Francisco banned plastic bags to advance its goal to become a zero-waste city by 2040. You can support that goal by bringing a reusable bag – and save yourself the city-mandated 25¢ bag fee.

Composting

Next to blue recycling bins in SF cafes and restaurants, you'll spot a green bin – that's for compostables, including food scraps, paper napkins and compostable takeout containers, cups and straws (San Francisco banned plastic straws in 2019). Since San Francisco introduced mandatory composting in 2009, the city has provided over 2 million lb of compost to local farms, orchards and vineyards.

THE ULTIMATE UPCYCLING

Since 1990 SF's employee-owned Recology waste-removal company has sponsored more than 300 artists with residencies at the dump.

Scan this QR code for upcycled art inspiration:

Climate Change & Travel

It's impossible to ignore the impact we have when traveling; Lonely Planet urges all travelers to engage with their travel carbon footprint, which will mainly come from air travel. While there often isn't an alternative, travelers can look to minimize the number of flights they take, opt for newer aircrafts and use cleaner ground transportation, such as trains. One proposed solution – purchasing carbon offsets – unfortunately does not cancel out the impact of individual flights. While most destinations will depend on air travel for the foreseeable future, for now, pursuing ground-based travel where possible is the best course of action.

The **UN Carbon Offset Calculator** shows how flying impacts a household's emissions

The **ICAO's carbon emissions calculator** allows visitors to analyze the CO2 generated by point-to-point journeys

Accessible Travel

Accessible Attractions

San Francisco is considered wheelchair-friendly for its ADA-compliant sidewalks, accessible public-transit options and accessible park trails. Top wheelchair-accessible attractions include Exploratorium, SFMOMA, Alcatraz, Presidio and Asian Art Museum. Nonprofit **SF Travel** *(sftravel.com/accessibility-san-francisco)* offers tips for accessible travel in SF – including tours, accessible venues and Golden Gate Park guides.

Support for Families

San Francisco's **Support for Families** *(supportforfamilies.org)* provides essential resources and community for families of kids with disabilities, covering specific disabilities and a wide range of ages. Get support by phone at 415-920-5040. Volunteers are welcome.

RENTALS

Cloud of Goods *(cloudofgoods.com)* rents wheelchairs and mobility scooters. Major car rentals can usually supply hand-controlled vehicles with a couple of days' notice, and **Wheelchair Getaways** *(wheelchairgetaways.com)* rents ramped vehicles.

Accessible Transit

San Francisco Bay Area Regional Transit Guide *(511.org/transit/accessibility)* covers accessible transit options for people with disabilities. Detailed information on wheelchair-accessible bus routes and streetcar stops is available from **Muni** *(sfmta.com/muni-access-guide)*.

For accessible outdoor adventures, San Francisco's **Environmental Traveling Companions** *(etctrips.org)* organize top-notch white-water rafting, kayaking and cross-country skiing trips in California for people of all ages with disabilities. Founded by people with disabilities in 1971, **Bay Area Outreach and Recreation Program** (BORP; *borp.org)* organizes 20+ adaptive recreational activities weekly around the Bay Area, including group outings like hiking and Sonoma wine-tasting.

TAXI & ROBOTAXI

Uber WAV *(uber.com/us/en/ride/uberwav)* offers rides in wheelchair-accessible vehicles. **Waymo** *(waymo.com)* provides driverless robotaxi service for people with guide dogs.

Resources

- **Independent Living Resource Center of San Francisco** *(ilrcsf.org)* provides helpful travel tips, including information about accessibility in hotels and public transit.

Nuts & Bolts

Opening Hours

Hours are often nonstandard in San Francisco neighborhood businesses – check online or call ahead. In general, opening hours include the following.

Banks 9am–4:30pm or 5pm Monday to Friday

Offices 8:30am–5:30pm Monday to Friday, though many locals work remotely

Restaurants Breakfast 8–10:30am; lunch 11:30am–2:30pm; dinner 5:30–9pm weekdays; Saturday and Sunday brunch 10:30am–2:30pm

Shops 11am–5pm or 6pm Monday to Saturday, sometimes noon–6pm Sunday

Bars and clubs Most stay open until 2am on weekends. Weeknights they may close before midnight; some open Sunday afternoons

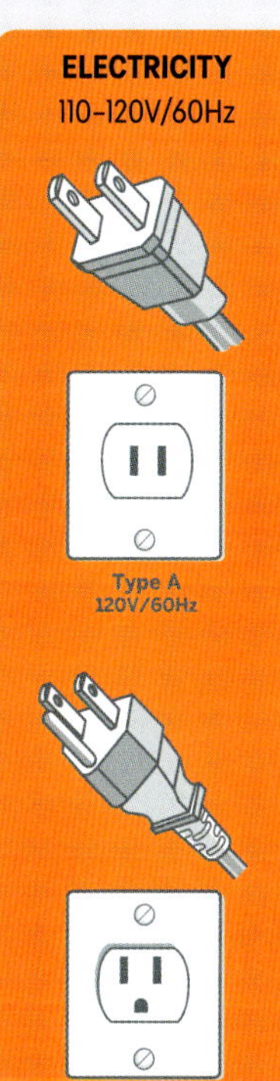

Public Holidays

Holidays that may affect business hours and transit schedules in San Francisco include the following.

New Year's Day January 1

Martin Luther King Jr Day Third Monday in January

Presidents' Day Third Monday in February

Easter March or April

Memorial Day Last Monday in May

Juneteenth June 19

Independence Day July 4

Labor Day First Monday in September

Indigenous People's Day/ Columbus Day Second Monday in October

Veterans Day November 11

Thanksgiving Fourth Thursday in November

Christmas Day December 25

Smoking

Smoking and vaping are prohibited in most SF gathering places, including restaurants, bars, cafes, theaters, museums, stadiums, workplaces, public-transit vehicles and stops – plus outdoor areas where food is served, farmers markets and parks. Some bars have designated smoking patios – otherwise, find a sidewalk spot away from doorways of open businesses.

QUICK INFO

Time zone PST/PDT (GMT/UTC -7/-8 hours)
Country calling code +1
Emergency number 911
Population 842,000

Index

Sights p000 Map pages **p000**

See also separate subindexes for:
Eating p205
Drinking p206
Shopping p207

Drinking

Shopping

Send Us Your Feedback

We love to hear from travelers - your comments help make our books better. We read every word, and we guarantee that your feedback goes straight to the authors. Visit lonelyplanet.com/contact to submit your updates and suggestions.

Note: We may edit, reproduce and incorporate your comments in Lonely Planet products such as guidebooks, websites and digital products, so let us know if you are happy to have your name acknowledged. For a copy of our privacy policy visit lonelyplanet.com/legal.

Acknowledgements

Cover photograph: Volkswagen Beetle parked in front of an orange town house.
Tom Windeknecht/Stills

Back photograph: Golden Gate Bridge (p46).
vichie81/Shutterstock

THIS BOOK

The 10th edition of Lonely Planet's San Francisco guidebook was researched and written by Alison Bing, Dylan Lalanne-Perkins and Margot Seeto. The previous edition was written by Alison Bing. This guidebook was produced by the following:

Destination Editor
Melissa Yeager

Cartographer
Jennifer Johnston

Production Editor
Aileen Cudmore

Image Editor
Eoin T Loughney

Coordinating Editor
Mani Ramaswamy

Cover Researcher
Katelyn Perry

Thanks to
Janet Austin, Imogen Bannister, Vojtech Bartos, Alison Killilea, Kellie, Langdon, Darren O'Connell, Katerina Pavkova

Published by Lonely Planet Global Limited
CRN 554153
10th edition - Jan 2026
ISBN 978 1 83869 916 1

10 9 8 7 6 5 4 3 2 1
Printed in China